The Economics of Hope

FOR DAISY

The Economics of Hope

Essays on Technical Change, Economic Growth and the Environment

Christopher Freeman

Pinter Publishers

London and New York

Distributed exclusively in the USA and Canada by ST. MARTIN'S PRESS

Pinter Publishers
25 Floral Street, Covent Garden, London, WC2E 9DS, United Kingdom

First published in 1992

Distributed exclusively in the USA and Canada by
St. Martin's Press, Inc., 175 Fifth Avenue,
New York NY 10010, USA.

Christopher Freeman is hereby identified as the author of this work as provided under Section 77 of the Copyright, Designs and Patents Act, 1988.

British Library Cataloguing in Publication Data
A CIP catalogue record for this book is available from the British Library.
ISBN 1 85567 083 6

Library of Congress Cataloging-in-Publication Data

Freeman, Christopher
      The economics of hope: essays on technical change, economic
   growth, and the environment/Chris Freeman.
         p.   cm.
      Includes bibliographical references and index.
      ISBN 1-85567-083-6
      1. Economic development.   2. Environmental policy.
   3. Technological innovations—Economic aspects.   4. Research.
   Industrial—Economic aspects.   I. Title.
   HD74.5.F74   1992
   338.9—dc20   92-15155
                                                                                   CIP

Typeset by GCS, Leighton Buzzard, Bedfordshire
Printed and bound in Great Britain by
Biddles Ltd, Guildford and King's Lynn

Even apart from the instability due to speculation, there is the instability due to the characteristic of human nature that a large proportion of our positive activities depend on spontaneous optimism rather than on a mathematical expectation, whether moral, or hedonistic, or economic. Most, probably, of our decisions to do something positive, the full consequences of which will be drawn out over many days to come, can only be taken as a result of animal spirits—of a spontaneous urge to action rather than inaction, and not as the outcome of a weighted average of quantitative benefits multiplied by quantitative probabilities. Enterprise only pretends to itself to be mainly activated by the statements in its own prospectus, however candid and sincere. Only a little more than an expedition to the South Pole, is it based on an exact calculation of benefits to come. Thus if the animal spirits are dimmed and the spontaneous optimism falters, leaving us to depend on nothing but a mathematical expectation, enterprise will fade and die—though fears of loss may have a basis no more reasonable than hopes of profit had before.

It is safe to say that enterprise which depends on hopes stretching into the future benefits the community as a whole. But individual initiative will only be adequate when reasonable calculation is supplemented and supported by animal spirits, so that the thought of ultimate loss which often overtakes pioneers, as experience undoubtedly tells us and them, is put aside as a healthy man puts aside the expectation of death. (J.M. Keynes: *General Theory of Employment, Interest and Money*, pp. 161–2)

Hoffnung

Es reden und träumen die Menschen viel
   Von bessern künftigen Tagen,
Nach einem glücklichen goldenen Ziel
   Sieht man sie rennen und jagen.
Die Welt wird alt und wird wieder jung,
Doch der Mensch hofft immer Verbesserung!
Die Hoffnung führt ihn ins Leben ein,
   Sie umflattert den fröhlichen Knaben
Den Jüngling begeistert ihr Zauberschein,
   Sie wird mit dem Greis nicht begraben,
Denn beschließt er im Grabe den müden Lauf,
Noch am Grabe pflanzt er—die Hoffnung auf.

Es ist kein leerer schmeichelnder Wahn,
   Erzeugt im Gehirne des Toren.
Im Herzen kündet es laut sich an,
   Zu was Besserem sind wir geboren,
Und was die innere Stimme spricht,
Das täuscht die hoffende Seele nicht.

F. Schiller

Contents

List of figures

List of tables

Preface

This set of chapters was written at various times over the past twenty-five years. During this time I was extremely fortunate to be associated with the Science Policy Research Unit in the University of Sussex (SPRU) and more recently with the Maastricht Economic Research Institute on Innovation and Technology (MERIT) in the Netherlands. I owe a great debt to all of my colleagues in both these organisations. Many of the ideas developed in these chapters were the result of joint projects with a variety of colleagues, although of course they are not responsible for the views which I express.

Both groups were founded in the belief that technical change is the main source of dynamism in economic development. Although this proposition is not seriously challenged by any school of thought in economics, the study of innovations and their diffusion was until recently a neglected area of theoretical and applied economics. This is no longer the case, as can be seen from the new journals established in the 1980s, the so-called 'new growth' theory and many other developments, such as the success of the Schumpeter Society and a number of other new research centres in many different countries.

It was in fact a natural scientist, J.D. Bernal, who gave the first big impetus to the study of research and development activities in industry, government and universities with his book *The Social Function of Science* (1939). The first essay in the book makes clear my debt to him by reviewing critically the lasting contribution which he made. It was Bernal who made the first systematic attempt to measure R&D activities in Britain, long before governments were involved. It was his example which I followed when I worked on the first major survey of industrial R&D in Britain by the Federation of British Industries (now the CBI) in the 1950s and worked with the Organisation for Economic Co-operation and Development (OECD) on the standardisation of R&D Definitions and Measurements (the so-called Frascati Manual) in the 1960s.

Measurement of scientific and technical activities has always been and remains an essential task for researchers in this field and the Epilogue indicates some directions in which new initiatives are required. I am especially happy that this piece was written jointly with Geoff Oldham, the co-founder with myself and Jackie Fuller of the Science Policy Research Unit, and my successor as Director. As colleague and friend over twenty-five years at SPRU he embodied the co-operation between natural and social scientists, which we both believe to be essential. We share the conviction that progress in both the natural and the social sciences is often related to improvements in measurement, although of course these are no substitute for analytical insights and theories. Chapters 2 and 3 are examples of two areas where progress in measurement has facilitated understanding: innovations in industry and international trade performance. Both SPRU and MERIT have been at the forefront in the original use of scientific and technical indicators to improve the analysis of the role of innovation in the competitive performance of companies and countries in international trade. Once more I wish to acknowledge my debt of gratitude to three friends and colleagues who have made such an outstanding contribution to the role of technology in international trade theory and to many other aspects of evolutionary economics: Giovanni Dosi, Keith Pavitt and Luc Soete.

Another research area in which they have all participated is the relative contribution of large and small firms to innovative performance. Again, improved measurement through the SPRU Data Bank was of invaluable help. However, before that the contrasting views of Galbraith and Jewkes were the subject of heated discussion and the OECD Seminar in 1967 gives the flavour of the early debates in this field and provides the opportunity to assess the contribution made by the classic study of *Sources of Invention* by Jewkes, Sawyers and Stillerman.

The second part of the book comprises three more recent papers which attempt to synthesise the findings of a great deal of empirical research on innovations and their diffusion over the last quarter of a century. They make clear that it is impossible to understand diffusion without considering the systemic features of innovation. Technological interdependencies are just as important as economic interdependencies and have to be considered together in their interaction. Moreover, some technologies are so pervasive and have such powerful 'lock-in' effects and scale economies that they dominate the behaviour of the entire global economy for considerable periods. Chapters 4, 5 and 6 argue that an evolutionary theory of economic growth must pay special attention to the origin, development and diffusion of such dominant technology systems. They make clear my debt to Carlota Perez with her highly original theory of changes of 'techno-economic paradigm'.

Finally, the chapters in Part III of the book take up the even more fundamental problems of *Limits to Growth*. Together with many colleagues in SPRU I took an active part in the debates in the 1970s on the MIT 'world dynamics' models. Chapters 7 and 8 reflect the intensity of those early debates. Despite the many reasons for pessimism advanced by the MIT modellers and by Heilbroner, we took a more optimistic view of the future of the world. A combination of technical and institutional change could in our view avert the neo-Malthusian catastrophes foreseen by the MIT modellers. Economics need not be the 'dismal science' which Malthus propagated. On the contrary, the economics of technical change still demonstrate the possibility of a bright future for human beings in the twenty-first century, including all those who will inhabit the Third World. Economic theory and economic policy can be and should be the economics of hope.

In editing the volume for publication minor changes have been made to the original papers. These are largely confined to the avoidance of repetition, consistency of publishing conventions and clarification of language.

Finally, I should like to thank especially Susan Lees without whose help in a thousand ways it would have been impossible to complete this book.

Chris Freeman

List of abbreviations

CAD	computer-aided design
CBI	Confederation of British Industry
CIM	computer-integrated manufacturing
CNC	computer numeric control
EC	European Community
EITB	Engineering Industry Training Board
ERA	engineering research association
FAST	future applications of science and technology
FMS	flexible manufacturing system
GNP	gross national product
ICT	information and communication technology
ILO	International Labour Office
IMF	International Monetary Fund
IT	information technology
JIT	just in time
MERIT	Maastricht Economic Research Institute on Innovation and Technology
MIT	Massachusetts Institute of Technology
MNC	multinational company
NASA	National Aeronautics and Space Administration
NC	Numerical control
NEDO	National Economic Development Office
NIC	newly industrialising country
NIESR	National Institute of Economic and Social Research
NSF	National Science Foundation
OECD	Organisation of Economic Co-operation and Development
OPEC	Organisation of Petroleum-Exporting Countries
OTA	Office of Technology Assessment
RA	research association
R&D	research and development
RITE	Research Institute for Innovative Technology for the Earth
S&T	science and technology

SPRU	Science Policy Research Unit
STINFO	Scientific and Technological Information Services
STP	science and technology policy
STS	scientific and technical services
TA	technology assessment
TEP	techno-economic paradigm
TNO	Netherlands Technological Development Organisation
TRE	Telecommunications and Radar Establishment
UN	United Nations
UNEP	United Nations Environmental Programme
VAN	Value-added network
VLSI	very large scale integration

Part I
Policies for allocation of resources to scientific and technical activities

1 Bernal and the 'social function of science'

This chapter discusses Bernal's seminal book *The Social Function of Science* (1939). It was seminal in the full meaning of the word: it gave rise not only to many new ideas in the social sciences and a new subject—the 'social studies of science', but also to new policies and indirectly to many new institutions both inside and outside government. To go through the contents list at the beginning of the book is to draw up the agenda of most of the debates on policies for science and technology since the Second World War.

Although much of the detailed discussion is of course now dated and of interest mainly to historians, the issues which the book raises are still the fundamental issues half a century later. The main reason for this is that Bernal was the first to see 'science' clearly as a social subsystem, to attempt to define and measure its boundaries, to assess the problems of managing and planning the subsystem as a whole, and to relate all this to the wider social system in its historical development and possible future.

This was an ambitious objective and it is not surprising that the book is open to criticism on many points of detail, as well as on major judgements of contemporary and future social developments. Nevertheless it remains an outstanding original intellectual achievement and perhaps Bernal's greatest single contribution to our understanding of the contemporary world. Its quality was widely recognised at the time of publication (1939) and was never confined to Marxist circles, although the response was most enthusiastic there.

This chapter represents a personal evaluation of Bernal's book (and other closely related work) rather than the account of an historian or a definitive biographical study. For this reason it begins and ends with personal comments on the *Social Function of Science*. In the introductory remarks I try to convey the central message of the book and its significance for the social sciences as it appeared at the time and in retrospect. I then follow Bernal's subdivision of his book into two parts: 'What science does' and 'What science could do'. These sections attempt to demonstrate Bernal's achievement in rather more detail in the light of subsequent developments in the theory and practice of science policy.

The discussion of 'What science could do' leads inevitably to the fundamental political problems of the 'planning of science' which aroused intense controversy at the time of the book's first appearance and have continued to do so ever since. In the fourth section of the chapter I attempt to relate this controversy to subsequent debates on the freedom of science and civil liberty more generally. In this endeavour I do not subscribe to the view that there was more than one Bernal, nor to the more widely held view that there is more than one science.

This entails finally some attempt to put the *Social Function of Science* in the context of his life and work as a whole and in particular its relationship to its brilliant forerunner, *The World, the Flesh and the Devil* (1929). Even if there was only one Bernal and even if (as I believe) there was a fundamental consistency in the pattern of his life, he constantly responded to new developments in science and in society. The direction in which he modified his views is therefore of importance not as a demonstration of a split personality, but as the learning process of an outstanding scientist striving to implement his youthful ideal in a complex and changing world.

As a student at the London School of Economics I was fortunate enough to hear Bernal lecture several times before, during and after the Second World War on the *Social Function of Science* and related topics. These lectures were not part of the regular curriculum; they were events organised by various student societies. Nevertheless, I learnt more from them than from any lectures in the regular curriculum with the exception of some by Harold Laski.

One lecture in particular stands out in my mind. It was in 1947 and as an ex-service student I was dissatisfied with much of the regular economics curriculum which seemed to me and most of my fellow students to be even more remote from the real world than when I started economics in the 1930s. Keynesian economics was still only grudgingly accepted and even young lecturers such as Kaldor, who taught the full range of economic theory brilliantly, scarcely mentioned 'research and development'. It was therefore extraordinarily refreshing to hear Bernal talk about the role of scientific research in the economy and in war from firsthand knowledge of government, the armed forces and industry.

Even more stimulating was his discussion of the future role of scientific research in the civil economy. It was from Bernal and not from any economist that I first learnt about the concept of 'research intensity'—a measure of the relative scale of resources committed to R&D by different industries and different firms. In his lecture Bernal described the differences between the 'research-intensive' industries such as electronics and chemicals for whom new product development was an accepted part of firm behaviour and other industries which had not yet internalised the functions of research, invention and development. It was an elaboration of Chapter 6 of the *Social Function of Science* based on the new developments during the war.

His picture of the growth of industries and the competitive behaviour of firms made far more sense to me than any of the orthodox models of perfect competition which were the staple diet of undergraduate economics students at that time. Only in our courses on economic history and the history of economic thought did we get some notion of a more dynamic and realistic picture of the rise and decline of industries and firms related to the progress of science and invention. These ideas were of course not original to Bernal—they were the central theme of Schumpeter's (1912 and 1943) model of economic development and of the Marxist model from which this was derived.

However, Bernal went beyond Schumpeter and Marx in his perception of the extent to which the R&D function had become professionalised and internalised within both industry and government. It was this theme which was the organising principle of the *Social Function of Science* and enabled him to describe, measure and criticise the social subsystem of science and technology. In Marx's time this specialisation and professionalisation of the science subsystem had hardly begun and even for Schumpeter before the First World War research and invention were still largely exogenous to the firm. By the 1920s, however, the 'invention of a method of invention', as Whitehead called the R&D laboratory, was generating a 'research revolution'.

Bernal's principal contribution to economics and to the other social sciences was his clear perception that the allocation of resources to the various branches of organised R&D and related scientific and technical services and their efficient management had become crucial for the development and performance of nations and enterprises in war and peace alike. Around this central idea he was able to build up a critical analysis of the use and misuse of science and technology in Britain and in other countries and thereby to establish 'science policy' and 'technology policy' as an important issue of public debate and government intervention.

'What science does'

A quarter of a century after the publication of *The Social Function of Science* a group of his admirers published a set of essays under the title *The Science of Science* to commemorate Bernal's achievement (Goldsmith and Mackay, 1965). They also set up the 'Science of Science Foundation' to attempt to continue his work. So far as I am aware, Bernal rarely if ever used the expression 'science of science' in connection with his own work, although it had already been used in connection with other social studies of science.

Personally I am unhappy with the expression, although this is partly a simple question of semantics. The Anglo-Saxon usage of 'science' to mean 'natural science' is so ingrained that the legitimate claims of the social sciences to be included (as they are in the continental conception of

Wissenschaft or *Nauk*) have never made much headway. In the English language 'social studies of science' is still a far more intelligible description of what Bernal was about than 'science of science'. (Presumably the Science of Science Foundation itself took the same view as the name was soon changed to Science Policy Foundation.)

Perhaps it was the fragmentation of the social sciences which prevented social scientists from attempting to do what Bernal did in his book—to analyse how the science subsystem actually worked in contemporary society. Or perhaps, as Jewkes (1958) suggested when he came to study 'the sources of invention' twenty years later, they were put off by the seemingly intractable measurement problems. Or as he again suggested, they may have thought that their other preoccupations were more urgent. A physicist or a biologist might be less bogged down by the traditional preoccupations of social science disciplines and bolder in charting a new course.

Bernal certainly made errors in economics and in politics. He had the physicist's determination to understand the behaviour of the system as a whole and to build order from a complex mass of detail by generating simplified fundamental laws and abstract models as a first approximation of the system's behaviour. He remained throughout his life first and foremost a natural scientist, although in relation to social systems this was a strength rather than a weakness, for whereas many social scientists never saw the wood for the trees, Bernal did see more clearly than any of them some features of social change which they largely or completely ignored. It also led him into some very big errors of judgement about the system's behaviour.

Whatever the reason or combination of reasons it was in fact a zoologist (Julian Huxley) and a physicist (Bernal) and not economists or sociologists who made the first attempts to measure the scale of resources committed to scientific research in Britain in the 1930s, to examine the sources of financial support and to point out the political, social and economic implications of the pattern which emerged from this analysis. Bernal produced one of the first good maps of science as a social system and the first good guidebook too.

Before Huxley and Bernal of course it was not a blank sheet of paper. Many little pieces of information existed and parts of the map had been drawn. The situation was rather like maps of the world in the fifteenth century. Bernal's achievement was to establish a global perspective, to put the continents more or less in the right places and to give some valuable advice about the problems of navigation. As he knew only too well, much of his detail was inaccurate, being based on incomplete survey data and in some areas on unreliable observations. He did not have the resources of a national or an international organisation to commission full-scale survey work. Nor was he able to resolve the definitional problems which abound in the field. Nevertheless he made remarkably good use of the sources at his

disposal and used intelligent guesswork to fill in some of the gaps.
After reviewing the available statistics he remarked:

From what has already been said it can be seen that the difficulties in assessing the precise sum annually expended on scientific research are practically insurmountable.... It could only be done by changing the method of accounting of Universities, Government Departments and industrial firms.... Nevertheless it is necessary to obtain some idea, however rough, inside which expenditure on research is likely to lie, in order to see the position of research in the national economy'. (Bernal, 1939, p.62).

The estimate he came up with was that in 1934 Britain was spending about £4 million on scientific research. His upper limit which he called 'gross' was £6.7 million and included applied research, and in some cases routine testing work. Definitions differed between government and industry. His lower limit which he called 'net' was £1.9 million and corresponded fairly well to what would now be termed 'fundamental research'. He estimated that his figure of £4 million was about 0.1 per cent of the national income at that time (then being estimated unofficially by almost equally amateurish techniques). Comparing this with what was known about research in the United States and the Soviet Union he came to the conclusion that both of these countries were spending a significantly higher fraction of their national income on scientific research than Britain—0.6 per cent in the case of the United States and 0.8 per cent in the Soviet Union (1939, p.65).

It was not until nearly twenty years after Bernal's original work that the first official survey of research and development expenditure was undertaken by the British government in 1955–56. A few years earlier the National Science Foundation had initiated annual R&D surveys in the United States. Since the 1950s almost all industrialised countries have adopted R&D surveys as part of their regular statistical procedures and many developing countries have done so too, so that the type of statistics which Bernal pioneered in the 1930s have now become an almost routine business in most parts of the world. The OECD has acted as a focus for standardisation of definitions and international comparisons (OECD, 1963).

The major difference between Bernal's work and that of the OECD surveys lies in the approach to development (now more precisely described as experimental development). Bernal did not use the expression 'R&D' in the *Social Function of Science* and nor did other scientists at that time. Even in the very incomplete surveys in British industry in the 1930s information was collected about 'industrial research' or 'scientific research' and 'development' was not mentioned. This was still true even in the early post-war surveys. Bernal's estimates therefore should be regarded as estimates of R rather than of R&D. The definitions were imprecise in any case, so it is impossible to know the degree of underestimation if we are thinking of R&D on contemporary definitions. Probably D in the 1930s was about twice as big as R so that Bernal's figures would have to be trebled to make them comparable with current R&D survey data.

The same point affects Bernal's international comparisons. The US industrial surveys of the 1920s and 1930s were more complete than the British and took more account of D. The combined R&D Department was more characteristic of US industrial practice and the expenditure figures available in firms reflected this. The Soviet surveys were even more comprehensive and included many scientific and technical services (STS) as well as R&D, such as geophysical exploration, project design and feasibility studies, scientific information services and so forth. The Soviet Union led the world in measurement of all these activities although any reliable international comparison would have to take account of these differences in the scope of measurements. Thus a closer approximation to the 'true' comparable figures of R&D as a fraction of national income would probably be 0.3 to 0.4 per cent in 1934 in the United Kingdom, 0.6 to 0.7 per cent in the United States in the same year, and 0.2 to 0.3 per cent in the early 1930s in the Soviet Union rising to 0.4 to 0.5 per cent by the late 1930s.

Bernal's 'upper' estimate for Britain probably included all R, a little D, and some miscellaneous STS, while his 'central' estimate was fairly near the mark for R alone. His figures for university research and government research were more reliable than those for industry where he had to rely on very sketchy and incomplete data.

It might be tempting to infer that Bernal shared the disdain for technology or development which is often supposed to be a characteristic of British university scientists. However, this would be remote from the truth. Although it is true that he does quote from Huxley's earlier report which uses the expression 'mere development', Bernal was aware both of the importance and the difficulties of development. He always insisted strongly on the importance of the interactions between science and technology in the historical development of science, and he was of course intimately involved in development work and applications research during the Second World War. The exclusion of D from his measurement system was a largely pragmatic issue.

However, it probably would be true to say that he always regarded basic research as the heart of the whole science–technology system and that he saw the advance of fundamental science as the most dynamic element. After discussing the limitations of incremental rule of thumb improvements in traditional techniques he goes on to remark:

The most complete integration of industry and science is, however, only reached when the knowledge of the fundamental nature of the processes is so extensive that it is able to lead to the development of entirely new processes unthought of, or indeed unthinkable, by traditional methods; as for example in the chemical synthesis of new dye-stuffs or specific drugs. The same result follows even more directly when a purely scientific discovery of a new effect is turned to some industrial use as, for instance, in the telegraph or the electric light. In these cases, we have an industry scientific through and through, an industry which owes its inception as well as its development to science. (Bernal, 1939, p.129)

Bernal's vision of the future was that this tendency towards industries which were 'scientific through and through' would predominate but would only reach its ultimate fruition in a socialist world. Much of Part I of the *Social Function of Science* is concerned with demonstrating the inadequacies and shortcomings of the organisation and management of science in a capitalist society. Two of his most telling points are as important today as they were when he wrote: the diversion of a great deal of scientific and technical effort into armaments development and production, and the tendency for industrial R&D to achieve much better results in capital goods than in consumer goods and services.

Bernal's indictment of the failings of science policy in the 1930s thus comprised three main elements: first, the inadequate scale of resources for research and other scientific activities, second, the misdirection of those resources which were available, and third, the inefficient use of the resources committed. Much has changed with respect to the first point since he wrote his book both in the capitalist world and the former socialist world. The period from 1940 to 1970 was one of extremely rapid growth in the R&D system and in other STS. A part of this change must be credited to the influence of Bernal in both Britain and elsewhere.

The second and third problems remain the focus of intense debate and controversy and many of the issues of misallocation and inefficiency which Bernal identified are still very much with us today. In particular the problem of a satisfactory scale, direction and effectiveness of consumer-oriented R&D is more crucial than ever and the related problem of military R&D is far more serious and far larger in scale than it was even in the 1930s.

The socialist countries were unable to improve matters much in either of these areas and were unable to fulfil Bernal's hopes that the planned use of science and technology for social welfare would enable these societies to advance much more rapidly than the capitalist countries. Bernal did not discuss the limitations and problems of science and technology policy in the socialist world. He had an idealised vision of 'What science could do' which has not necessarily been falsified by the experience of the last fifty years, although obviously requiring much re-examination and debate. As a result of Bernal's work and the subsequent developments there is fairly widespread agreement now on 'What science does' but there is even greater controversy on 'What science could do', to which I now turn.

'What science could do'

The first part of Bernal's book was analytical and descriptive, the second was mainly prescriptive. Having measured roughly the scale of resources committed to scientific research, their approximate distribution in terms of objectives and sector of performance and the inefficiency of the system as he saw it, he went on to propose a series of radical changes and reforms which he believed would enable science to fulfil its true potential for human welfare.

This method of tackling the subject was entirely characteristic of Bernal. He insisted always, both in this book and in all his other work, on the importance of the social implications and applications of any branch of knowledge. He believed profoundly that the interactions between science and the economy were mutually beneficial and his main criticism of contemporary social science was that it was too much of an abstract 'spectator' subject and did not participate sufficiently in policy-making and real-world testing.

It was equally characteristic of Bernal that he never took up the sterile position that nothing could be done in a capitalist society. Although he argued in 'What science could do' that most of the reforms and changes which he proposed depended upon a socialist transformation of society, this did not stop him from advocating a great many reforms and improvements straightaway. Whether he was looking at air raid precautions or building technology or policies for fundamental research, he was always ready to make constructive practical proposals for immediate action as well as fundamental criticisms and proposals for long-term structural change.

Unlike Keynes he was always a committed socialist, although like Keynes he was ready to offer advice to governments and various political parties and even to work for governments both in official and unofficial capacities. Like Keynes of course he was often *persona non grata*; however, especially during the war he was very much *persona grata*. For this reason many aspects of the programme of reform which Bernal proposed in the second part of the *Social Function of Science* have had an appeal not only to Marxists but also to many others who shared his concern for using science more effectively for human welfare, although they did not agree with him that the Soviet Union represented a good model for such policies, or even that socialist planning of the economy was desirable at all.

The first major point which Bernal makes in the second part of his book is that there is a need for a massive increase in the scale of commitment of resources to research and other scientific activities. At the time it appeared an incredibly bold proposal to suggest that support for research should be increased by an order of magnitude (tenfold), as he himself acknowledged (Bernal, 1939, p.242).

Nevertheless, such an increase was in fact achieved over the next twenty-five years, both in Britain and a good many other countries. As we have seen, Bernal overestimated the scale of Soviet R&D in the mid-1930s, and as part of his justification for a tenfold increase in British research he argued that the Soviet Union was already spending 1 per cent of national income, whereas Britain, according to his estimate, was spending only 0.1 per cent. Consequently he maintained that there was already a precedent for the scale of commitment he was proposing.

Although he was wrong about the precise figures and understandably did not resolve the problems of international comparability of definitions, he was right about two fundamental points. It *was* possible to expand the scale of R&D at approximately the rate he suggested for a considerable period and this was already happening in the 1930s in the Soviet Union. Other countries did indeed follow the Soviet example in this respect, in the first place because of the impetus of the Second World War, and later on a more sustained basis in the 1950s and 1960s, largely because the kind of arguments which Bernal evoked in the 1930s carried widespread conviction far beyond Marxist or socialist circles.

As a result of this rapid and sustained expansion the leading industrial countries were spending about 2–3 per cent of national income on R&D by the end of the 1960s, and on a comparable basis the Soviet Union was spending 3–4 per cent of national income. Typically about a quarter or a third of this total was R and the remainder was D. In Bernal's terms, therefore, R had increased from his estimate of about 0.1 per cent of national income to about 0.7 per cent in the United Kingdom in the 1960s, whilst combined R&D had increased from about 0.3 per cent to about 2.3 per cent of a much larger national income. In Britain national income had doubled in this period and elsewhere it had grown even more. In absolute terms, therefore, the increase over twenty-five years may have been rather more than tenfold.

Since the 1960s the rate of increase has slowed down substantially and even gone into reverse for some years, especially in the United Kingdom. Bernal expressed alarm when this tendency first became apparent and described the arguments then advanced for zero growth in the Science Budget as 'voluntary underdevelopment'. He continued to believe that still further expansion of scientific activities was desirable throughout the world and at an especially high rate in the developing countries. In *World Without War* (1958) he visualised a long-term change in the distribution of employment over the next century in which scientific and technical occupations would come to employ about a third of the total labour force. Many of these would be in STS and only a minority in R&D. Nevertheless in Bernal's view it would be desirable to expand R&D well beyond the 2–3 per cent fraction of national income which had been realised during his own lifetime and of which he had been the principal prophet and instigator. Long before Daniel Bell (1973) and other apostles of the 'information revolution', Bernal had recognised the probable future evolution of occupational structure in advanced industrial societies and had projected the probable decline of manufacturing employment to a level comparable to that of agriculture in these societies today.

However, although the tenfold expansion of research which Bernal proposed was realised within a period not much longer than that which he projected, neither in Britain nor in the Soviet Union, nor in any other countries did the consequences of this expansion quite live up to his expectations and hopes. He had believed that there would be a very high rate of return to the massive increase in R&D which he advocated, i.e. that national income would grow more rapidly and that other welfare benefits would accrue, not necessarily measured in national income statistics.

Of course, he would have certainly agreed, there were many other factors affecting the growth of national income as well as the increased scale of investment in research, development and other scientific activities. Nevertheless, during the 1950s and 1960s the evidence of empirical research by both economists and engineers increasingly favoured Bernal's view that technical change associated with professionalised scientific and technical activities is the single most important element in the complex process of economic growth.

So far as R&D is concerned this is not quite so straightforward as it might seem. Clearly rapid growth is quite possible simply on the basis of the diffusion of existing best-practice techniques. The differences in productivity between 'best-practice' and 'worst-practice' enterprises are so great that a doubling of national income would be feasible anywhere without completely new knowledge. Moreover, it is also true that a very important part of the technical improvements which are continually introduced into production do not depend on formalised professional research or even on R&D: they result directly from the activities of workers and engineers more directly concerned with production. Although these considerations are especially relevant to the circumstances of developing countries with very limited scientific resources, they are important everywhere. In practice it has proved possible for a good many countries to achieve high growth rates of national income with a quite low fraction of that national income devoted to professional R&D, even as low as 0.1 to 0.3 per cent.

When growth is based to a considerable extent on the assimilation of best-practice techniques first developed elsewhere in the world (and this must be true of most technical change almost everywhere), then local R&D may still be very important as the experience of Japan and South Korea has shown, since it enables the adaptation and improvement of imported technology to be carried through with maximum efficiency. Moreover, as a country industrialises and catches up with best-practice techniques, it will increasingly face the need to make original contributions to industrial R&D if it is competing in international trade. Consequently the fact that other countries have achieved higher growth rates with a much lower commitment to R&D than Britain since the Second World War certainly cannot be taken as invalidating Bernal's arguments for a massive increase from the pre-war level of British R&D. Most of those countries successfully competing on a significant scale in world trade in manufactured goods (as opposed to oil or primary commodities) now spend a higher fraction of industrial net output on non-military R&D than Britain.

However, these considerations do serve to emphasise some aspects of the 'returns to R&D investment' problem which were rather neglected in the *Social Function of Science*. Bernal recognised of course that the dissemination of scientific and technical knowledge was extraordinarily important. There is very great emphasis throughout his book both on education and on what is now called STINFO (scientific and technical information services). Some of the best chapters are concerned with reforms in science education, the science curriculum, and scientific publication and documentation. Moreover, he went further than most contemporary reformers in his proposals for popularisation of science and technology on an enormous scale. He cannot therefore be charged with any failure to appreciate these aspects of the problem of widespread introduction of technical change. Where he was perhaps open to criticism was in the neglect of other complementary aspects of the process which are embraced in the concept of STS, although not the narrower concept of R&D, still less in R by itself.

In particular the *Social Function of Science* has little or nothing to say about some aspects of engineering and investment which are extremely important both for the effective implementation of much R&D work and for the efficient adaptation and exploitation of imported technology. Even fifty years after Bernal we are still very far from measuring (or even satisfactorily defining) the full range of STS, although we have made some progress with R&D measurement, thanks largely to his original impulse. However, we do know enough about STS as a result of the work of Martin Bell (1985) and others to accept that 'project engineering' activities, design engineering, production engineering and similar functions are extraordinarily important complementary activities in efficient technical change. A fuller understanding of the efficient management of technical change will have to embrace the entire range of STS and not only those on which Bernal concentrated in his pioneering work.

This leads on to a wider consideration of 'What science could do'. Whereas Bernal has been at least partly vindicated in his belief in the importance of a massive increase in research and research-related activities for the future growth of national income, neither the extent of the increase nor its composition and distribution have been satisfactory. I do not share the view that the improvement in living standards in Britain since the war is trivial or unimportant. On the contrary, even though it was less than that achieved in most other European countries, and even though its fruits have been unevenly distributed, I do believe that it was a very important social gain just as it was in other countries in both Eastern and Western Europe.

However, the returns to the vastly increased investment in R&D and other scientific and technical activities have been less than Bernal had hoped for and have been a source of disappointment to many others including those who shared his political ideals and those who did not. The simple explanation of this disappointment is of course that whilst the *scale* of R&D was increased in the way which he suggested, the fundamental social changes which he advocated and believed to be essential to realise the full benefits of the increased scale of research have not been made. However, in the Soviet Union and other socialist countries which increased their commitment to research and related activities on an even greater scale than Britain, and which also implemented many of the other reforms and changes which Bernal suggested, there was still greater disappointment with the results. The plain fact is that in the 1970s growth rates for national income declined in *both* Eastern and Western Europe and that this decline in growth rates occured *after* the most massive expansion in scientific and technical activities which the world has ever known. Moreover, it is also the case that the bias in technical change in the direction of capital goods and materials, rather than consumer goods and services, has persisted world-wide.

Socialists, including Bernal, would have no difficulty in explaining the situation in capitalist economies. They would argue, as Bernal did in the 1930s, that the decline in growth rates, or the absolute fall in output which then occurred, was a failure of the economic system which could not make satisfactory use of the fruits of science and technology. The decline in the rate of growth in many of the socialist countries and their failure to surpass the growth rate of many capitalist countries in the 1960s are more difficult phenomena to explain in Bernalian terms. A satisfactory explanation would have to include *either* a much more fundamental critique of social, economic and scientific systems of the Soviet Union than Bernal was willing to make in the 1930s, *or* a hypothesis of diminishing returns to R&D investment, at least temporarily both in capitalist and in socialist economies, possibly based on a theory of change in 'technological paradigms' as suggested by Carlota Perez (1983).

Such a phenomenon of diminishing returns is of course quite consistent with strong emphasis on the two other major aspects of Bernal's programme stressed in 'What science could do' dealing respectively with the misallocation of scientific resources and the inefficient use of those resources even where appropriately allocated. Whilst the scale of total resource commitment has increased much as he advocated, the major misallocations which he identified have not been rectified and may even have worsened, and the inefficiencies which he identified may well have persisted despite some attempts to improve matters.

The greatest single misallocation of resources which Bernal identified was of course the diversion of scientific and technical effort into military R&D. Although the scale of this misallocation vastly increased since the 1930s both in Britain and in the Soviet Union and the United States, the proportion of total scientific activities devoted to military objectives may not be so very different now as then—perhaps about one-third of total R&D. There were periods during and after the Second World War when this proportion was even higher—probably more than a half at one time in all three countries, and it seems likely that it remained well over half in the Soviet Union. However this may be, the enormous waste of resources is even more evident today than it was in Bernal's time. He himself returned to this theme again and again after the Second World War, most notably in *World Without War* (1958), in which he argued cogently that the most straightforward way to increase rapidly the scientific resources available for global development was through world disarmament and the reallocation of military R&D resources.

From time to time voices have been raised in support of the 'spin-off' hypothesis—that the civil economy benefits to a great extent from the technical advances won through military R&D. None the less, the weight of the evidence supports the view that the effect of spin-off is slight, that by far the greater part of military R&D has little or no civil application, and that in so far as there is any genuine spin-off, this is an extraordinarily inefficient way to make technical progress, quite apart from all the other overwhelming arguments about the dangers of a technological arms race. A particularly alarming feature of the present massive misallocation of global R&D resources is the tendency for a growing number of poor developing countries to invest a high proportion of their extremely limited scientific resources in military areas.

Those who naively imagine that this process may ultimately enhance their economic performance should contemplate the experience of Britain and also that of the United States and the Soviet Union. The evidence is now very strong that the opportunity cost of the diversion of a high proportion of the best *industrial* scientific and engineering talent into military projects in the 1950s was quite unacceptably high. The two strongest countries in world trade in manufactures since the Second World War, West Germany and Japan, did not suffer from this disability. They were able to concentrate their scientific and technical efforts almost entirely on civil objectives until recently and the consequences are there for all to see. In those industries which really matter for international competition, such as vehicles, engineering and chemicals, they have outstripped not only Britain but increasingly also the United States, both in new product design and in productivity. As Pavitt (1980) and Mary Kaldor (1980) have shown, the strength of the United States and Britain in a very limited area of defence-related industries, such as aircraft, has not compensated for this deterioration in competitive power across a much wider range of industries. The same point applies *a fortiori* to the Soviet

Union, although it is perhaps not one which Bernal would have made himself.

Bernal's analysis of this major resource misallocation must therefore be accepted as a large part of the explanation of the relatively disappointing results of the increase in sheer scale of R&D, particularly so far as Britain is concerned. Other types of misallocation identified in the *Social Function of Science* pale into insignificance by comparison with the military R&D problem, although undoubtedly some of them have also continued to be important. Among these are the greater effort put into consumer goods R&D compared with capital goods, the relative neglect of the life sciences and the social sciences compared with physics and chemistry, and the substantial effort devoted to product differentiation in industrial R&D as opposed to more fundamental technical advance.

Planning and science

The central argument of 'What science could do' is not merely one of gross under-investment in science and technology, and serious misallocation of resources. It is also the more fundamental one that these deficiencies, together with many other sources of inefficiency in the system, really require some form of socialist planning to rectify. It was this argument which provoked the main attack on Bernal both at the time and since, on the grounds that planning would destroy freedom and would be even more inefficient. Since the *Social Function of Science* was published in 1939 the crude anti-planning standpoint has lost ground, although it remains a very important influence. However, the view which identifies socialist science planning with authoritarian orthodoxy and bureaucratic repression has made considerable headway not because of anything in the *Social Function of Science*, but because of events since that time especially the Lysenko controversy and its aftermath.

Hardly any government in the world, whatever its formal ideological complexion, has accepted the simple view of abdicating central government responsibility for science and technology and leaving these areas to the free play of market forces to determine resource allocation and scale for the simple reason that even the most extreme advocates of the virtues of the free market have recognised that according to the pure principles of a *laissez-faire* world there has to be public investment in basic science, science education and scientific and technical information systems. Most of those classical and neo-classical economists who have examined the issues at all closely, from Adam Smith to Kenneth Arrow, would add to this list various other parts of the science–technology system, such as the promotion of new technologies, technical advisory services in agriculture and other branches of the economy, military-related aspects of science and technology, and so forth.

Even if only the first group of activities is accepted as an area of public responsibility, primarily financed from central government funds (as it is in almost every country in the world), then there is already major government involvement, which requires some form of science policy. It is partly a matter of semantics whether this policy is described as 'planning'. Some countries which do not describe their system as a planned one pay much attention to aspects of policy-making and execution normally associated with planning.

When the *Social Function of Science* first appeared it was strongly attacked by J.R. Baker (1945) on the grounds that planning meant the suppression of freedom in science and the regimentation of scientists. Since then the rationalisation and idealisation of 'muddling through' is certainly one of the continuing sources of opposition to 'planning' in both theory and practice. However, a more sophisticated theoretical justification of *laissez-faire* in science was developed as part of the critique of Bernal, especially by Polanyi (Bernal and Polanyi, 1949).

In his article on the 'Republic of science' in the very first issue of the journal *Minerva*, Michael Polanyi (1962) attempted to develop a doctrine of pure *laissez-faire* in relation to fundamental scientific research. He did this by making a direct analogy between a pure competitive economy and the fundamental research system. Just as the individual entrepreneurs were the only ones qualified to respond to market signals of price and demand, so, Polanyi argued, only the scientists directly involved had the specialised expertise to make decisions about a particular field of science. Unfortunately for Polanyi and his supporters there were three fundamental flaws in this argument in so far as it was designed to limit government participation in science or exclude it altogether.

The first and most important flaw was that Polanyi himself (and everyone else concerned in the argument) conceded at the outset that government must provide most or all of the money for fundamental research, however it might subsequently be distributed. This inevitably means that somehow or other government must develop a policy on the total budget for science and its growth (or reduction), just as Bernal had insisted. This was and still is often an unwelcome responsibility for some governments and one which they usually attempt to devolve to various scientific advisory bodies, although few have been able to escape it altogether.

The second basic difficulty with the Polanyi approach is that unlike the market economy, where the criterion of profitability can at least superficially be applied to every form of activity, quite irrespective of the actual products or services, the criterion of scientific merit has no such interchangeable recognition. Polanyi may well be right (and Bernal thought so too) that the specialists in a particular field of high energy physics may be the only ones competent to decide on the relative merits of alternative research projects in that field, and the same goes for any other specialised branch of science. Nevertheless, there is absolutely no reason to expect that the specialists in high energy physics can decide on the relative merits of competing claims in, say, cell biology, geophysics, medieval history and colloidal chemistry. In fact, the contrary is the case on Polanyi's own theoretical arguments. This means that the Polanyi model breaks down at the most important level—the subdivision of a global budget between various disciplines and subdisciplines. As long as the total science budget was both small and steadily expanding this was not too serious, and the Polanyi 'autonomy of science' system appeared to work. However, once budgets became large and more seriously constrained, this problem became much more acute and is a critical one in all science policy bodies today, irrespective of whether they talk about planning or not.

Moreover, the problem has become greatly accentuated by the development of 'big science'—areas of investigation where the capital cost of instrumentation or other types of equipment has become so high that it may pre-empt a large part of the total funds available for science. The extreme example is space exploration, although there are many other cases where the issue is very important: accelerators and telescopes are two obvious ones. This problem may be partly circumvented by separating these decisions and funding them under separate budget headings, for example, National Aeronautics and Space Administration (NASA) or military or nuclear power budgets. This is only a pseudo-solution, however, since the development of science is then affected by many different budget decisions and co-ordination or some form of mutual consultation becomes necessary.

Finally, a third difficulty is that government participation inevitably includes not only responsibility for the total level of funding of science (and some areas of technology) and for the principal subdivisions within that total, but also for the 'health' or 'efficiency' of substantial parts of that system. Even under highly decentralised management systems such as the universities this remains true, and it is a much more direct responsibility in the case of government laboratories, research stations, libraries, patent offices and the like.

In the 1930s even the idea of 'science policy' was still unfamiliar and the notion of a long-term plan for science was regarded as far-fetched and Utopian. As with the Keynesian heresy in economics, with which Bernal's ideas have many parallels, it was the Second World War which made possible the more widespread acceptance of the notion of explicit overall central government responsibility for the healthy development of science and technology as for a healthy state of employment, investment and growth in the economy more generally. Partly for this reason Baker's initial attack was never very effective and its revival by Polanyi after the war was hardly more successful.

If the area of public responsibility is more widely defined (and in almost every country central governments are as a matter of fact involved much more widely), then government policy extends to technology policy as well as science policy more narrowly conceived as policy for fundamental research. In these areas too, it is much easier to point to the shortcomings and inconsistencies of government policies or 'plans' (when they are described as such), than it is to destroy the argument for some degree of government responsibility. Even if 'planning' is regarded with great distaste and reluctance as an inevitable residual obligation, in practice it has been found difficult to dodge the responsibility entirely. This means of course that as Bernal insisted, the job is often done half-heartedly and incompetently.

This can be confirmed by simply examining the history of public administrative and legislative activity in the United States or any other industrialised society during and since the Second World War. There has been a bewildering succession of different committees, councils, centres, departments and administrations; but the underlying trend has clearly been towards a more extended participation not only in the funding of basic science through the National Science Foundation, but also in many other directions. The disavowal by the Rothschild Report (1971) of any central system of priorities for science or technology in Britain was accompanied by a substantial increase in departmental 'planning' of science and technology and the re-entry of *de facto* central priorities by the back door.

All of these problems were clearly recognised by Bernal in the 1930s, and it is hardly surprising that in subsequent issues of the journal *Minerva* and elsewhere the Polanyi school had distinctly the worst of the argument. They really did not have a leg to stand on and could only score points by pointing to the inefficiency and incompetence of government policy-making and planning. Here they were on stronger ground, for progress in developing a more efficient way of managing the science–technology system has not been conspicuous since 1939, whether under socialist 'planned' systems or others.

Thus, although since the *Social Function of Science* government responsibility for scientific activities has been greatly extended in both scale and range, it remains true that many of the sources of inefficiency identified by Bernal are still evident. Some of these relate to the management and planning of work in individual institutions, others to the co-ordination of groups of institutions and their joint action, and finally some relate to the management, co-ordination and planning of the entire system or network of institutions.

It is by no means the case that when he identified the sources of inefficiency, waste and misallocation in British science in the 1930s, Bernal confined his strictures to the influence of the market or its failings. On the contrary he stressed very strongly bureaucratic government mismanagement and waste, as well as the deficiencies of the private market system.

He was particularly insistent that the whole style of work in government laboratories was often inimical to creative work and emerged as an early and extreme advocate of what would now be called 'flexi-time':

The special difficulties which beset scientific research carried out under government control are largely due to bureaucratic methods. Civil service and army methods of administration are essentially unsuitable for the carrying out of research. Research is always an exploration of the unknown, and its value is not to be measured by the amount of time spent on it but by the output of new ideas thought of and tested out. Regularity of hours or days, clocking in and clocking out, with an annual fortnight's holiday, is not conducive to original thought. The work of a scientist requires the most irregular hours. Sometimes it may be a matter of wanting to work sixteen or twenty-four hours a day for weeks on end; at others all the time spent in the laboratory is useless and the best results would come from going to parties or climbing a mountain. (Bernal, 1939, p.106)

He also realised clearly the dangers of an authoritarian or autocratic style of management both at the laboratory level and higher up. All the post-war discussion among sociologists about the most efficient way to manage laboratories and the empirical investigations of management techniques have served only to confirm the conclusions which he reached. He pointed out that:

We have to balance, as in all political affairs, the dangers of arbitrary or incompetent action of a single individual against the possible lack of unity, inconsistency and general obstructiveness of any corporate body. According to the temperament and abilities of the people available for the work at any particular time or place, one or the other method may be the more suitable. In a scientific laboratory an individual, who with his guiding ideas markedly leads the way, will be willingly chosen as a personal director; in other cases it may be a small group who combine in a harmonious way a set of ideas which they can realise effectively only by working in close collaboration. (Bernal, 1939, p.268)

Whether the responsibilities of the director were exercised by an individual (which he thought generally the most effective way) or by a small group, he saw the need to guard against arbitrary power, ageing and incompetence by including the whole staff of an institution in discussion of major issues: 'Any new organisation of science, if it is to be vital as well as effective, must bring with it the democratic principle which will ensure adequate participation in responsible control by scientific workers of every grade of seniority' (Bernal, 1939, p.116).

At higher levels of management and planning he thought the same principle was valid although he recognised the need for some delegation of power and responsibility. However, it is at this level of decision-making that Bernal's analysis becomes more vulnerable and he sometimes underestimates the problems created, both in the political power structure and the content of the decisions themselves. Nevertheless he can hardly be faulted for his clear recognition that some method of determining central government priorities for science and technology must be established, and that there was merit in deliberately debating these priorities and encouraging new initiatives, especially in the areas between established disciplines. The idea of a publicly discussed flexible plan remains the most suitable approach despite our greater awareness of all the pitfalls involved. Even if experience so far suggests that it is much more difficult to eliminate inefficiency and waste and to achieve 'optimal' use of resources than Bernal supposed, through any planning system, this does not destroy his basic argument.

Moreover, the very difficulties which have been encountered in all types of economy surely strengthen his case for public criticism and debate and for not concealing these problems by a conspiracy of silence:

If we try to examine more clearly the inefficiency of science as a method of discovery, we find that it originates in two major defects. The first is the totally inadequate scale of finance . . ., the second is the inefficiency of organisation which ensures that these small resources shall to a large extent be wasted. This last remark may seem to the scientist something approaching treason. Even if it were true it should not be publicly stated, for the little science gets now it gets as the result of the belief in its effectiveness. Once it is suspected that scientists waste the money that is given to them, they will not even be able to get even that much. Yet the gentleman's agreement to gloss over the internal inefficiencies of science is bound to be disastrous in the long run. However carefully concealed such things are, they are always suspected and give rise to an attitude of vague distrust on the part of possible benefactors and the public at large, which is far more damaging to science than openly brought charges. (Bernal, 1939, p.99)

Ironically, since the wasteful misuse of resources reached a much vaster scale in government military and prestige projects, scientists often actually found it easier to acquire more money. Nevertheless, Bernal was right about the long-term damage brought about by this type of situation, whether publicly or privately financed.

Thus in his critique of science under capitalism, he was not simply contrasting 'public' and 'private' and arguing that public operation and responsibility was somehow always better, rather he was contrasting an idealised model of socialist planning with the private and public decision-making of a capitalist or mixed economy. Unfortunately for his case, he chose to identify such an idealised model of socialist planning very largely with the actual workings of the science-technology system in the Soviet Union. This was the most vulnerable part of the whole argument of the *Social Function of Science*, and the remainder of this chapter discusses the reasons for Bernal falling into the trap, if trap it was.

The extent to which Bernal idealised the operations of the Soviet science-technology system can be seen especially clearly in his discussion of the relationship between basic research and industrial technology. Since the Second World War and especially in the 1960s and 1970s much of the internal debate in the Soviet Union was concentrated on the weaknesses of this relationship and the failure to achieve a satisfactory two-way flow between academy (basic research) institutes, industrial research institutes and factory-level development and implementation of technical change. It has been widely recognised both inside and outside the Soviet Union that the organisational separation of the various institutions led to major communication failures and other deep-seated problems in the system, including much duplication and waste of resources. Yet Bernal wrote in the *Social Function of Science*:

From the scientific point of view the research institutions in industry and agriculture are closely linked with the Academy, and the separation which exists in Britain between academic and industrial science is largely non-existent. The idea behind the organisation is that there should be a two-way flow of problems and solutions. The problems of industry put in a precise form by works laboratories are passed on to the technical institutes. In so far as their solution falls within the scope of existing knowledge they are solved there. But if some more fundamental ignorance of the working of nature is revealed, this is passed on to the Academy. Thus industry serves to present science with new and original problems. At the same time any fundamental discoveries made in the universities or the Academy are immediately transmitted to the industrial laboratories so that anything which can be turned to useful purposes may be used in practice as soon as possible. (Bernal, 1939, p.227)

It may be that the system worked rather better in the 1930s, nevertheless the description here contrasts strongly with his greater sense of realism, balance and sophistication in discussing those political and organisational structures with which he was more familiar. The naivety of the phrases: 'the problems of industry put in a precise form' and 'fundamental discoveries . . . are immediately transmitted' is rather surprising for someone who perceived so clearly in his chapter on scientific information and documentation that direct personal contact was the most important form of communication and advocated interchange of people as essential to achieve efficiency and avoid bureaucracy, and who was in general so well aware of the complexity of the science–technology relationship.

One of the reasons that he misjudged the real situation in the Soviet Union may have been that he was inclined to distrust the accounts of more critically-minded colleagues and outright opponents of the Soviet system because of the very large amount of prejudicial comment on Soviet affairs which was characteristic of the inter-war period and which he suspected biased the general view in an anti-Soviet direction. It is important to remember too that the Soviet Union really was the first political system in the world to accord science high priority in its economic policies in a deliberate and systematic way. It was also the first to give the highest priroty to science and technology in its education system, and to promote the growth of the science system and the science education system more rapidly than any backward country had previously ever attempted. It is not surprising that these very positive features of Soviet policy made a considerable impression on Bernal and many other scientists at a time in the 1930s when science was being cut back in many other European countries or mutilated and militarised as in fascist Germany.

Nevertheless, there was clearly something more fundamental in the relative suspension of his critical judgement in relation to Soviet affairs. In part it was a failure which was common to the whole communist movement and sympathisers like the Webbs. Bernal was certainly no more gullible than many others. Even if the general tenor of his remarks about Soviet science in the *Social Function of Science* was rather uncritical, he did point out in an important passage:

.... the great disadvantage is the lack of sufficiently rigid criticism, but this again is to be expected. A critical attitude is the fruit of long experience and well established schools, its absence one of the faults of youthful enthusiasm which only time and experience can correct. A certain part is played here by the long period in which Soviet science was cut off from the rest of the world and the degree to which political, financial and language barriers still cut it off today. It is only by the comparison of the work of a very large number of scientists in different places that a fully critical attitude can be developed. (Bernal, 1939, p.230)

This, together with other passages which have already been quoted, shows that Bernal was certainly not entirely unmindful of the importance of open debate and criticism and restraints on the exercise of political power in any social system. However, he was sufficiently confident that the socialist countries were developing in general on what he regarded as the right lines that he was almost always inclined to give them the benefit of the doubt and to abstain from any public criticism of their shortcomings. It was only after this approach led to the tragic episode of his support for the official Soviet line on Lysenko that he came to realise that there were more fundamental problems than simply those of 'youthful enthusiasm' and maturity.

In addition to the more general political problem of the uncritical approach of part of the Left to the Soviet Union in the 1930s and 1940s, there was clearly a specific reason for Bernal's identification with official Soviet views in this period. After all, both Bertrand Russell and Rosa Luxemburg, both greatly respected figures among left-wing intellectuals, had clearly recognised as early as 1918 the fundamental political problems of the Soviet system: the monopoly concentration of power in the party as opposed to the soviets, trade unions and parliament; the concentration of power within the Central Committee of the party, and the tendency towards an even further concentration of power within a small group or one single individual. Both Russell (1920) and Luxemburg predicted quite clearly that the emergence of an authoritarian 'socialist' orthodoxy was just as inevitable within the confines of the Soviet system as it was in similar political systems of power concentration throughout the ages, whatever the initial ideals and scientific intentions of the founders.

Although Bernal clearly recognised the analogous problem in capitalist countries and in his brilliant indictment of fascism, there was some mental block which prevented him thinking equally clear-headedly about the Soviet Union and later about other socialist countries. The additional peculiarity in Bernal's case was his identification of 'science' with 'socialism' and his readiness to accept one version of Marxism as 'social science'. He idealised science not just as knowledge but in a political sense too, believing that the management of human affairs could also be more scientific by virtue of being 'socialist'. He was thus particularly inclined to accept the claims of Soviet Marxism to represent science in general, and to accord it the same degree of respect. This is a strong claim and it can be substantiated only by considering not just the *Social Function of Science* but also some of his earlier work.

The *Social Function of Science* was not his first book. It was preceded by his extremely daring, imaginative and provocative essay on *The World, the Flesh and the Devil* written ten years earlier and published when he was only 28 years old. This first book is important in giving us an insight into some basic values and ideas which affected his approach to science and society throughout his life. As Bernal himself said forty years later in writing a foreword to the second edition:

This short book was the first I ever wrote. I have a great attachment to it because it contains many of the seeds of ideas which I have been elaborating throughout my scientific life. It still seems to me to have validity in its own right. (Bernal, 1970)

In the final section of this chapter I therefore turn to the consideration of this book in relation to the central weakness of the *Social Function of Science*.

The World, the Flesh and the Devil

Enthusiasm for science is evident throughout Bernal's entire life and work. Sometimes even in the *Social Function of Science* he seems to forget the wider social and political system and subconsciously to identify the interests of 'science' with the interests of society. It is not too much to say that his position sometimes came very close to 'What's good for science is good for the world'. This must be qualified by the recognition that he saw science as the instrument for overcoming poverty and war and promoting welfare on a vast scale.

Many years later in some notes for the Russian novelist Boris Polevoi, Bernal traced his enthusiasm for science to his boyhood in Ireland. When he was only 5 years old, his sister was taken to be X-rayed in the hospital in Limerick 13 miles away. Tremendously impressed by the talk in the family about the X-ray machine he tried to simulate it in his bedroom with a paraffin lamp. Although he did not set the house on fire, the lamp was knocked over and his father gave him 'a very bad beating' which he said he had remembered ever since: 'But it fixed firmly in my mind the determination to find out what those x-rays were and what to do about it.'

When he was 7, he read Faraday's *Chemistry of the Candle* and was excited by the prospect of making oxygen and hydrogen. He succeeded in persuading his mother to write a letter to the local chemist requesting various chemicals for experiments:

My mother, who knew less science than I did, because she had not even read Faraday on *The Chemistry of the Candle* obediently wrote it all down and the chemist handed the stuff over, which of course if he had had any sense, he would not have done, because what he gave me in fact was a small bottle of concentrated sulphuric acid—oil of vitriol—with which I could have done myself and the house very much damage'.

The experiments (conducted just outside the house) ended with a 'magnificent explosion' and Bernal continues:

'I was more frightened than hurt because in fact I kept my hand fairly far away . . . . But I was absolutely convinced of the truth of science. So you see, these two stories together were sufficient to start me off on a scientific career, though it was a difficult career to follow in Ireland, and it was not for many years that I was to learn about the chemical actions of sulphuric acid, and to find that my life's work lay in the use of x-rays for determining crystal structures. Strangely enough I was later to take on Faraday's old job, Assistant at the Royal Intitution in London, and to work in the cellar he worked in.

Psychologists may make of these stories what they will; what is certain, however, is that Bernal's boyhood enthusiasm for science was to continue undiminished throughout his life. The most outstanding characteristic of *The World, the Flesh and the Devil* is the total commitment to science, and the subtitle *The Three Enemies of the Rational Soul* indicates the basic approach of this brilliant essay in futurology. It is also better written and gives the impression of greater spontaneity than anything else that he wrote later.

The extent of his faith in science can best be described as religious devotion. (He comments himself: 'The same type of mind that would now make a physicist would in the Middle Ages have made a scholastic theologian.') This can be seen most of all in those passages in which he looks beyond the short-term problems of scarcity and poverty (which he expected to be overcome at the latest within a few centuries) to the long-term perspectives for the human race. Here he makes clear his own preference for a society of interlinked disembodied minds devoted to the pursuit of research and control of the universe. He accurately foresees space travel and contemplates not merely reaching the stars but using them as 'efficient heat engines'. A characteristic comment is that the 'stars cannot be allowed to continue in their old way'. He is fully prepared to make the ultimate Faustian bargain, although he saw no need for bargaining.

Looking back forty years later he was entitled to some self-congratulation for the way in which he anticipated developments in rockets and space travel, as well as other more mundane developments in synthetic materials and industrial technology. Indeed the prophetic 'technological forecasting' is both bolder and more accurate than that in the *Social Function of Science*. Even his vision of space colonies does not sound anything like so implausible as when it was written half a century ago.

The boldness of his speculation about technology is, however, far exceeded by his speculation about the future of human beings and their social systems. Although the book should be regarded of course to some extent as a form of science fiction, he is ready to ask the question: 'What is to be the future of feeling? Is it to be perverted or superseded altogether?' And to give the answer: 'Feeling, or at any rate, feeling tones, will almost certainly be under conscious control: a feeling-tone will be induced to favour the performance of a particular kind of operation' (Bernal, 1929, p.63).

Yet Bernal himself is obviously not satisfied with cold rationality, for he comments that one of the advantages of the interconnected superbrains of the future which he envisages would be that 'feeling would truly communicate itself, memories would be held in common, and yet in all this, identity and continuity of individual development would not be lost' (1929, p.44). Moreover, he recognises the strength of the revulsion against technical changes which might be considered dehumanising and confesses to sharing it himself:

It is not sufficient, however, to consider the absence or presence of desire for progress, because that desire itself will not make itself effective until it can overcome the quite real distaste and hatred which mechanisation has already brought into being. This distaste is nothing to what the bulk of present humanity would feel about even the milder of the changes which are suggested here. The reader may have already felt that distaste, especially in relation to the bodily changes: I have felt it myself in imagining them. (Bernal, 1929, p.55)

He is not so intolerant as to wish to compel humanity to follow the scientists to the stars. Indeed he takes seriously the possibility of 'dimorphism' for future humanity, i.e. division into one section which colonises space and pursues the scientific enterprise to the ultimate, and the other—'the old mankind—would be left in undisputed possession of the earth, to be regarded by the inhabitants of the celestial spheres with a curious reverence' (Bernal, 1929, p.73). One is reminded irresistibly of the biblical prophecy: 'Blessed are the meek, for they shall inherit the earth.'

Bernal comments that this prospect should satisfy both the scientists with their unending quest for knowledge and experience, including observation of the 'human zoo' on earth and the humanists with their desire for idyllic happiness on earth. The zoo would be so well-managed that the inhabitants would not even be aware of it.

The point of this brief consideration of some of the basic ideas in *The World, the Flesh and the Devil* is not to dispute Bernal's vision of the future, which he was first to recognise is inevitably speculative and highly uncertain. Characteristically he rejected the 'dimorphic' perspective outlined above because it was too probable and 'we do not really expect or want the probable'. The aim is rather to demonstrate some basic features of Bernal's way of looking at the world which shaped also his approach to the *Social Function of Science*. These may be summarised as follows:

1. Science is seen as the most important activity of human beings both in the short-term and in the long-term. It is its own justification.
2. It is seen as the specialised activity of a social group—the scientific community—which, however, has a dual function: 'to keep the world going as an efficient food and comfort machine, and to worry out the secrets of nature for themselves' (Bernal, 1929, p.69).
3. The scientific community has already increased in number and compactness, so that the world may be run more and more by the scientific experts. Real sovereignty will tend to shift to advisory bodies composed of scientists, as the influence of force diminishes and the world becomes more rational.
4. The problems of overcoming poverty could be fairly quickly solved on a historic time-scale to leave humanity free to pursue other goals. Scarcely anything would ultimately be beyond the powers of organised human scientific intelligence: 'the motions of stars and living things could be directed'. Although God may not exist, science has become God.

When he came to reconsider his book years later, he did not retract on his vision of brains interlinked to form a complex hierarchical system, although he does allow that the Devil was overinfluenced by the Freudian ideas of the 1920s. Apparently this refers to the notion of sublimation of sexual desires into science and art. In considering the significance of *The World, the Flesh and the Devil* for the *Social Function of Science*, it is not so much the small dose of Freudianism in the book which is of interest as the faith in planned scientific social organisation on a vast scale.

This dream was of course not a new one. Armytage (1965) has demonstrated that it has a long intellectual lineage and has been a recurring theme of Utopian and science fiction literature for centuries. It is not surprising that a brilliant young scientist like Bernal should be attracted by this vision in the atmosphere of the 1920s and 1930s. In his own work and in that of his colleagues he could see the frontiers of science changing so rapidly as to appear almost limitless. Perhaps more than any other scientist of his generation he was aware of the new implications of scientific discoveries in relation to biology as well as to physics. Nor is it surprising that he should share the dissatisfaction of the post-war generation with the time-serving politicians of the 1920s and the depression and poverty of post-war Europe and contrast this with the achievements and the potential of science. It was an obvious step to link this Utopian idealism about the future with what appeared as the one hopeful attempt to apply science systematically for human betterment—the young Soviet state.

As Bernal himself says, he remained in some ways true throughout his life to his Utopian dream of the future. Personally I do not criticise him for this, rather the reverse. However, it would be ridiculous and quite unjust to him to make no distinction between brilliant speculative semi-fiction and the political programmes which he actually advocated in his numerous later books. I am not suggesting that he did not distinguish between long-term speculation and everyday politics, only that there was an important connection. Although he came down to earth from the stars, he never lost sight of the stars.

Whatever he may have said in *The World, the Flesh and the Devil,* in the *Social Function of Science* he unequivocally dismisses the notion of government by scientists:

The solution that is most often and most persuasively put forward, from Plato to H.G. Wells, has been the ideal one of placing the management of affairs in general in the hands of the philosophers or scientists. Unfortunately it suffers from two radical objections: first, that no-one can think of any way of transferring control into their hands; and, second, that most existing scientists are manifestly totally unfitted to exercise such control. The reluctance of democracies to choose people who appear, at least to themselves, so eminently suitable for controlling the community has led most of the proposers of these schemes to turn to authoritarian or, in modern language, Fascist solutions. But in fascist states it happens that the scientists are used merely as tools for war preparation and propaganda. Nevertheless, though we may dismiss as fantasy the prospect of the scientist ruler, the scientist will certainly have a large and critically important part to play in the formation and development of the social organisation of the future. (Bernal, 1939, p.398)

However, in the light of *The World, the Flesh and the Devil* one can far more readily understand why in the *Social Function of Science* he so easily accepts the notion of the perfectibility of organisational systems and does not see the need for pluralism and the toleration of organised groups of dissent and disagreement in the way that Laski, Luxemburg and Russell so clearly did. In trying to ask the question 'Need science be organised?' he says:

A quite opposite objection to the reorganisation of science is based on the recognition of this very danger of control by elder scientists. The existing anarchic state of science gives many opportunities to avoid particularly obnoxious control.

If objections are taken to the policy of one committee, another can be formed to do the same work under different auspices. It is felt that organisation might put an end to these possibilities and perhaps more effectively than ever block unorthodox developments in science, through the danger of carrying over to that organisation the principles of autocratic control. But this is not so much an objection to organisation as one against existing abuse of such organisation. (Bernal, 1939, p.116.

This passage is particularly interesting because it shows that Bernal was missing the main point of the Russell–Luxemburg–Laski argument, which was precisely that a 'margin of contingent anarchy' was absolutely essential to avoid the 'abuse of such organisation', and that pluralistic political and social arrangements which deliberately tolerate organised criticism and opposition and the expression of alternative approaches were not evidence of irrational waste but essential features of a civilised community, and of an efficient system of developing and testing new ideas.

Bernal saw 'participation' as the answer to the danger of intellectual and political orthodoxy, although he failed to see how easily 'participation' could be manipulated in centralised power structures. Some of Bernal's contemporary 'radical' critics still miss this point. Whilst highly critical of Bernal's behaviour over the Lysenko issue they have not recognised how easily the insistence on a 'socialist science' in opposition to a 'capitalist science' can degenerate into the suppression of unorthodox and unwelcome ideas from whatever source. The best way to criticise and expose reactionary ideas in science surely remains to demonstrate that they are unscientific, not to rely on political labels to discredit them, or fail to perceive the common human basis of most of our science and art.

The lesson which I personally draw from Bernal's *Social Function of Science* is not that he was wrong in his enthusiasm for the ambitious and well-organised use of science and technology for human welfare. On the contrary, I still share this ideal, and believe that in varying degrees it is being realised in many parts of the world, partly as a result of Bernal's impulse. But this ideal needs to be complemented by an equally explicit commitment to political and social institutions which promote open critical debate appealing to fact, experiment, experience and logical argument. Bernal did recognise this in his *Social Function of Science*, although as I have tried to show he misspecified the basis on which it could be realised. The most important debt which I believe we owe to Bernal is to try and realise both these ideals simultaneously, not one without the other.

References

Armytage, W.H.G. (1965), *The Rise of the Technocrats: A Social History*, Routledge, London.

Baker, J.R. (1945), *Science and the Planned State*, Allen & Unwin, London.

Bell, D. (1973), *The Coming of Post-Industrial Society: A Venture in Social Forecasting*, Basic Books, New York.

Bell, R.M.N. (1985) 'The great experiment: harnessing science and technology to Third World development', Science Policy Research Unit, mimeo, Sussex University.

Bernal, J.D. (1929), *The World, the Flesh and the Devil: The Three Enemies of the Rational Soul*, new edition, Cape, London, 1970.

Bernal, J.D. (1939), *The Social Function of Science*, Routledge & Kegan Paul, London.

Bernal, J.D. (1958), *World Without War*, Routledge & Kegan Paul, London.

Bernal, J.D. and Polanyi, M. (1949), 'Can science be planned?', *Bulletin of Atomic Scientists*, Vol.5, No.1, pp. 17–20.

Goldsmith, M. and Mackay, A. (eds) (1964), *The Science of Science: Society in a Technological Age,* Souvenir Press, London.

Jewkes, J. *et al.* (1958), *The Sources of Invention*, Macmillan, London.

Kaldor, M. (1980), 'Technical change in the defence industry', in K. Pavitt (ed.) *Technical Innovation and British Economic Performance*, Macmillan, London.

Organisation of Economic Co-operation and Development (1963), *The Measurement of Scientific and Technical Activities*, OECD, Paris.

Pavitt, K. (ed.) (1980), *Technical Innovation and British Economic Performance*, Macmillan, London.

Perez, C. (1983), 'Structural change and the assimilation of new technologies in the economic and social system', *Futures*, Vol. 15, pp. 357–75.

Polanyi, M. (1962), 'The republic of science', *Minerva*, Vol.1, pp. 54–73.

Rothschild Report (1971), *A Framework for Goverment Research and Development*, Cmnd 4814, HMSO, London.

Russell, B. (1920), *The Practice and Theory of Bolshevism.* Allen & Unwin, London.

Schumpeter, J.A. (1912), *The Theory of Economic Development*, Duncker & Humboldt, Leipzig.

Schumpeter, J.A. (1943), *Capitalism, Socialism and Democracy*, Allen & Unwin, London.

Whitehead, A.N. (1946), *Science and the Modern World*, Macmillan, London.

2 Science and economy at the national level*

I certainly cannot answer all the questions that Mr Gass has thrown up, but one of them I can answer immediately and unequivocally and that was his first question. No economist, whether he is left-handed, right-handed or ambidextrous, can possibly determine the ends of society in pursuing research and development. The really big choices in science policy—or in that part of science policy which goes under the heading of research and development policy—are political questions or politico-moral questions, and there is no economic magic formula to resolve these issues.

There are many different reasons for which society finds it useful to support research and development. Among the principal reasons one can distinguish five main categories. First of all, military reasons. Monsieur Salomon reminded us yesterday that war was the mother of science policy, and certainly military motivation has played a very big part indeed in the whole development of modern science and research policy. A second main group of reasons for supporting research and development is to do with prestige. A third main category can be classified as broadly economic, to do with either economic growth or competitiveness.

It is important to bear in mind that questions of survival may be just as important as questions of growth. Very often a firm may be in a position where it has no choice except to innovate if it wishes to stay in business. An example of this was Rolls-Royce. The Chief Executive, Sir Denning Pearson, in justifying the expenditure of £20 million of private venture funds on the development of the Spey engine, said: 'Building a new engine would not guarantee that we stayed in business. Not building one would certainly guarantee that we went out of business.'[1] Even so, it was not an easy decision and they went through a very difficult period of extremely low profitability in order to finance this new development.

A fourth group of reasons for supporting research and development, closely related to the economic reasons although not identical, can be grouped as welfare reasons. Society may decide to support research in

---

*This chapter was originally a paper prepared for the OECD Experimental Working Session on Science Policy at the École des Hautes Études Commerciales, Jouy-en-Josas (France), 19–25 February 1967.

public health, medical research, air pollution, water pollution, and so forth, for reasons which are not directly economic and which may even hinder economic growth, at least as it is measured by statisticians at present.

A fifth main reason for supporting research and development, which is often emphasised very strongly by scientists, is the pursuit of science for its own sake—what Lord Bowden yesterday described as one of the supreme achievements of the human intellect. A comparison is sometimes made, as Lord Bowden made it, with the opera. This is science for science's sake.

Although there are other reasons for supporting research and development, I think that these five main categories—military, prestige, economic, welfare and science for its own sake—probably cover the main purposes of research and development. In any country's science policy, the specific weight of each of these objectives will be determined by political considerations. The political balance will change in the different circumstances confronting different countries at different times. From 1938 to 1955, in many European countries, in the United States and in the Soviet Union, the military motivation was undoubtedly predominant in science policy. More recently, in the last decade and over a much longer period in many of the smaller countries of the world, other motives have been dominant, principally economic motives.

I think it is probably true to say that in most countries the last two categories—welfare reasons for supporting R&D and science for its own sake—have always ranked rather low in strategy-making. This may at first sight appear paradoxical because scientists sometimes tend to exaggerate the extent of social support for science based on the theory of science for its own sake—for the intrinsic value of science. Our work at Sussex University, as far as it goes, suggests that the main motives, even for the support of fundamental research, have been utilitarian, prestige or military. Schmookler has also emphasised this view in his paper on 'Catastrophe and utilitarianism in the development of science'.[2] And the fact that fundamental research leads to practical economic results by a rather roundabout route does not mean that the motive for supporting it is not utilitarian. This is quite clearly shown by the example of the Soviet Union. The Soviet Union, from 1917 onwards, categorically rejected the whole idea of science for its own sake, or pure science, just as they rejected the theory of art for art's sake. Nevertheless, Soviet science policy has always found it very well worth while to allocate substantial funds to fundamental research for purely utilitarian reasons.

The fact that the welfare and 'science for its own sake' motives for the endowment of scientific activities have usually ranked rather low in national science policies does not mean, of course, that these priorities would be my own personal priorities. If one ranked the motives in order—military, prestige, economic, welfare, science for its own sake—and if one acknowledges that in several countries this has in fact often been the order of priority, my own personal ranking might be the complete reverse of this. I am not talking about my own personal scale of preferences but about that scale of preferences which has been expressed in the political process in some of the countries which allocate large funds to research and development.

I certainly should not claim that an economist, just because he is an economist, has any right to determine these political, strategic priorities. They must be the outcome of the political process. This is not to say that the political process could not be very much improved; undoubtedly it could be improved and I shall make various suggestions by which it might be done. Although the economist's vote counts only as one along with all other citizens in determining the main political objectives of society, he does nevertheless have a special responsibility in contributing to the discussion in formulating these objectives.

The economist has the responsibility of measuring the cost of attaining these objectives, to show the alternatives open in choosing them and to help in the more explicit formulation of the likely benefits which may follow from attaining certain research and development goals. It was Field Marshal Montgomery who said that he never wanted any officer to give an order to take an objective 'at all costs'. Montgomery maintained (along with most of the greatest generals in history) that no military leader should think on these lines, that every military decision must take into account the cost in men and in supplies. Logistics is fundamental to military science. The expression 'at all costs' is not only bad economics, it is also extremely bad military strategy. Partly for this reason, military research and development have been important in the development of science policy because military planning has run up against the fact of limited resources, and has made an important contribution to cost effectiveness analysis and to the management of research and development projects. No one can escape the limitations of the available resources in any economy, and therefore there always will be problems of choice, of measuring alternative costs, confronting policy-makers.

Second, economists have a special responsibility in so far as society sets the objective of economic growth as a primary or important objective. Here again, of course, it is important to remember—and no one has reminded us of this more forcibly than Galbraith—that economic growth is not an end in itself: it is only a means to other ends. Nevertheless, rapid economic growth does very often make it possible to fulfil a great many other social goals, such as greater leisure or better social services, and indeed it may make it possible to fulfil military goals more easily. The economist, then, does have this special responsibility in the discussion which leads to the political process weighting the different main objectives of science policy.

The first elementary step towards improving the rationality of this process, towards making these choices more conscious and more carefully considered, is the systematic collection of statistics on the deployment of scientific manpower, and on the expenditures on different branches of scientific activity. These statistics must be collected in a great variety of breakdowns. They must show the distribution of scientific effort between industries, between firms, between sectors of the economy, between government agencies, between different universities, between different sizes of research establishments, between different disciplines in science. Although this is a very elementary requirement for rational policy-making, it is only recently that such statistics have begun to be available in any quantity, and as we all know, in many countries they are still deficient. I think the OECD has played a very valuable role in stimulating this flow of statistics. Trying to follow a science policy, to choose objectives and to count the cost of alternative objectives without such statistics is equivalent to trying to follow a full employment policy in the economy without statistics of investment or employment. It is an almost impossible undertaking. The chances of achieving rational decision-making are very low without such statistics.

Not only those who are immediately responsible for formulating science policy need to have such statistics, but also all the interested members of society need to have them. In my view, it is an essential of rational policy-making that the knowledge of these figures should be very widely diffused in society. For example, I should maintain that it is possible to have a useful and rational debate in the United States on the space research programme. Because NASA publishes full and detailed figures of its activities every year, a great deal of information is available to the public in the United States on NASA's research programme. However, it is very much less possible to have such a debate in the Soviet Union because only a small circle of people know the extent of the commitment of resources to space research. Although one can make a guess—the amount is obviously very large—a rational debate is extremely difficult unless statistics and information are fairly widely available in society.

The point made yesterday in our discussion by Dr Leddy is extremely important. There is a strong bias in science policy-making in most countries at present towards an expertocracy or an aristocratic form of decision-making. Dr Krauch in his paper on 'Expertocracy in science policy'[3] calls urgently, as a very important task in improving political decision-making in science policy, for what he calls a *Kritik-fähige Öffentlichkeit*—a very good expression in German, although difficult to put into English. In a much longer form of words it means a 'public opinion capable of making serious criticism about science policy'. This has, of course, very big implications for parliamentary machinery in relation to science policy, for the press, for specialist science journals and for the educational system, especially the universities.

The fact that a science policy debate which has available a much greater volume of statistics and information is likely to be more fruitful than one in which there are few or no statistics does not mean necessarily that policy-making will be a rational business. Far from it. Nor does it mean that the figures which we now have, for example for the United States or in some West European countries, are satisfactory. Very far from it. We have a long way to go before we have the necessary degree of accuracy in our statistics. One of the biggest problems confronting policy-makers or anyone concerned with science policy is that the figures which we have, useful though they are, are mainly figures of *inputs* into research and development: that is, numbers of people working on research and development, the amount of money expended, sometimes some figures on capital investment, instrumentation, and so forth. We have no systematic series of *output* figures, and some economists think that we may never have any. This means that we are confronted with an extremely serious problem in any rational policy-making, and in fact the difficulty in relating output to input in research and development activities is the biggest problem of science policy.

Machlup in his paper at the Conference on *The Rate and Direction of Inventive Activity*,[4] in discussing this question of a 'production function' (in economists' jargon), says:

One might take the position and defend it on good grounds that it is impossible even to define invention, let alone to identify, count and weight inventions, and if it is meaningless to quantify the output, it must be meaningless to assert or posit the existence of a quantitative relationship between input and output.

Or, [he says,] one might take a less negative position and grant the possibility of quantifying input and output at least roughly or for the purpose of constructional reasoning, but at the same time hold that the incidence of accidents in making inventions is too great to legitimise even provisionally the assumption of a production function.

These views are in fact fairly characteristic of a number of economists and scientists. The weight of Professor Jewkes' argument on inventions tends very much to the second position that Machlup mentions.[5]

Lord Bowden mentioned nuclear energy in Britain as an example of the difficulty of decision-making in science policy. He mentioned the errors made by economists in their estimates of the costs and the returns from nuclear energy. One might conclude that if input and output cannot be related, we might as well all pack up and go home. So it is worth while to spend some time on the question of the relation between input and output and whether indeed the whole process is too arbitrary for any rational decision-making.

I shall deal here mainly with applied research and development and not with fundamental research. I think what I have to say is relevant to fundamental research, although partly for reasons of time and partly because Harvey Brooks will be talking tomorrow about fundamental research, I shall limit myself now mainly to applied research and development. First of all I should like to make a few obvious points about the relationship between input and output.

The first point is that all production functions, all relationships between input and output in the economy, entail a probability distribution with a fairly wide deviation from the norm. This is quite obvious, for example, if one considers agriculture. When the farmer commits certain inputs, he uses seed, he uses fertilizer, he uses land, he uses his own and maybe hired labour; he does so in the expectation of certain output that will follow from his inputs. Of course he knows that this output may vary enormously from season to season. He knows in some countries that the return may be nil in certain years, or it may be a very high yield in other years. However, the fact that there are these enormous variations in output, owing to weather conditions or pests and other accidents which he cannot control, does not mean the farmer cannot take rational decisions about his investment and his inputs. Although he has to take into account the variability of outputs, the deviations from the norm, he can nevertheless follow a rational strategy for his inputs.

The second point I want to make is that in fact most research and development managements and most science policy-makers, whether they are in government or industry, behave as though they were farmers. They act 'as if' there were a production function in scientific activities. They act as if, when they increase the resources to research and development, they will get a higher output and if they diminish them the output will fall, although of course most of these policy-makers are very well aware of the accidental factors and the difficulties in science policy.

The third point that is extremely important to bear in mind in the whole discussion of inputs and outputs in research and development, and one that is often forgotten, is the very important distinction between discoveries and inventions on the one hand, and innovations on the other. Strictly speaking, and it is important to speak strictly on this question, the output of research and development is a flow of information: it is blueprints, models, research reports, scientific papers, sketches. Sometimes it may be prototypes or pilot plant. To have economic effects, military effects, or welfare effects, to achieve all the policy goals except the goal of science for its own sake, then this output of R&D is not sufficient. If the output of R&D simply remains at the stage of a prototype or a sketch or a model and never goes to the next stage of innovation, then so far as policy-making is concerned it is almost useless. To move from invention to innovation, whether it is military or economic, requires a chain of further steps before the R&D output is converted into a useful economic output.

We owe this distinction between invention and innovation primarily to Schumpeter. He was one of the few economists who gave innovation and invention a central place in his economic doctrine. However, Schumpeter, and most of the other economists of his time, assumed that inventions were exogenous to the economy and not the result of organised work in industry. Primarily he was concerned in his economic theory with innovation in the economy and the way in which innovations spread. This was fairly typical of economic thinking until after the Second World War, and even since then there are still many economists and some scientists who still fundamentally adhere to this view.

A very important example is the book by Jewkes *et al* on *The Sources of Invention*.[6] This might be held to justify the view that the incidence of accident is so great in invention that it is not sensible strategy to allocate large resources to research in industry, although Jewkes concedes that development is a different problem. He makes the distinction between corporate R&D or corporate invention, and private inventors, and he tries to show in his book that of sixty-one major inventions of the twentieth century the majority came not from the industrial R&D departments of firms but from private inventors acting on their own account, very often in the face of considerable opposition from business enterprises. I regard his book as a classic in science policy and it has had a very considerable influence on both economists and scientists in Europe and in the United States. It is important to see how much validity there is in the argument.

Taking first of all the major twentieth-century inventions which Jewkes attributes primarily to individual inventors, as opposed to corporate invention, he includes among these the following: air-conditioning, Bakelite, the ballpoint pen, catalytic cracking of petroleum, Cellophane, cinerama, the cyclotron, electric precipitation, the electron microscope, the Gyro compass, the helicopter, insulin, the jet engine, Kodachrome, magnetic recording, penicillin, the Polaroid camera, power steering, quick-freezing, the radio, the safety razor, the self-winding wristwatch, streptomycin, the Sulzer loom, titanium, xerography and the zip fastener. Among those inventions which he attributes mainly to corporate inventive effort in organised industrial research and development laboratories, he includes acrylic fibres, hot-strip rolling, DDT, the diesel electric locomotive, fluorescent lighting, methyl methacrylate polymers, neoprene, nylon, polyethylene, synthetic detergents, television, Terylene, tetraethyl lead and the transistor. Six of the sixty-one inventions Jewkes regards as indeterminate or as primarily government R&D inventions. He emphasises that the essential feature of invention is that the path to it is not known beforehand. In his view, therefore, the less

an inventor is precommitted in his speculations by training and by tradition, the better the chance of escaping from the grooves of accepted thought. The history of invention provides many examples of the advantages, if not of positive ignorance, at least of a mind not too fully packed with existing knowledge or the record of past failures.[7]

As examples he quotes the first success in the use of short-wave radio for long-range transmission, achieved by sceptics who refused to be deterred by the formal proof of mathematicians that this was impossible: 'The first use of the controllable pitch propeller evoked in Europe theoretical proofs that such mechanisms had no advantages.' Other examples are Gillette, the inventor of the safety razor, who was a travelling salesman in Crown corks; the joint inventors of Kodachrome, who were musicians; Carlson, who invented xerography, was a patent lawyer. The inventor of the ballpoint pen was, at various times, a sculptor, a painter and a journalist. Two Swedish technical students were responsible for the invention of domestic gas refrigeration; a 20-year-old Harvard student for success in producing the first practical light polarising material; and so on.

In considering Jewkes' theory, there are four main possible lines of criticism. One would be to accept as valid, for purposes of arguments at any rate, his list of sixty major inventions as a method of assessing approximately inventive output in the twentieth century, and to criticise his conclusions on this basis. A second line of criticism would be to accept his method of listing sixty major inventions, but to criticise the actual selection of the inventions: to argue, for example, that he left out certain very important ones or that he included too many in one industry. A third method of criticism would be to deny that his method has validity in assessing R&D output for the stages of development and improvement of inventions. A fourth line of criticism would be to deny altogether the validity of his method.

Let us take these four lines of criticism in turn. First of all, if we accept for the moment that Jewkes' list of inventions is a fairly good one, representative of the principal inventions of the twentieth century, even on this basis it is possible to make some serious criticisms of his conclusions. The first important point to remember is that these sixty inventions cover the whole period from 1900 to about 1956, and nearly half of them were made before 1928. So that if one breaks up the list of inventions into two groups, those made before 1928 and those made since 1928, then a somewhat different picture emerges. It is important to do this because although we have very few statistics of research and development in industry before the Second World War, we do know that there were fewer industrial R&D laboratories before 1939 and the scale of their expenditure was far lower. From the results of a survey by the Federation of British Industries, we know that in Britain the majority of industrial firms who have R&D laboratories started them only after 1939,[8] although many large firms did of course have R&D departments even then. The same is probably true of other industrialised countries. There were still fewer industrial R&D laboratories before 1928. It is worth while remembering also that in the United States it was not until 1930 that corporate patents exceeded the number of individual private patents. Breaking down the period into pre- and post-1928, one finds that of those inventions which Jewkes attributes primarily to individual inventors, twenty were made in or before 1928 and thirteen after 1928. If one takes those inventions which he attributes to corporate industrial R&D or to 'mixed' R&D, one finds that eight were made before 1928 and nineteen after 1928. It is difficult to classify some of the inventions because the process was spread out through the 1920s.

Taking only those inventions made after 1928, even on Jewkes' own list there were actually nineteen which could be attributed primarily to organised government and industrial R&D, and a smaller number, thirteen, which could be attributed mainly to private inventors. However, taking up the second line of criticism, there is reason to believe that even on this basis of breaking down the inventions before and after 1928, the list of sixty major inventions is somewhat biased in its selective method against corporate or industrial R&D and in favour of the private inventor. To make a more thorough analysis would require a very big research effort. I hope that ultimately at Sussex University we shall make a very much more comprehensive list of inventions, covering hundreds rather than tens of inventions. The criticism I make now is a partial and very limited one in those areas of invention where we have already done some research and have some special knowledge.

There are two areas where I think Jewkes' list is open to criticism. One is synthetic materials. He includes amongst synthetic materials two, Bakelite and Cellophane, which he attributes primarily to individual private inventors, and two, polyethylene and methyl methacrylate, which he attributes primarily to corporate inventions; and he includes three more, synthetic fibres, all of which he attributes to corporate invention. However, if one takes a list of plastic materials in the 1950s or in the 1960s and rates them in order of their volume utilisation in the economy or in the value of their output in the world or in the United States or in Western Europe, then one finds that two of the plastic materials with the highest volume and value of output, PVC and polystyrene, both exceeding Cellophane or Bakelite in volume and value of output, were not included in Jewkes' list. And if one made a comprehensive list of all synthetic materials, one would find that the corporate inventive method, particularly that in I.G. Farben, played a very great part in the invention of this group of materials. However, Jewkes himself does emphasise that the contribution of organised industrial R&D has been considerable in the chemical industry.

A second criticism, of detail, I should make of Jewkes' list concerns the cracking of petroleum, of the heavy fractions in crude oil. Jewkes includes as his only invention in the cracking of petroleum the Houdry process, as an example of a brilliant individual inventive effort with only very little backing at a late stage from the oil companies. If one looks at the history of process innovation in petroleum cracking, however, as Enos did very thoroughly in his book on the history of the petroleum industry,[9] one can distinguish six major process innovations in this industry. Jewkes was absolutely right to include the processes in this industry as very important inventions. Table 2.1 shows what tremendous gains were made in the reduction of inputs per unit of output in physical terms from process innovation.[10]

The first column, the Burton process, was the first thermal cracking process at the beginning of the twentieth century. The fluid catalytic cracking process was introduced mainly in the 1940s and 1950s (and was predominant in the 1950s and early 1960s), and the difference is quite spectacular in capital and labour inputs. It is an extremely good illustration of the gains to be made from technical progress and from organised research and development. If one took Jewkes' example of the Houdry process, which was intermediate between the Burton process and the fluid process, then one might conclude that this kind of gain in technical progress was primarily due to the effort of an individual inventor—to more or less accidental random factors in the whole process. However, at the time when the book was written, the Houdry process actually accounted for less than 5 per cent of refinery output in the United States, and less than 5 per cent in world output. It had already been almost entirely superseded by the fluid catalytic cracking process, which was very much more efficient. The fluid catalytic process was the result of the largest organised corporate research and development effort before the atom bomb. It entailed an enormous expenditure on research and development by Standard Oil, Shell, the big petrochemical contractors and consultants in the United States, Kellogg and UOP; in the early period, it also used important know-how from I.G. Farben. It is true of course that the borderline between invention and innovation is important here although it is often difficult to draw. Enos himself certainly recognised the greater contribution of individuals to inventions.

Table 2.1 Comparison of the productivity of the Burton and fluid cracking processes

	Consumption of inputs (per 100 gallons of gasoline)		
Input	Burton process	Fluid process, original installation	Fluid process present installation
Raw material (gallons)	396.00	238.00	170.00
Capital (1939 $)	3.60	0.82	0.52
Process labour (man-hours)	1.61	0.09	0.02
Energy (millions of BTUs)	8.40	3.20	1.10

Notes: Capital costs include construction, maintenance, royalty, and, for the fluid process, catalyst. The unit capacities are 88.5 bpcd for the Burton process, 12,750 bpcd for the original fluid installation, and 36,000 bpcd for the most recent one. In this table, no allowance has been made for quality improvement.
Source: J.L. Enos, *Petroleum Progress and Profits*, MIT, 1962.

However, if one took only the Houdry process, which in its time of course was very important, one would have quite a wrong picture of the history of process innovation in the petroleum industry. Of the six processes which can be distinguished as making a major contribution to technical progress in this industry, only two, perhaps even only one—the Houdry process—can be described as primarily individual inventive effort rather than organised corporate R&D. So there may be some substance in the second line of criticism of Jewkes' method—that the list of sixty inventions is not entirely representative of inventive effort in the twentieth century. The discussion of inventions and innovation in petroleum refining points to another issue.

A third main line of criticism is to say that even though it is useful to list major inventions, to examine their origin and to discuss case studies of the history of invention, nevertheless the method is fundamentally a very limited one because it is concerned with only the very early part of the inventive process: with the first most original ideas. It is not concerned with the vast number of secondary and improvement inventions which are necessary to achieve technical progress and economic growth. If one considers not just the primary inventions but the whole vast number of subsidiary secondary inventions, then one would have to attribute a far greater weight to organised industrial research and development. Cellophane is a good example of this point. This is attributed by Jewkes to an individual inventor but its applications were very limited as a packaging material until Du Pont developed moisture proof cellophane in their R&D laboratories. Jewkes himself concedes that development work is mainly the prerogative of industrial research and development departments. Taking into account the expenditure figures which are available, probably between two-thirds and three-quarters of total expenditure on industrial research and development is on development activity.

A fourth possible line of criticism, which was in fact explicit in the work of some American sociologists before Jewkes' book was written, is the rejection of the whole personalised or 'heroic' theory of invention. This school would maintain that it is not possible to attribute, for example, the invention of the radio or the telephone or television to any single inventor or even to a very few inventors: that invention is so complex that it makes sense only when viewed as a fairly prolonged social process. Typical of this view is Alfred Kahn, writing in the *American Economic Review*. He says:

Strictly speaking, no individual makes an invention in the usual meaning of the term, for the object which, for linguistic convenience, we call an automobile, telephone or a radio is as a matter of fact the aggregate of an almost infinite number of individual units of invention, each of them the contribution of a separate person. It is little short of absurdity to call any one of the interrelated units the 'invention' and its creator the 'inventor'.[11]

This was put more briefly by *The Economist* in 1851: 'Nearly all useful inventions depend less on any individual than on the progress of society.'[12] This view is the opposite extreme of the method of listing individual inventions.

Taking into account, although not necessarily accepting, all these criticisms of Jewkes' analysis, perhaps we need not be so pessimistic about the possibility of relating inputs to outputs in research and development. The allocation of large sums to organised inventive work in industry does not appear quite so unrewarding as it might appear on a first reading of Jewkes' book. Decision-making in industrial research and development is not entirely irrational and has in fact led to a very useful flow of outputs. This conclusion is fortified by the researches of Edwin Mansfield in the United States, who has made some very thorough studies of invention and innovation in a series of American industries. Mansfield says:

Although the pay-out from an individual R and D project is obviously very uncertain, there seems to be a close relationship over the long run between the amount a firm spends on research and development and the total number of innovations it produces.[13]

In spite of the fact that in my view Jewkes' book cannot be used to sustain the view that rationality is impossible in R&D decision-making, I nevertheless think that his book is extremely important for science policy. I think this for three reasons.

First of all, it does show that very often in the history of invention, major advances have been made with very limited resources, that it is possible to achieve very significant returns, in favourable circumstances, from small inputs.

The second reason is because it shows, I think fairly conclusively, that fresh minds (not necessarily ignorant minds, but fresh minds) often do make very important contributions to inventive activity. I think that this has extremely important implications for mobility of engineers and scientists between firms and between sectors of the economy, between government, universities and industry.

The third reason that I think Jewkes' book is extremely important is because it shows, especially in the case studies, the very great importance of the social barriers, not so much to invention, but to innovation. It also shows the tremendous importance of the enthusiasm of inventors, whether private or corporate, as a driving-force to overcome these social barriers and these inertias. All of these things are of the greatest importance for R&D decision-making.

The problems in deciding on the allocation of resources at different levels (government, industrial, university, and that of the individual inventor) vary enormously between different countries and at different times. It is not possible to lay down a universal model or a universal panacea or formula which can cover all the tremendous complexity of circumstances which exist, and I certainly shall not attempt to do this. What I intend to do briefly is to indicate three very important factors which I think must be taken into account, if not in every R&D decision at any level, then in a very large proportion of them. Moreover, these three factors, which might perhaps be regarded as part of a check list in decision-making, are factors which are very often overlooked or ignored, even in those decision systems which depend on very elaborate or sophisticated mathematical formulae. These three factors are, first of all, the question of scale of the activity; second, the question of structure of the activity in relation to the policy aim of innovation. The third point is consideration of alternative methods of achieving the desired policy goal.

Taking first of all the question of scale, it seems to me essential in almost any R&D decision-making to ask the questions posed by any economist in an ordinary investment decision. There is no simple answer, of course, to these questions of scale. If one is considering investment in any industry, whether it is in brewing, chemicals, iron and steel, electric power, clothing, the catering trade, the tourist trade, etc., there is a different answer in every industry at different times. The economies of scale are always varying and depend on a wide range of factors which differ between industries, and the same is true of R&D. There is no absolute rule about the scale of R&D. Each case must be considered on its merits. One also has to consider, in assessing each R&D project or each science policy allocation, the most appropriate scale. In particular, is there a threshold factor? Is there a critical level below which we are wasting our time and money? Quite often one finds, both at national level and at the level of the firm, research projects in progress which are sub-threshold, which cannot conceivably yield results which will achieve the policy goal.

In 1960 the Shirley Institute, which is the main organisation in Britain concerned with cotton and rayon research, with a much smaller budget than it has today, was conducting 213 different research projects, many of them below the threshold level needed to achieve results. Today, although they have a far larger budget—more than double the size and double the manpower employed—they have reduced the number of projects from 213 to ninety, and of those ninety they have given first priority to thirty-nine.[14] This seems to me good decision-making. It is the kind of way of looking at the allocation of resources which is needed in any research institute. It would not necessarily follow, of course, that having looked at the scale of allocation of resources, one would decide to reduce the number of projects; one might decide to increase it. There may be diminishing returns to scale or there may be increasing returns to scale, depending upon the industry and the project and the resources available.

Another example was a chemical firm which had put about thirty development engineers on to developing an important new process. They had come to the conclusion, after about eighteen months' work, that they could not achieve results in the development of this process because they could not solve the technical problems of scaling-up the plant size. Immediately, they cut back on the development work and shifted the engineers to a completely different project with greater prospects of success, although they continued the other work with only two scientists working on the fundamental problems of the process. This again, I think, is often the kind of strategy and thinking that is required.

The second point concerns the question of *structure* of research and development in relation to the goal of innovation: too often science policy decision-making is confined to the research and development, and somebody else is left to consider the innovation aspect, above all the marketing. In my view this is an almost certain recipe for failure. Lord Bowden said yesterday, talking about the Atomic Energy Authority, that Britain had had very little, or nil, or negative returns to our enormous investment in our nuclear energy programme, that we were not generating nuclear power even now at a cost below oil-fired power. I think he implied from what he said about the role of the economist in this decision-making that the whole thing was a very big waste of money. This is not the only kind of analysis which needs to be made of the British nuclear power programme. The weaknesses which existed in that nuclear R&D programme, and which to some extent still exist, were structural; they were not only to do with the estimates made by economists, although of course the estimates were wrong. Incidentally, they were wrong mainly for other reasons than those mentioned by Lord Bowden. The main reason for the economic estimates going wrong, so far as I understand the figures, was that the reduction in generating costs of power by conventional means, through R&D on conventional power generation, were very much underestimated.

However, these kinds of errors were far less important than the errors made in the organisation of the whole innovation. The R&D was conducted, I think, on the whole quite efficiently by the Atomic Energy Authority and led to very important new types of reactor, technically very well advanced, although this was very largely separated from those organisations (the consortia of contracting firms) who would be responsible for marketing these nuclear power-stations. The biggest difference that I see between the American and German nuclear power programmes, which have apparently been more profitable, and the British lies in this: that they were better able to integrate the research, development, production and marketing aspects into one whole and the chain was not broken through structural weaknesses. To take another example, I would maintain that on any, certainly on any industrial, research and development project, it is usually necessary from the very outset to include people who are responsible for marketing the ultimate product, and this would apply also in the military case, by analogy—from the very outset in military R&D one must include representatives of the people who are going to use the weapon or weapons system.

There were several cases in Britain of innovations of important plastics materials which have been successful and profitable, in all of which the man who ran the whole project from start to finish was the sales manager. When I mentioned this to some Russians, I found that they were astonished. They had never considered that marketing people should have any say in research and development policy-making. I think it is significant that there are now beginning to be voiced in the Soviet Union big criticism by Kapitza and others, not so much of the technical merits of Soviet research and development or of their technical achievements, but of the structural weaknesses, the fact that the R&D institutes are centralised for each industry and are not merely divorced from marketing but are divorced from the plant production level to a large extent. So it might very well be, in considering disparities between input and output in research and development, that the real disparities are not in the output of the research and development. It could very well be that Soviet industry or Soviet industrial institutes or West European industrial firms compare favourably with their American counterparts in what is strictly speaking the output of R&D—in the generation of scientific information, blueprints and so on—although where they fall down is on the next step in the chain, in the innovation. From the point of view of the economy and the policy-maker, what matters really is the innovation.

This emerges from an extremely interesting secondary analysis of Jewkes' statistics by Professor Ben-David, in a paper prepared for the OECD.[15] Professor Ben-David listed those inventions on Jewkes' list which from start to finish were made entirely in the United States. On the other hand he listed those which from start to finish were invented in Europe—in Britain, France and Germany. He found that ten major inventions were initiated almost entirely, or entirely, in Britain, France and Germany; nineteen were initiated entirely in the United States. However, the significant thing is what happened next. Of the ten which were initiated in the West European countries, only seven emerged into final product innovations in those European countries, whereas in the United States twenty-two emerged into finally developed products. So that, if one takes the disparity at the first stage, one finds nineteen in the United States, ten in these three West European countries: a 2:1 disparity in originating inventions. If one takes the disparity at the next stage, that is, commercial innovation, one finds twenty-two successful innovations in the United States and seven in Western Europe: a disparity of 3:1. This, I think, is probably illustrative of the kind of thing which tends to happen because of structural weaknesses in the invention/innovation chain, not only in Western Europe but in Eastern Europe too. So that it seems to me an extremely good rule in science policy decision-making to consider the structure of the whole process in relation to the goal of the project, and in particular to consider the investment, production and marketing decisions which will necessarily follow from R&D success. These decisions must be integrated with the R&D decision-making. This means, incidentally, that since science policy decision-making, or R&D decision-making, is essentially the constant development of technical and economic forecasts and relating them to one another, the work of Dr Jantsch, which Mr Gass mentioned, is of critical importance for this whole process. Technical and economic evaluation, as a continuous process, is vital to successful innovation.

The third point I want to mention is the question of considering alternative routes to the policy goal which is sought. Sir Leon Bagrit, the Chairman of Elliott-Automation, has a slogan: 'Never re-invent'. The reason that he adopts this formula is that in his view, and I think he is right, it is a waste of time simply to repeat what has been done elsewhere in the world. Therefore, it is essential to consider, in starting any R&D project, whether the results are already available, and if they are not already available, whether the results may very shortly be available from an alternative source. No country and certainly no industrial firm, however large, can possibly rely on its own research and development to provide all the answers. Everyone stands to gain by an inflow of research results and technical know-how from other countries. This is true even if one takes the very largest American corporations. For example, Muller in his study of Du Pont took twenty-five major Du Pont innovations,[16] and showed that two-thirds of them came from outside the Du Pont R&D laboratories, despite the fact that Du Pont is one of the most research-intensive firms in the world and prides itself on its own R&D capacity as a source of its main innovations, and was indeed the source of such major innovations as nylon. The same is true, for example, of IBM. Although IBM has a very big revenue from other computer companies through its patent portfolio, it also has paid out very large sums to companies like Univac for know-how and for licences. The same is true of a firm like Pilkingtons, who developed one of the major process breakthroughs in the last decade: the float glass process for plate glass. Although they have a very strong R&D capacity, perhaps the strongest in the European glass industry, nevertheless, in the field of glass fibres, they rely primarily on licensing and know-how agreements from outside their own organisation. This is a very sensible strategy. Every organisation should be alive all the time to the possibilities of acquiring know-how and research results more cheaply from outside its own R&D laboratories; and it is a very good rule in embarking on any project to ask: 'Can we find the know-how elsewhere or could we acquire it very soon by licensing or know-how agreements or by consultancy, or some similar arrangement?'

However, although I think it is essential to compare the cost of trying to achieve a goal by one's own research and development with the cost of achieving the goal by a licensing agreement or a know-how agreement, I nevertheless think that there are very grave dangers in limiting the analysis on this point to simple direct comparison of alternative costs. One must take into account a number of complex factors which would not appear in the first approximation which is made. One must consider, for example, if one is taking a decision about an industrial development project, the effect of licensing the product on the morale of our own R&D engineers and scientists. This is an extremely important question, especially in relation to the problem that Lord Bowden illustrated so graphically yesterday, the brain drain problem. It is especially obvious, for example, in the aircraft industry in Britain, where the cancellation of development projects could have very important repercussions on the already large emigration of aircraft engineers from Britain to the United States. One has to consider also, not only the short-term costs of know-how purchase by comparison with R&D costs, but also the long-term economic effects on the bargaining position of the firm, or the country in the cases of national decisions, in subsequent technical policy decisions. If, for example, Rolls-Royce had decided in the 1950s not to develop the Spey engine with their private venture R&D resources, it is probably not strictly true to say, as the Chief Executive did say, that they would have gone out of business—probably they could have gone into sub-contracting and licensing. Nevertheless, what would have been the consequences of this strategy for the long-term competitive position of Rolls-Royce in the world aero-engine industry? One cannot examine the effects of only one agreement, one must also take into account the whole long-term posture of a firm or a country. This applies, for example, also to such considerations as the position of Bull in the computer industry in France.

Third, one must bear in mind that in a developing country which wants to start new industries and new areas of research and development work, one will always, by definition, be in a position of inferiority to the established leading countries and leading firms. It has been recognised for a long time by economists in such questions as international trade that there is a very powerful argument for the so-called 'infant industry' policy: that every developing country will need to take special measures to protect its industries in the early years because otherwise they could never become established in world competition. This is a commonplace now of development economics: that all the developing countries almost without exception give special protection to infant industries. This applies *a fortiori* to research and development: there is a strong case, in making R&D decisions, for deciding sometimes to invest in a project even if the first cost comparison shows a higher cost from own R&D to a policy of buying a licence. It is not a simple, straightforward decision, and in the long run this kind of consideration—what weight one gives to developing one's own problem-solving capacity—goes back to the political and cultural decisions with which I began. In the long run, how much one wants to rely on imitation, licensing and purchasing know-how, and how much one wants to rely on one's own problem-solving capacity, will depend partly on what kind of society one wants to live in. It is conceivable that one could rely as a matter of policy entirely on imported know-how, and not attempt to do research. Although this is a possible line of argument, on economic grounds it has obviously enormous implications for cultural and political results flowing from such a policy.

It seems to me, speaking quite personally, and I emphasise that this is partly a question of value judgment rather than economics, that there are two equally big dangers in considering these kinds of questions. One is the danger of an inflated chauvinism, of an attempt at autarchy, of trying to go it alone in every single field of research and development, which is economic absurdity and is the kind of nonsense that Montgomery was talking about when he said: 'Do something at all costs'. This can lead only to wasted resources, to uneconomic projects, to disillusion and failure in a large number of prestige R&D projects. This is one danger, and a number of countries have been guilty of this kind of 'go-it-alone-itis'. Lord Bowden mentioned the example of nuclear power in India. Some people would say the same about the aircraft industry or nuclear power in Britain although I should not say it myself. Obviously there are cases where it is absurd to try to go it alone, taking into account the limitation of resources in a given country. I think it is also important to remember that there is another danger, and that is the danger of voluntary underdevelopment. Indigenous R&D and imports of technology are complementary not alternative strategies.

Notes

1. A. Bambridge, 'The real thrust at Rolls Royce', *Management Today*, November 1966, p. 58.
2. J. Schmookler, Paper at the Ohio State Conference on *The Economics of Research and Development*, ed. R. Tybout, 1962.
3. H. Krauch, 'Kritik an die Expertokratie', Paper at the Berlin Conference on Science Policy, 1963.
4. National Bureau of Economic Research, *The Rate and Direction of Inventive Activity*, Princeton, 1962, p. 152.
5. J. Jewkes *et al.*, *The Sources of Invention*, Macmillan, London, 1958.
6. Ibid.
7. Ibid., p. 116.
8. FBI and NIESR, *Industrial Research in Manufacturing Industry, 1959–60*, London, 1961
9. J.L. Enos, *Petroleum progress and profits*, MIT, 1962.
10. Ibid.
11. A.E. Kahn, 'Fundamental deficiencies in the American patent law', *AER*, 1940, p. 478.
12. *The Economist*, 26 July 1851, quoted by Edith Penrose in *Economics of the international patent system*, Johns Hopkins University Press, Baltimore, 1951.

13. E. Mansfield, 'Industrial research and development expenditures', *JPE*, 1964.
14. Dr Douglas Hill, Director of the Cotton, Silk & Man-Made Fibres Research Association, The Shirley Institute, in lecture to Science of Science Foundation, 25 January 1967, part of series entitled 'Formulating a programme for research and development'.
15. J. Ben-David, *Fundamental Research and Government Policy*, SP(66)8, Committee for Science Policy, OECD, Paris, 1966.
16. W.F. Muller, Paper in *The Rate and Direction of Inventive Activity*, National Bureau of Economic Research, Princeton, 1962.

3   Design and British economic performance*

This chapter first of all considers some problems of the definition and measurement of design activities in relation to research and development. It then considers the relationship between a range of scientific and technical activities (including design) and competitive international trade performance. Finally, it discusses the reasons for German and Japanese success in world markets over the past thirty years and some of the implications for British policies in relation to technical innovation and design.

The chapter considers design from the standpoint of an economist who has hitherto been mainly concerned with research, development and technical innovation and their influence on economic performance. Whilst working on definitions and measurement of research and development in the 1960s one frequently encountered the view that what should be measured in industry was not R&D, but R, D&D—Research, *Design* and Development. This seemed at first sight a reasonable point of view, since a new product or process must be designed and good design is a condition of success in technical innovation.

However, anyone who looks more closely at this immediately encounters the problem that there is no satisfactory definition of design. Some emphasise intellectual and technical originality in the same way as definitions of R&D. For example De Bono maintains that design goes beyond styling or optimisation and contains an element of originality. Other definitions emphasise styling or optimisation and some are so broad as to include almost any activity which is concerned to influence the future. For example, Christopher Jones suggests that design is 'to initiate changes in man-made things',[1] a definition that would include at least some politicians, poets and economists as well as many managers, scientists and engineers.

A big opportunity was missed in the 1950s and 1960s when the present official definitions of R&D were first formulated and standardised. At that time there were proposals to measure not just the rather narrow range of

---

*This chapter is based on a lecture given at The Design Council, The Haymarket, London for the Royal College of Art on 23 March 1983.

activities presently defined as research and development under the OECD 'Frascati' definitions, but also a much wider range of scientific and technical activities which are collectively described as 'scientific and technical services'. These include (in addition to R&D), scientific and technical information services, geophysical exploration activities, project feasibility studies and surveys, and a range of activities described as design and engineering. The last are generally taken to include most of the work done in drawing offices, engineering departments and design bureaux, which could not be classified as R&D, and sometimes also the work of architects, textile designers and other types of designer whose work is predominantly an artistic activity.

All of these activities are important for the efficient conduct of technical change and for a high level of economic performance. The one-sided emphasis on the research and development end of the spectrum can give rise to a distorted view of the process of innovation and its efficient management, and as I shall hope to show, can also give rise to difficulties in the interpretation of the available statistics relating innovation to trade performance and other indicators of economic performance.

The East Europeans do measure a much wider range of scientific and technical activities than we do, which makes for big difficulties in international comparisons, since at first sight the Russians and other East Europeans appear to have far more R&D than we do, until we remember that we have either to enlarge our own range of measurements to match theirs, or to cut off many of their activities to match our own much narrower definitions of R&D.

Unfortunately, the attempts which were made in the 1960s to establish international comparability in this field through the agency of the United Nations were stillborn, so that until there is another major push forward we shall have to make do with the present unsatisfactory definitions and statistics. In relation to design, this means that we have to recognise at least four distinct types of design activity, which are as yet not measurable, which may overlap in organisational structures and the work of particular individuals, all of which are essential for a satisfactory economic performance.

First of all, there is that activity which is at present included in the rubric of research and development, described as 'experimental design'. Although the design of prototypes and pilot plants is already part of the activity of R&D departments, the present definitions insist that after this phase of experimental development, the subsequent activity of detailed elaboration of production drawings and other preparations for commercial production do not constitute bona fide R&D.

Thus we have a second type of design activity, which in this scheme of things follows the R&D phase and consists of routine design-engineering, which would be typical of most of the design work in large plant contractors for the oil and chemical industries, or many engineering firms.

As we shall see, there are some big dangers in this conceptualisation, since it does violence to the real complexity of technical innovation in many sectors of industry. Nevertheless, we have to understand the limitations of our present R&D statistics (which are the only ones we have) if we wish to make intelligent use of them.

Third, there is a type of design activity in which aesthetic and fashion considerations tend to predominate and which is also essential for competitive economic performance. It is most apparent in textiles and clothing, although it is obviously important in construction and many other industries. Fashion design is again excluded from the official definitions of research and development. The use of this expression to describe a distinct range of design activities neither implies that aesthetic considerations are absent from other types of design work, nor gives any derogatory view of the importance of changing fashions.

Finally, there is a type of design activity, which almost coincides with the management of innovation. This covers the creative synthesis of the work of R&D, design engineering, fashion design, production engineering, marketing and market research to design, produce and launch a new product on the market. It is a planning, co-ordinating and managerial activity which is sometimes called design management, although in much of the literature it is described as innovation management or broad management.

Having distinguished between: (1) Experimental design (included in R&D); (2) Design engineering (largely outside R&D); (3) Fashion design (also outside R&D); and (4) Design management (partly outside R&D), I shall now proceed to discuss the results of some of the work which has been done by economists attempting to relate measures of R&D to economic performance. It will become apparent that these attempts have often suffered from a failure to take into account a wider range of activities which affect innovation, including especially the four types of design which I have distinguished. In the first place I shall concentrate particularly on international trade performance, since success in international trade competition is generally regarded as crucial for our future prosperity and economic performance generally.

What I shall hope to show is that where our existing R&D measures are a good surrogate for the full range of activities devoted to the introduction of new products and improved products and processes, then there is also a strong statistical relationship between such R&D figures and various measures of competitive trade performance. Where design and other technical activities associated with successful innovations are not satisfactorily captured or represented by R&D measures, then such statistical correlations are weak or non-existent. Although this applies mainly at the level of the individual industries or product groups, it also applies at the level of some countries, such as Italy. Italian industry has been very successful in exports of some classes of manufactured goods, where even if formal R&D is not very high, design activities have been at a high level.

International trade theories and technology

During the post-war period the traditional theory of international trade has proved incapable of providing a satisfactory explanation of the observed patterns of commodity trade. Following the demonstration in 1953 of the 'Leontief paradox',[2] it became difficult to sustain explanations of the trade performance of such countries as the United States and the German Federal Republic in terms of the relative costs of labour and capital. Posner's seminal paper in 1961[3] opened the way to the development of an alternative paradigm, or at the very least a substantial revision of the established theory. Starting from the self-evident fact that a firm which introduces a new product may enjoy an export monopoly from the country of origin at least until imitators come into the market, he developed a set of concepts which became the basis for various 'technology gap' theories of foreign trade. As long as the 'imitation lag' was longer than the 'demand lag', technology gap trade could persist. Posner identified several mechanisms which might tend to maintain this gap for fairly long periods, including the quality and scale of commitment to R&D, the 'clustering' of technical innovations and dynamic economies of scale.

A few years after the appearance of Posner's paper, Hufbauer[4] provided an excellent empirical illustration and validation of the theory with his study of international trade in synthetic materials. He measured imitation lags for many countries for some sixty synthetic materials and demonstrated a clear-cut relationship between trade performance and innovative leadership. He recognised, however, that, as a new technology matured, traditional cost elements could become increasingly important, so that 'low wage' trade could take over from 'technology gap' trade in mature technologies. Although he showed convincingly that innovation and early imitation explained the predominant position of the German and US chemical industries in trade performance in the early decades of the new synthetic materials industry, he did not attempt to investigate the source of these innovations other than by identifying the firm of origin.

This question was taken up in a series of studies at the National Institute of Economic and Social Research (NIESR) in the 1960s.[5] These attempted to relate both the innovative and the comparative trade performance of firms and countries to various factors which Posner had identified, particularly the scale, location and quality of their R&D and the outputs from that R&D, as measured by various indicators such as patents. The results of this work lent support to the view that the innovative leadership of German chemical firms over a long period was related to their exceptionally heavy investment in R&D and the same point also emerged in relation to the leadership of US firms in the world market for electronic capital goods. Patent statistics showed that technological leadership in these industries was broadly based and did not rest simply on a few chance inventions or discoveries. However, it was never suggested that the innovative successes of leading firms or countries could be explained simply by the quantity of R&D performed. The studies also attempted to take into account firm strategies, institutional factors, such as the role of government research, the education system and the interdependent relationship between various groups of firms, such as chemical firms, chemical process plant contractors and machinery suppliers. In the case of chemical process plant the research took particular account of design engineering as well as R&D and attempted some measurements of this activity. This chapter represents an attempt to extend and generalise this approach, taking into account the results of more recent work. In particular, it tries to provide a very crude answer to the question: 'How did Germany and Japan manage to gain a lead in the world competition in so many areas of design and technical innovation?'

Both the NIESR studies and Hufbauer's work were important in demonstrating the relationship between the growth of new industries, dynamic economies of scale, process innovation, and a wide range of scientific and technical activities including all types of design. Imitation lags could be prolonged if R&D thresholds costs were high and the best competitive efforts of would-be imitators could be repeatedly frustrated if the innovators could maintain a flow of process design innovations related to scale economies and new generations of products. Such mechanisms were later shown to be extraordinarily important in the semi-conductor industry by the studies of Golding, Sciberras and Dosi.[6] All of this empirical evidence pointed to the conclusion that technology gaps could be sustained over long periods, and our own British experience with INMOS emphasises both the importance and the continuing difficulty of closing gaps in the semi-conductor industry. However, this evidence related only to a few specific industrial sectors and could thus be dismissed as irrelevant for the greater part of foreign trade.

The first attempts to relate trade performance to some measure of technical innovativeness across a wide range of industries were made by Vernon, Keesing and their colleagues at Harvard in the mid-1960s.[7] Their work pointed the way to a resolution of the Leontief paradox, inasmuch as it demonstrated that there was a fairly strong statistical association between the ranking of US shares of world export markets by product group, the R&D intensity of those industries and other measures of the participation of highly qualified manpower. World export performance of the United States was exceptionally strong in several industries, which although they were certainly labour-intensive rather than capital-intensive in the traditional sense, were characterised by very large inputs from highly skilled personnel. However, this work related only to the

United States and attempts to extend it to a wider range of countries at the OECD in the late 1960s ran into severe difficulties because of the limitations of the R&D data, the problems of reconciliation of the R&D classification with trade classifications, and international comparability problems. Measures of total input of scientists and engineers often appeared to suggest stronger correlations with trade performance than R&D alone, which may have been an indication of the importance of other scientific and technical activities.

In any case, it was always conceptually unsatisfactory to use an input measure (R&D expenditure or manpower data) as a surrogate for technological innovativeness. In the absence of any direct measures of innovative achievement (except those laboriously constructed for individual industries such as synthetic materials), patent statistics seemed to offer the best available output indicator, since they were universally available for long periods. Some of the main problems associated with their use (lack of comparability of different national systems, variations in propensity to patent) were ingeniously overcome by Pavitt and Soete through their use of the new statistics which became available through the Office of Technology Assessment and Forecasting of the United States Department of Commerce.[8]

The first systematic attempts to relate international trade performance to some measure of technological output across the board and for a large number of OECD countries were made by Soete.[9] In his 'General test of technological gap trade theory' he regressed variations in export performance across twenty-two OECD countries on variations in innovativeness for each of forty industrial sectors. His results demonstrated the crucial role of the technology variable in explaining inter-country variations in export performance in the great majority of industries. Non-significant results were obtained for some industries such as food, petroleum and stone, clay and glass, in which natural resource endowment clearly plays an important role. A second group of industries where results were also sometimes not significant were the typical mature industries of fairly low research intensity, such as textiles and clothing. In these industries the element of fashion design is clearly of great importance. Nevertheless, the results were significant for 70 per cent of the product groups at the 5 per cent level and for half of them at the 1 per cent level of significance. The twenty industries which showed a high statistical correlation included all those of high R&D intensity, where R&D measures are quite a good surrogate for the whole complex of activities devoted to product and process innovation and improvement including design.

In the face of such evidence and the lack of any comparable support in the empirical work to justify the traditional factor proportions theory of comparative advantage, it has become difficult'[10] to ignore the importance of technology for trade performance. Indeed, already in the 1960s some of the leading traditional trade theorists had begun to acknowledge the need for some revision of the mainstream theory, notably Harry Johnson, who developed the concept of 'human capital' within neo-classical trade theory.[11]

This major revision of the theory by its leading exponent meant that after the Montreal Conference of the International Economics Association, both believers and heretics could agree up to a point in stressing the importance of such factors as investment in education and industrial technical training, as well as R&D, design and other scientific and technical services. In the 1970s a number of economists provided further strong support for this view (see for example the works of Horn and Wolter).[12]

This did not necessarily mean of course that technology gap and human capital trade theories were in agreement about other fundamental issues such as the assumptions of perfect competition, attitudes to government intervention and so forth. In practice, despite Harry Johnson's revisionism, a significant body of trade theory continued to neglect or ignore the issues raised by the neo-technology debate and to make somewhat unrealistic assumptions about the role of relative prices and government in trade competition.

However, statistical studies of international trade continued to suffer from the lack of satisfactory measures of product quality and the varied activities which contribute to a competitive design in world markets: in any case, statistical correlation studies have their own limitations and are only really convincing if they are reinforced by detailed case studies of sufficient depth, rigour and quality to demonstrate the mechanisms supposedly proven by the statistics.

All the more importance therefore attaches to the other stream of empirical and theoretical work which operates at this level. One stream of such work has concentrated on the relevance of 'non-price factors' in the explanation of trade competitivity and international trade performance. Almost all such studies, whether based on interviews with buyers and sellers, or on other techniques, point to the conclusion that price is only one element in effective competition. It is of course of decisive importance for homogeneous primary commodities and bulk chemicals traded in internationally competitive markets or subjected to fairly simple processing or refining. However, in most capital goods markets and for many consumer goods, empirical research points unambiguously to the conclusion that factors such as real or perceived quality variables related to design, technical service, reputation and marketing play an extremely important role, along with non-technical factors such as credit availability.

In their analysis of price competitiveness in German–American trade, Kravis and Lipsey[13] report that their questionnaires showed that only 28 per cent of US exporters attributed success to lower prices, whereas 37 per cent suggested that the critical factor was product superiority and a further 10 per cent said product uniqueness. Of German importers, only 7 per cent said they were buying in America because of lower prices, whereas 63 per cent explained their imports by non-availability of products at home. Rothwell's results for textile and agricultural machinery showed an even greater emphasis on non-price factors.[14] Only 4 per cent of UK companies importing textile machinery in the 1970s gave lower prices as the reason, whereas over 80 per cent gave reasons such as 'superior overall performance and design' or 'technically more advanced' or 'no suitable UK alternative'. In his study of the success of Japanese exporters in the world colour television industry, Sciberras[15] reported that evidence from consumer organisations in both Europe and the United States in the 1970s stressed superior product quality over a great part of the product range. For example, Juran reported in the *Journal of the Electronics Industry* (March 1979) that US sets failed at least five times as frequently as Japanese sets at that time.

Technological leadership and trade performance

These and other studies confirm that long-term shifts in world export shares between the leading manufacturing countries are not primarily explicable in terms of traditional price competition theory, but must be explained in other terms. The studies which have been discussed so far have, in my view, provided fairly conclusive evidence that 'technology' broadly defined has played a very important role. However, that evidence relates mainly to competitive performance sector by sector. This applies even to studies, such as those of Soete, which have examined all sectors of industry. His results and those of similar studies show that firms (and the countries in which they are based) tend to do well in their trade performance if they are more successful than their competitors in developing and designing new products and improving old ones, and in improving the manufacturing technology by which such products are made. They do not show why it is that in certain historical periods particular countries tend to do exceptionally well in export performance not just in one or two industrial sectors, but in many simultaneously, indeed sometimes in almost all of those sectors which are not dominated by natural resource availability or long-term traditional fashion-based factors.

It was such general shifts in country performance which lent credibility to such general explanations as relative prices (sometimes brought about by deliberate exchange rate policies) or low wages. However, if such older general explanations do not stand up to empirical testing or explain only a small part of the observed long-term changes in international trade patterns, then what can technology theories offer which might help to explain shifts in world technological leadership—shifts which are not just randomly distributed across industries or between the various industrial countries or in proportion to their earlier shares of world production or world trade, but occur in waves over long historical periods? What too can they offer to help explain why, when many countries are striving to catch up with the world technology leaders, only a few succeed and then only after a very long time?

What has already been said about Posner's theoretical framework and about the NIESR studies of innovation and trade performance have suggested that catching up with and overtaking established technological leaders could pose formidable problems for imitators and aspirants to leadership, since they must aim at a moving target. It is no use simply importing today's technology from the leading countries, for by the time it has been introduced and efficiently assimilated, the leaders have moved on and the relative position of the various countries may be unchanged or even worsened from the standpoint of the followers. It cannot be simply assumed that catching up is an easy and almost costless process, based on the simplistic assumption that new technology is equally and freely available to all comers. This is one of several very unrealistic assumptions of perfect competition theory which must be finally discarded if any progress is to be made in understanding the diffusion of new technologies.

We must start, not from such unrealistic assumptions, deriving from general equilibrium theory, but from the evidence of empirical research on the dynamics of technological competition. The findings of such research are virtually unanimous, whether they originate in applied economics, management studies, sociology, or the work of historians, in pointing to several characteristics of innovation, which must be clearly recognised if we are to understand it. Design activities of one kind or another are closely associated with all of these characteristics.

Some features of the process of technical innovation are inherent in the very nature of innovation itself. What changes in successive historical periods and in different countries is the mode of dealing with these basic characteristics, i.e. those social changes which permit and stimulate a particular society to introduce specific new technologies and to achieve technological and economic leadership in a range of products and services associated with those technologies.

Some basic characteristics of technical innovation

If it is accepted that success in technical innovation and design is a crucial element in competitiveness and if we wish to place it at the heart of our analysis, instead of relegating it to a peripheral or residual role, then it follows that these basic characteristics of innovation must be taken into account. They may be summarised as

1. coupling (of changing technology, production and markets);
2. creating (new products, processes, systems and industries);
3. clustering (of groups of related innovations);
4. comprehending (new skills, new technologies, new markets); and
5. coping (with the technical and market uncertainty of innovation).

We shall consider each of these briefly in turn and their relationship to design before going on to discuss the ways in which Germany and Japan modified and changed the institutional framework in which they dealt with these characteristic features of innovation and design in successve cycles of economic development.

1. *Coupling*

This aspect of innovation may be considered as definitional or purely tautological. Nevertheless it is a feature of the process which is often forgotten in practice (thus leading to failure in attempts at innovation both in market and in planned economies). Its implications for theory are often also overlooked. Following Schumpeter, innovation is usually defined as the commercial realisation or introduction of a new product, process or system in the economy. This may be contrasted with invention, which is simply the bright idea for such a new product, process or system. Schumpeter pointed out that there is a world of difference between the two. Most inventions never become innovations since there is many a slip between cup and lip. Scientists and inventors may be unaware of the needs of the market. It is mainly designers who build this bridge and keep it in good repair. This requires a special type of creative ability which at the highest level Schumpeter defined as entrepreneurship, reserving this term for the management of innovation rather than everyday management. It follows from this definition of innovation that the most important role of the entrepreneur or innovation manager or designer is to match technical and scientific possibilities with the needs of potential users of the innovation. These three categories may be combined in one individual. If not, they must work closely together. Indeed, all four types of design, as defined earlier, are concerned with matching techniques and markets. This interpretative role of design is not limited to matching inventions and markets. It is equally important in relation to production techniques. Many new products also require a new process to produce them. They all require attention to the method of production. As we shall see, the ability to redesign the entire process of production to achieve higher product quality and a greater capacity to introduce new and improved products, has been one of the main strengths of Japanese design engineering. The key role of design lies in this integration of R&D, production and marketing. Designers have to provide integrated solutions in organisations which may divide these functions into completely separate worlds with very little communication.

2. Creating

Creativity is of course an essential element of innovative entrepreneurship and design, since it entails the bringing together of what were previously disparate and scattered pieces of knowledge to create something new. Sometimes the term 'creativity' is reserved for those abilities of the scientist which lead to new discoveries or of the artist which lead to new works of art. These kinds of creativity are important for innovation too. However, when we are considering national innovation systems (as opposed to global civilisation and the world economy), then at least in the past they have not been so central to innovative success as those types of creativity which are characteristic of the engineer and the designer in the work of invention and design. In these design/engineering types of creativity the *synthesis* and creative application of information from a variety of sources (including the arts and sciences) is critical. The capacity for such creative synthesis has become increasingly related to more effective modes of coupling with the arts and sciences and their creative initiatives, and with the capacity to take advantage of information technology.

3. Clustering

It was Schumpeter again who observed that innovations, like troubles, do not come singly but in battalions. They are 'more like a series of explosions than a gentle though incessant transformation.'[16] They are not distributed at random, instead tending to concentrate in certain sectors. This clustering is related to diffusion which leads to further innovations as the bandwagon starts rolling. These observations of Schumpeter have been amply confirmed by much empirical research since his day. All statistics of the inputs and outputs of the R&D system illustrate the point. They show heavily skewed distributions of research, inventive and innovative activities. Moreover the research-intensive industries and activities tend to be the same throughout the world, with certain exceptions related to military R&D and to the small size of many countries. This suggests that the common underlying factors are the progress of world science and technology and new market opportunities based on income growth. There are a number of mechanisms which might explain the clustering in terms of world technology. A major new material would need many applications innovations to take advantage of its new properties for various uses. A new piece of equipment, such as a computer, would lead to both component and applications innovations, which are an obvious feature of the contemporary industrial scene. Most product innovations lead to further process and product innovations as their scale of manufacture increases and as competitors strive to gain some cost of production or quality improvement advantage. The expression 'natural trajectory' has been coined by Nelson and Winter[17] to describe this process of the cumulative exploitation of new ideas, and clearly the role of designers is again crucial in the rapid and efficient exploitation of such trajectories in many different markets.

Changes in world technological leadership may be associated with the emergence of new techological systems and the associated changes in industrial structure. Some countries might fall behind through a failure to adapt sufficiently quickly to the new natural trajectories. If the new technological systems have very widespread applications—for example, electricity or computers—then they could help to explain the tendency for countries to succeed (or fail) in many different sectors in the same period. It is the contention of this chapter that the capacity to exploit a natural trajectory or a new technological system rapidly and efficiently is strongly related to various types of infrastructural investment, especially education and design, as well as to the modes of interaction between industrial firms themselves and their own arrangements for design, education and training.

4. Comprehending

In whatever country and in whatever institutions the original scientific and technical ideas which underlie a new technological system may have originated, the ability to innovate successfully and continuously depends upon the number and quality of the people who have assimilated these ideas and the depth of their understanding. These in turn depend upon monitoring, information and education systems as well as upon the general 'openness' of a society and the movement of people and ideas. Clearly the receptiveness of industrial designers to new technologies is a key element in the whole system.

5. Coping

Again this is in part a mattter of definition. Innovation inevitably includes uncertainty of technology and markets. By definition it is not possible to make accurate predictions of the costs, duration and consequences of technical innovation. If it is possible, then what is being done is not innovation. One can, of course, speculate, make informed guesses, and anticipate some of the problems and consequences. The less radical the innovation, the easier this is, and in the simple imitation of an innovation made elsewhere the uncertainty may be minimal. Nevertheless, the ability to cope with uncertainty and to live with it is an essential element in design and the successful management of innovation. This has many implications for technological leadership. It puts a premium on flexibility in ideas and institutions. It puts a premium on 'management slack' of some kind or other in innovating organisations. It puts a premium on long-term patience with radical new ideas and inventions, and long-term strategies generally as opposed to the apparent near-certainties of short-term profit maximisation. I now turn to consider some historical examples of major shifts in world technological and trade leadership in the light of the above discussion, and in particular the rise of two countries which have shown a phenomenal growth of exports of manufactures and have successively displaced Britain in the twentieth century as a world leader in trade, productivity, and technology—first Germany, and then Japan.

Friedrich List and Technology

Friedrich List[18] is known today in Britain mainly as the advocate of protection of infant industries. Hardly anyone reads List in the original, so that a central part of his teaching is completely ignored—that is his emphasis on the role of technology in economic progress and in international trade. List actually believed in free trade, although he thought the ideal was feasible only when a number of countries were almost equal in terms of wealth and technology. Britain appeared in the first half of the nineteenth century, much as Japan appears today, as a country which dominated most world markets for manufactured goods. List therefore insisted that Germany had first of all to catch up with Britain in technology. Since, by the irony of history, the roles have been reversed, the main protectionist school in economic theory now being located in England whereas German economists preach the virtues of free trade, it is worth examining the policy conclusions which List drew from his theoretical analysis. They may be summed up as a long-term national technology policy closely linked to industrial and education policy.

The fundamental points in List's spirited defence of national technology strategies were the following:

1. The importance of 'mental capital' ('intellectual capital' might be a better rendering today than the English translation of that time). There can be no doubt whatever what List was talking about in this passage:

    The present state of the nations is the result of the accumulation of all discoveries, inventions, improvements, perfections and exertions of all generations which have lived before us: they form the mental capital of the present human race, and every separate nation is productive only in the proportion in which it has known how to appropriate these attainments of former generations, and to increase them by its own acquirements.

2. The recognition of the importance of the interaction between 'mental capital' and 'material capital' (or as we might put it today: 'intangible' and 'tangible' investment or 'hardware' and 'software'). List clearly recognised both the importance of new investment embodying the

latest technology and the importance of learning by doing from the experience of production with this equipment.

3. The importance of importing foreign (especially English) technology and of attracting foreign investment and the migration of skilled people as a means of acquiring the most recent technology.

4. The importance of skills in the labour force. He argued that Smith did not follow up his clear insight into the importance of 'productive powers', skill, knowledge and education, concentrating only on the division of labour aspect of the problem. He ridiculed the classical school for regarding teachers and doctors as 'non-productive', and completely underestimating the role of scientists, engineers and designers by reducing all inputs of labour to a common denominator.

5. The importance of the manufacturing sector for economic progress and the necessity for investment in manufacturing as a means of stimulating the development of the entire economy, especially agriculture although also including services.

6. The importance of taking a very long-term historical view in developing and applying economic policies. He clearly regarded the development of manufacturing, the appropriate institutions and 'mental capital' to enable manufacturing to flourish as a matter of many decades. He ridiculed J.B. Say for accepting the argument that infant industry was the exception to free trade only in those cases where a branch of industry would become remunerative after a few years.

7. Finally, List stressed very strongly the importance of an active interventionist economic policy to promote long-term development, and decisively rejected the philosophy of the 'night-watchman state'.

It was because he believed that the entrenched authority of a school was such a powerful influence on national economic policies that Keynes in his day launched an attack on the classical school no less vigorous (and some might say no less exaggerated) than that of List. And, at least for a generation, if not longer, both were successful in establishing a new orthodoxy. The economists who influenced most of those rising to authority in Germany in the latter half of the nineteenth century were not the classical school, as in Britain, but the school of Friedrich List. This was of decisive importance for the evolution of German economic policies and German approaches to technology. Its first and most important consequence was the early development of an education and training system capable of putting the acquisition and dissemination of world technology on a regular and systematic basis.

The advantages which German industry and the German economy gained through the development of what is by general consent a first-rate system of educating and training craftsmen, technicians and technologists would be difficult to overestimate. It was recognised, though belatedly, by the British when they began to realise that the ever-increasing effectiveness of German trade competition in the period leading up to the First World War was related to superior technology and quality of products, based on the achievements of the Technische Hochschulen and the other institutions devoted to the advance of knowledge and its dissemination.

This belated British recognition, although it was important in various attempts at educational reform in the nineteenth and twentieth centuries (such as the establishment of Imperial College), was never sufficiently widespread as to overturn the dominant influence of the classical school on industrial, economic and education policy. So much was this so that the majority of British engineers down to the middle of the twentieth century had no professional academic qualifications, only a part-time qualification based on evening class study. British industry paid the penalty for national complacency resulting from the early predominance of Britain in the first two Kondratiev waves. Although in that period the method of training engineers 'on the job' on a part-time amateur basis was probably rather effective, it was not capable of coping with the increasingly sophisticated technologies of the third and fourth Kondratiev cycles. The German system, on the other hand, was based on thorough and deliberate professional development and on the recognition of *Technik*—design and engineering— as a 'third culture' at least equal in status to the arts and sciences. This was of the greatest importance for the general management culture in German industry. Since there were rather few professional academically trained engineers in British industry (and for other socio-cultural reasons), the dominant management tradition was amateurish and inclined to give weight to accountancy considerations on a short-term basis. The German management tradition was much more heavily influenced by professional engineers and designers who had both high status and high rewards. The type of long-term strategic thinking necessary for long-term success with new technologies was therefore far more characteristic of German than of British industry, as well as an insistence on high quality and good design on the technical side.

The importance of this long-term way of thinking was by no means confined to industry. It was also extremely important in government (for example in the finance of research and education, as well as in measures to promote strategic industries) and in financial institutions. British industry lagged well behind in the development and application of the newer technologies and in the growth of industrial R&D. This lag was reflected in the growth of American and German investment in Britain in the newer industries, especially electrical, as well as in Britain's declining share of exports of manufactures and her chronic imbalance of visible trade.

It has been possible only to sketch in the briefest and crudest outline some aspects of the displacement of Britain as the leader in world technology and trade. However, from what has been said it is clear that in their international competitive struggle, Germany (and the United States) relied not simply on tariffs (important though these were), but also on technology, and that in gaining that technological lead, the development of the education system and design capability for both products and processes was of central importance for almost all industries, and the role of professional R&D also became of growing importance for many. In sum, the German economy proved capable of assimilating (comprehending) the best available technology of the day, of improving upon it (creating), of organising the linkages through good design management between science, technology and markets (coupling) necessary for the efficient exploitation of new technological trajectories (clustering) and of coping with the long-term strategies of tangible and intangible investment which all of this implied. Japan in the twentieth century carried all these strategies to the nth degree in pursuing her own competitive advantage.

The case of Japan

When historians describe the intense Japanese efforts to overtake Western Europe and the United States, they usually start with the Meiji Restoration of 1868. Already in the nineteenth century many policies had been adopted to stimulate the growth of manufacturing industry and to import the best available technologies from wherever they might be available in the world.

The central point of interest from the standpoint of this analysis is that in the immediate post-war period, after an intense debate Japan specifically rejected a long-term development strategy based on traditional theory of comparative advantage, which was apparently at that time being advocated by economists in the Bank of Japan and elsewhere who subscribed to the free trade doctrines of the classical school. They had advocated a 'natural' path of industrial development, based on Japan's lower labour costs and comparative advantage in labour-intensive industries such as textiles. Although one of the central points at issue was whether Japan could hope to compete in the automobile industry and whether special steps should be taken to encourage its growth, the debate affected industrial and trade policy in its entirety. In the early days, according to G.C. Allen[19] (one of the few European economists who consistently attempted to study and learn from Japanese experience), the views of the Bank of Japan had some influence. They blocked loans in 1951 for a large new up-to-date steel works and 'Sony was obliged to postpone its imports of transistor technology because the officials in charge of foreign exchange licensing were doubtful both about the technology and about Sony's ability to make use of it'. On the whole, however, the bureaucrats and their advisers at the Ministry of International Trade and Industry (MITI) prevailed. They repudiated the view that Japan should be content with a future as an underdeveloped country with low productivity and income per head. Again, according to Allen (and many other observers):

Some of these advisers were engineers who had been drawn by the war into the management of public affairs. They were the last people to allow themselves to be guided by the half-light of economic theory. Their instinct was to find a solution for Japan's post-war difficulties on the supply side, in enhanced technical efficiency and innovations in production. They thought in dynamic terms. Their policies were designed to furnish the drive and to raise the finance for an economy that might be created rather than simply to make the best use of the resources it then possessed.[20]

The principal elements of this long-term techno-economic strategy were:

1. The ability to design and redesign entire production processes, whether in shipbuilding, colour TV, machine tools, or any other industry. The Japanese have been more successful than any other industrial nation in a systems approach to design, which recognises the integrative, coupling role of innovation management, relating product design and process design to world technology and world-wide markets. The Japanese system sets great store on the participation of employees in system changes, affecting as they do the entire work-force. The 'quality circles' are a social innovation designed to maximise the specific contribution from the lower levels of the work-force and to assign to the lower management levels a responsibility for technical change. We should also note that the Japanese policy of mainly rejecting foreign direct investment as a means of technology transfer, automatically places on the enterprise the full responsibility for assimilating imported technology and is far more likely to lead to total system improvements than the 'turnkey plant' mode of import or the foreign subsidiary mode.
2. The capacity at national government level to pursue an integration strategy which brings together the best available resources from universities, government research and private or public industry to solve the most important design and development problems, whether these relate to the use of integrated circuits in colour TV, or to the fifth generation computers.
3. The development of an education and training system which goes beyond the German level in two important respects. First of all, in the absolute numbers of young people acquiring higher levels of education, especially in science and engineering. Japan is now, together with the United States and the Soviet Union, among the leading countries in the world in the extent of educational opportunity. Second, in the scale and quality of industrial training, which is carried out at enterprise level. One of its features is to encourage all-round capability at lower levels in the work-force so that problems of breakdown and maintenance are far more rapidly dealt with. Another advantage of this approach is a

much smoother assimilation and readier acceptance of new process technology.

4. The early recognition that leadership in the new technological trajectories—robotics, information technology and computers—would be decisive for world competition in the 1990s in many branches of the economy, and the gearing of R&D, investment and training strategies to meet the objective of world technological leadership in these areas.

Conclusions

The implications which flow from this analysis are many and varied and it would be quite impossible in a short chapter to do more than point to a few of the most important (1) at the international level, and (2) at the national level.

At the international level the analysis points to the conclusion that future reforms in the international trading and financial arrangements must start from the expectation that persistent disequilibria in international trade are likely to be the norm rather than the exception. The tendency for the 'strong' (technical leader) countries to run a surplus is likely to persist over long periods and to reassert itself repeatedly despite currency adjustments and other measures designed to restore equilibrium. Similarly, the tendency for the 'weak' countries to run into vicious spiral problems is likely to be persistent. This means that there are serious dangers of deflationary pressures in the system arising from competitive national attempts to restore short-term equilibrium, unless

1. international financial arrangements and credit arrangements clearly recognise the very long-term, structural (and developmental) nature of the underlying tendencies (the Brandt Reports are highly relevant here); and

2. surplus countries, with the help of the international community, have the imagination (and sense of history) to recognise that their own long-term interests depend not only on seeking exclusive national competitive advantages, but on the international transfer of technology as well as capital.

The Kiel Institute studies on long waves in the world economy have shown that protectionism is the *consequence*, not the cause of deep depressions.

So far as Britain is concerned, it is difficult to be enthusiastic about the way in which all the main political parties hark back to ideas and theories which were appropriate one or two centuries ago but are not much help today. The opposition appear to have forgotten that the white heat of a technological revolution is a matter of decades of patient effort, not an election gimmick for a few months. They have also regressed to a pathetic faith in devaluation and price competition as the major instrument of trade competition. The government are the victims of their own ideological rhetoric, which denies to central government its vital role as energiser, organiser and co-ordinator of that massive scale of public and private investment and initiative, vital to success in international technological competition in today's world, and also necessary to overcome the disastrous social and economic consequences of high and persistent levels of unemployment. What is needed is post-Keynesian, not pre-Keynesian economics. If we have to go back to the nineteenth century, there is more to learn from List than from the Manchester School.

Notes

1. J. Christopher Jones, *Design Methods, Seeds of Human Futures*, Wiley, 1970.
2. W. Leontief, 'Domestic production and foreign trade: the American capital position re-examined', *Proceedings of the American Philosophical Society*, September, 1953.
3. M.V. Posner, 'International trade and technical change', *Oxford Economic Papers*, October, 1961.
4. G. Hufbauer, *Synthetic materials in international trade*, Harvard University Press, 1966.
5. C. Freeman, J.K. Fuller and A. Young, 'The plastics industry: a comparative study of research and innovation', *National Institute Economic Review*, No. 26, pp. 22–60; C. Freeman *et al.* 'Research and development in electronic capital goods', *National Institute Economic Review*, No. 34, November 1965; Idem, 'Chemical process plant: innovation and the world market', *National Institute Economic Review*, August, 1968.
6. A.M. Golding, 'The semi-conductor industry in Britain and the United States', DPhil thesis, University of Sussex, 1972. E. Sciberras, *Multi-national Electronic Companies and National Economic Policies*, JAI Press, New York, 1977. Dosi, G. *Technical change and industrial transformation*, Macmillan, London, 1984.
7. R. Vernon, R. Gruber and D. Mehta, 'The R and D factor in international trade and international investment of US industries', *Journal of Political Economy*, February, 1967.
8. K. Pavitt and L.L.G. Soete, 'Innovative activities and export shares: some comparisons between industries and countries', in K. Pavitt (ed.), *Technical Innovation and British Economic Performance*, Macmillan, 1980.
9. L.L.G. Soete, 'The impact of technological innovation in international trade performance: the evidence reconsidered', OECD Science and Technology Output Indicators Conference, Paris, September, 1980. L.L.G. Soete, 'A general test of technological gap trade theory', *Weltwirtschaftliches Archiv*, (1981) 117 (4), pp. 638–66.
10. Not impossible, as we know from other cases of paradigm change in the natural as well as the social sciences that 'rationality' counts for less than the emergence of a new young generation of practitioners: Easlea, B. *Liberation and the Aims of Science*, Chatto and Windus, 1973.

11. H.G. Johnson, 'The state of theory in relation to the empirical analysis' in R. Vernon (ed.), *The Technology Factor in International Trade*, Columbia University Press, New York, 1968.

12. E.J. Horn, *Technologische Neuerungen und internationale Arbeitsteilung*, Kieler Studien No. 139, J. Mohr, Tubingen, 1976. F. Wolter, 'Factor proportions, technology and West German industry's international trade patterns', *Weltwirtschaftliches Archiv*, 1977, Vol. 113, pp. 250–67.

13. I. Kravis and R.E. Lipsey, *Price Competitiveness in World Trade*, Columbia, New York, 1971.

14. R. Rothwell, 'Innovation in textile machinery' in K. Pavitt (ed.), *Technical Innovation and British Economic Performance*, Macmillan, London, 1980.

15. E. Sciberras, 'Technical innovation and international competitiveness in the television industry', SPRU, University of Sussex, mimeo, 1981.

16. J.A. Schumpeter, *Business Cycles: a theoretical, historical and statistical analysis*, 2 Vols, McGraw Hill, New York, 1939.

17. R. Nelson and S.G. Winter, In search of useful theory of innovation, *Research Policy*, Vol. 6, pp. 36–76, 1977.

18. F. List, *The National System of Political Economy*, 1845, English trans. S.S. Lloyd, Longman, 1904.

19. G.C. Allen, 'Industrial policy and innovation in Japan', in C. Carter (ed.), *Industrial policy and innovation*, Heinemann, London, p. 69.

20. Ibid., p. 77.

Part II
The Theory of Innovation and Evolutionary Economics

4 The nature of innovation and the evolution of the productive system*

I. Introduction and summary

This chapter discusses the relationship between productivity changes and technical innovation. Whilst economists have always accepted that technical change is a fundamental driving-force of productivity growth, they have differed in their assumptions and theories about its sources and its impact. Some have stressed its 'exogenous' aspects, describing it as 'manna from heaven'. Others have argued, following Schmookler (1961), that inventions and innovations are endogenous activities within the economy, responding to demand pressures or changes in factor costs. These economists have tended to stress the smooth and continuous nature of technical change, whereas others, following Schumpeter (1912), have depicted it as a series of shocks or explosions, uneven in their incidence over time and space. They have stressed the unpredictable and largely autonomous developments in fundamental science in their interactions with technology and the creative pioneering role of innovative entrepreneurs, with characteristics differing from the ordinary routine managers and businessmen. Schumpeter's view is discussed in Section II.

The evidence from much recent research on technical change, as well as the evidence from the history of technology indicates that there is substance in both views and that a satisfactory theory of technical change must be based on a taxonomy of innovations, which includes both 'radical' and 'incremental' innovations. Although both are essential to the growth of productivity, their effects are quite different over a long period. This distinction is discussed in Section III.

When they are first introduced, just because they mark a break with past production practice and experience, by definition both management and work-force are unfamiliar with radical new products and processes and sometimes resist their introduction. Moreover, even with the best-

---

*This chapter was originally presented as a paper at the OECD International Seminar on Science, Technology and Economic Growth, Paris, 1989.

organised research and development, it is seldom possible to eliminate all 'bugs' in the R&D stage. There are almost always teething problems with radical innovations, which may last for many years. Case studies of radical inventions and innovations (e.g. Jewkes, Sawers and Stillerman, (1958) provide abundant evidence for this proposition. Consequently, even though imaginative entrepreneurs, scientists and engineers may be quite confident about the ultimate technical and economic benefits, early productivity and profitability are often disappointing. For this reason, 'me-too' or 'fast-second' strategies are often preferred to the tribulations of first innovators. For this reason too, as well as market acceptance problems, most diffusion studies and models start with the flatter part of the familiar 'S'-shaped curve.

Incremental innovations are usually needed to overcome the early teething problems with radical innovations, so that user and producer experiences are taken into account in the redesign of product and process. These improvements continue throughout the product life so that once fast diffusion commences, a combination of learning by doing, learning by using and economies of scale can yield strong productivity gains for a considerable period, even for several decades. Ultimately, however, further incremental improvements begin to bump up against both scale and technical limits (Wolf's Law). Although slower productivity gains may continue for a long time and even receive further stimulus from the competition of new radical innovations, in the end the focus shifts to radically new types of production which offer once more the *potential* scope for more substantial gains.

However, the analysis of productivity growth cannot be confined to the level of the single innovation. All the empirical evidence points to the interdependence of many radical and incremental innovations. Both historians of technology (e.g. Gille, 1978) and studies of diffusion (e.g. Gold, 1981) point to the importance of 'systems' of innovation and 'networks' of interdependent elements. Obvious examples are electric power, railways and telecommunications systems. Here, the success of any innovation is often dependent on modifications elsewhere in the system and imbalances are a powerful inducement to complementary innovations (Rosenberg, 1976, 1982). These system aspects of innovation are more widespread than is commonly realised for many radical innovations require new combinations of inputs, such as materials, instruments and machinery as well as new skills. New technology systems are discussed in Section IV.

System gains in productivity depend therefore on a combination of related innovations, so that the time required for the realisation of the potential major incremental productivity gains is even longer, normally extending over decades rather than years. If new infrastructural investment is also needed and the new technology system is so extensive and influential that it affects the performance of the entire economy, this amounts to a change of 'techno-economic paradigm' (Perez, 1983). The final section of this chapter (Section V) argues that such a shift to a new 'information and communication technology' paradigm underlies some of the paradoxical movements in productivity in the 1970s and the 1980s.

II. Schumpeter

Any attempt to discuss the role of technical change in economic theory must go back to Schumpeter. Almost alone among leading twentieth-century economists, he attempted to place technical innovation at the heart of his system. However, with Schumpeter, as with other economists, we find some dualism in his work. On the one hand in his *Theory of Economic Development* (1912), science and technology are treated, at least implicitly, as exogenous to the system. On the other hand, in his famous paper on the 'Instability of capitalism' (1928) and even more in his later work (e.g. 1943), he emphasised the role of 'bureaucratised R&D' which had become an internalised function of the large enterprises and the source of their supposed competitive superiority. So strong was this contrast that Almarin Phillips (1971) even spoke of 'two Schumpeters'—the young and the old. No doubt there is some validity in this distinction, but it is also possible to view the contrast as reflecting Schumpeter's own historical sense of the changes which were taking place in the process of technical innovation during his own lifetime (Freeman, Clark and Soete, 1982). Be this as it may, it is evident that any attempt to deal with the issues of exogeneity and endogeneity must start with a critique of Schumpeter's approach.

Ruttan (1959) has maintained that Schumpeter did not even have a theory of innovation. This is putting the matter too strongly. Schumpeter had a theory of innovation, although it was a one-sided theory subordinated to his theory of entrepreneurship. This led him on the one hand to neglect incremental innovation, and on the other hand to neglect the interdependencies between major radical innovations. His theory of innovation was based on his definition of the 'entrepreneur' as that individual (or combination of individuals) responsible for the business decisions which lead to the introduction of new products, processes and systems or the opening up of new markets and new sources of supply. In his view, such innovative entrepreneurship was an act 'not of intellect but of will', and this creative leadership was the source of the enormous dynamism in capitalist society. This led him to concentrate attention on the more spectacular, 'heroic' types of innovation, which were identified with outstanding individuals, reflecting the business climate of the years before the First World War. He recognised corporate and even state entrepreneurship (Schumpeter, 1939, p. 346) but they fitted less easily into his framework.

The *source* of the scientific and technical ideas, which were ultimately embodied in new products and processes by an act of entrepreneurship was never of very much concern to him. Although he consistently stressed the importance of history in the social sciences, he was in no sense a historian of science or technology and there is remarkably little about the technical aspect of inventions or innovations in the whole of Schumpeter's work. In this respect his approach was similar to that of the 'manna from heaven' economists. However, in no way did he regard the flow of technical and organisational innovations as a smooth, continuous process fed by a steady stream of exogenous developments in science and technology. On the contrary, no one emphasised more than Schumpeter the uneven, discontinuous, unpredictable aspects of technical change which is 'more like a series of explosions than a gentle though incessant transformation' (Fels, 1964, p. 75). Innovations are 'lop-sided, discontinuous, disharmonious by nature' and are not evenly distributed over time or space, but tend to cluster 'because first some, and then most firms, follow in the wake of successful innovation'.

His well-known distinction between 'invention', 'innovation' and 'diffusion', which has since been adopted in most economic analyses of technical change, served to highlight the role of the entrepreneur in the entire process and to put the main emphasis on the more radical innovations. Both invention and diffusion were relegated to a somewhat inferior status. The role of the inventor, although of course acknowledged, was not comparable to that of *innovator*, even though the roles might sometimes be combined in the person of the inventor-entrepreneur. Many inventions would never go any further than the laboratory or the proverbial attic or would gather dust in the patent office. Only an act of innovative entrepreneurship would bring an invention from the status of scientific curiosity to that of commercial artefact; for Schumpeter this was the true and only source of profit and growth in capitalist society, and its most characteristic feature.

Similarly, Schumpeter's sharp distinction between innovation and diffusion, was linked to a clear division between the creative entrepreneurs and 'mere' routine managers (normal businessmen) who simply followed in the wake of the business leaders. Rosenberg (1976) in particular has consistently emphasised the dangers of this Schumpeterian dichotomy (or trichotomy if inventors are included). He has repeatedly pointed out that the product or process which is diffusing through a population of adopters is subject to a continual process of improvement and modification, so that diffusion is seldom if ever a simple process of replication by unimaginative imitators.

To be fair to Schumpeter, he occasionally emphasised this point himself, as in relation to the history of the automobile. He pointed out that 'those who follow the pioneers are still entrepreneurs, though to a degree that continually decreases to zero' (Schumpeter, 1939, p. 414). Nevertheless, the main thrust of his argument undoubtedly tends to put the spotlight on the innovator-entrepreneur and to detract attention somewhat from the diffusion–improvement–learning-by-doing-and-using complex of events, as well as the science–technology–invention nexus leading up to innovations. Yet, it is precisely the interdependence of invention, innovation and diffusion which emerges from most of the empirical work on technical change which has been carried out in the forty years or so since Schumpeter's death. Most of the productivity gains associated with the diffusion of new technology do *not* come as an immediate consequence of the first radical innovation. On the contrary, they are usually achieved only as a result of a fairly prolonged process of learning, improving, scaling up and altering the new products and processes. This entails many follow-through inventions and innovations throughout the commercial life of the product or system. The steam-engine, the generation of electricity, the automobile and the computer are all obvious examples.

At this point, one might protest that these examples are a-typical. They are all extremely important innovations, which were systemic in nature and each put their stamp on an entire historical era in the development of technology. But this is precisely the point. It is *not* possible to treat all innovations as though they were isolated and equal separate events. A satisfactory theory of technical change must embrace a taxonomy of innovation which recognises the qualitative differences between different types of innovation and their systemic interdependencies. Although there are glimpses of this in Schumpeter, his basic approach prohibited its full development. Although he recognised the importance of Gilfillan's work, he deliberately chose to emphasise other features of the process.

III. Incremental and radical innovations

Schumpeter's work on the sociology of *innovations*, (and he was as much a sociologist as an economist) (Shionoya, 1986), differed from Gilfillan's (1934) work on the sociology of *invention*, despite his attempt (1939, p. 226) to reconcile the two. Gilfillan emphasised the continuous and often anonymous stream of discoveries, inventions and improvements and discounted the individual leaps of invention and entrepreneurship which were Schumpeter's main concern. Much recent empirical work on technical change has vindicated Gilfillan's emphasis on a fairly steady process of incremental innovations over long periods and on the great importance of learning by doing and using. These expressions, introduced by Arrow (1962), von Hippel (1976) and other post-Schumpeterian economists, have now become part of the accepted jargon of the analysis of technical change. More recently, learning by 'inter-acting' (Lundvall, 1988) has also become part of the common currency, serving to emphasise the mutual interdependence of 'suppliers' and 'users' of innovations within a national or international system. Although Gilfillan used none of these expressions himself, they are a logical development and refinement from the spirit of his work. Indeed they are essentially an elaboration of one aspect of the treatment of technical change already developed by Adam Smith and Karl Marx.

Although Smith stressed the combined role both of producers and of users of machines as the joint source of technical improvements, he also pointed to the scientists ('philosophers') whose role is to speculate and to combine the understanding of dissimilar objects. Marx, too, stressed the way in which users of tools and machines modified them to meet the innumerable and changing needs of specific applications, as in the example (Clark and Juma, 1988) of the large variety of hammers in use in British engineering workshops during the Industrial Revolution. However, Marx also recognised the ways in which science was increasingly pressed into the direct service of production.

Smith and Marx were interested in the detail of technical change and recognised the role of science as well as incremental modifications in changing the production system. But most of the neo-classical economists preferred to abstract from this nitty-gritty concern with innovation. Rogers (1962) could find only one case study of the industrial diffusion of innovations by an economist. However, since the 1950s there has been a resurgence of empirical research so that we now have far more evidence on which to base generalisations on the role of producers and users of innovation during diffusion.

Among many studies of technical change in specific industries, two in particular amply demonstrate the role of learning by doing and using in incremental innovation. These are Hollander's (1965) study of Du Pont's rayon plants and Townsend's (1976) study of the Anderton shearer-loader in the underground mechanisation of the British coal industry. Hollander's detailed longitudinal study showed that 90 per cent of the steady productivity gains achieved in Du Pont rayon plants over the 1950s could be ascribed to incremental improvements in the operation of the plant introduced by production engineers, systems engineers, and operators and could not be ascribed to the central R&D department of the firm. Townsend showed that after the original development and manufacture of the shearer-loader machine by Anderton-Boyes (itself based on prototype experiments at the coal-face initiated by a production engineer), hundreds of incremental improvements to the design were made during the 1950s and 1960s. These flowed from suggestions made at the coal-face and introduced by the manufacturers, just as Adam Smith had indicated. Here too, the process of incremental innovation led to very substantial productivity gains, particularly as the machine was modified to meet the wide variety of geological conditions and the exacting safety requirements of the Coal Board's tests.

These two studies are typical of many which have amply confirmed that the incremental improvements associated with learning by doing and using are indeed a major source of productivity gains in many industries. Such incremental improvement is not of course simply a process of *technical* change, it also involves *organisational* innovation and skill improvements based on experience. It is difficult to discern the role of Schumpeter's heroic entrepreneurs in this rather hum-drum process, except perhaps in creating an environment receptive to the innovative ideas of engineers, workers and users. As Pavitt (1984) has shown, it is a long process of accumulation of tacit as well as formal knowledge within enterprises.

Does all this mean then that Schumpeter's emphasis on major creative leaps was entirely misplaced and that Gilfillan-style incrementalism combined with Arrow's learning by doing gives us a sufficient account of innovation in capitalist society? By no means. Instructive though the Hollander, Townsend and similar studies are, they reflect only one part of the complex set of innovative activities which transform the production system. Studies of incremental improvement must be complemented by studies of more radical discontinuities in the economy. No matter how much the underground operation of the shearer-loader users improved, it could never lead to an automated moving coal-face system based on electronic sensing and electronic controls. Such changes cannot arise from the purely incremental improvements associated with doing and using. Or, as Schumpeter himself put it: no matter how many stage coaches you put together you will not get a steam locomotive or a railway system. A satisfactory theory of innovation must embrace both Gilfillan incrementalism and Schumpeterian entrepreneurship with its more radical discontinuities in both products and processes, on the lines which Enos (1962), Mensch (1975) and others have proposed.

Incremental improvement has its limitations. There are technical limits to the use of candles in illumination, the use of horses in traction, the uses of iron and steel as engineering materials, the use of the abacus in statistical processing or of the valve (tube) in electronic computers. No amount of experience, learning, organisational and technical improvements can ultimately overcome their limitations, even though the arrival of a radical (and discontinuous) innovation may sometimes stimulate a last surge of incremental innovations—the so-called 'sailing-ship effect' which should more properly be called the 'steam-ship effect', for it was the arrival of the radical innovation which led to the final wave of improvements in the design of sailing-ships. Both economists and technologists have demonstrated the tendency for any incremental improvements to asymptote towards limits which may be either economic or technical or both.

The scaling up of plant and equipment is a process which has yielded enormous productivity gains in such industries as steel, petrochemicals, oil refining (Enos, 1962), road, sea and air transport, in the post-war period. However, as technical limits are approached (Wolf's Law), there is an increasing cost for additional minor improvements. Similar limitations may affect both the management of very large units and the marketing of output in relation to transport and distribution. Thus, oil tankers and ethylene plants have probably reached the limits of their efficient scaling up. In many industries, such as steel, the trend towards larger capacity plants has even been reversed since the productivity gains from radically new technology, from electronic instrumentation and control systems and from computer-controlled marketing and distribution are greater than further gains from scaling up giant plants.

Schumpeter was not mistaken in stressing the importance of 'successive industrial revolutions' and of radical discontinuities in the productive system, or in recognising the enormous difficulties and risks confronting the innovative entrepreneurs in their attempts at radical innovation. The classic study by Jewkes, Sawers and Stillerman (1958) not only demonstrates the extraordinary persistence of inventors despite all kinds of discouragement, but also shows that the final development and commercialisation of major inventions does indeed depend on acts of entrepreneurship whether in large or small firms, and whether or not the inventor is also the entrepreneur.

A satisfactory theory of innovation therefore must embrace *both* the innumerable incremental improvements *and* the radical discontinuities. Even though the borderline is sometimes difficult to draw, as with all such distinctions, there really is an important difference between the introduction of nylon or electricity and the incremental improvement of rayon manufacturing or steam engines. In the case of incremental innovations the changes which take place can be expressed as change in the coefficients of the input–output matrix of the *existing* array of products and services. In the case of radical innovation, logically, new rows and columns would be needed as they change the array of products and services and not just the efficiency in use of existing commodities. In practice, of course, there are always long delays before the introduction of entirely new products, such as electronic computers, is recognised in established statistical systems, such as input-output tables. They appear first in rag-bag categories such as products 'not elsewhere classified', but this does not invalidate the basic point.

Radical innovations cause structural change in the economy and lead ultimately to entirely new branches of industry. They are indeed, as Schumpeter insisted, the main source of dynamic development, distinguishing capitalism from earlier production systems. Today they require different types of research and development, different relationships with basic science, different types of marketing and financing, different types of input and lead to a different pattern of productivity gain. By definition they need quite new skills and management organisation and different types of production equipment. Mensch (1975) defined radical innovations ('basic innovations') as those requiring a new type of facility for their production and/or a new market.

For productivity movements, the distinction between radical and incremental innovations is clearly of decisive importance. Major and prolonged productivity increases are likely to be achieved during the main incremental *improvement* phase or a radical innovation, but not in the early *introduction* phase, when the scale of production is too small to achieve scale economies, when standardisation of supply of new materials and components has not yet taken place and when designs of both product and process are still in flux. These considerations assume far greater importance when we take into account the *systems* aspect of most important radical innovations. The *potential* leap to much higher levels of productivity from a radical innovation may become a reality only when it is complemented by a wide range of other innovations, including especially organisational, managerial and social innovations. Keirstead (1948) was one of the first economists to recognise explicitly the great economic significance of these clusters, which he described as 'constellations' of innovations.

IV. Radical innovations and new technology systems

As Spike Milligan pointed out, one telephone was not much use without a switchboard to connect it to others. Innovations are not a set of isolated events but are inevitably linked together, both in their underlying technical and scientific foundations and in their physical connections to other parts of the economic system. They may often induce other innovations both directly and indirectly. Historians of technology such as Gille (1978), Hughes (1982) and Rosenberg (1976, 1982) have pointed to numerous examples. Hughes (1982) has shown that in complex supply networks, such as electric power, innovation in one part of the network can lead to intense engineering efforts to solve related problems or restore balance in its other parts. Rosenberg (1976) rightly insists that what is involved is not simply the inducement mechanism of relative factor costs, but also a complex interplay between new technological possibilities and 'trajectories', various cost pressures and bugs or imbalances in the system.

The expression 'generic technology' has been used to express the ways in which some new technologies open up a wide range of possibilities for further innovations in many sectors of the economy. Nelson and Winter (1977 and 1982) used the expression 'generalised natural trajectories of technology', to convey an essentially similar idea: that some developments in science and technology are so powerful that they set in train a number of chains of technologically related innovations.

For example, in the first Industrial Revolution, both Rosenberg (1976) and Rolt (1970) have demonstrated the critical role of machine tool technology for all kinds of other eighteenth and nineteenth-century capital goods innovations. Rolt (1970, p. 128) points out that Watt's steam-engine remained a good idea in the mind of its inventor until John Wilkinson had evolved a machine which could bore the cylinder accurately enough.

'From that time onwards it became plainly apparent that engineering progress would be governed by the ability of the machine shop to translate new ideas into hardware.' Rolt attributes to Henry Maudslay a number of the key innovations which facilitated this type of technical advance in other industries:

He was the first to realise that workshop precision depended upon four things: accurate screw threads; true plane surfaces; absolute rigidity in all machine tools and precise methods of measurement. The origins of the lathe, man's basic machine tool, may be traced back into prehistory, yet Maudslay's first screw-cutting lathe was the undoubted parent of the modern lathe because it was built on these principles.

Rolt shows that the accuracy of these early machine tools was largely self-propagating, once the necessary accuracy had been built into them. His innovation of the bench micrometer enabled detection of differences up to 1/10,000th of an inch and clearly these advances in machine tools technology affected productivity gains in every other part of the system.

In their turn, advances in machine tools technology were dependent upon and stimulated related advances in metallurgy, especially in steel technology. Towards the end of the nineteenth century, a new cluster of innovations in steel, heat treatment, electric motors, electric furnaces and cutting-tool speeds made possible enormous further improvements in the productivity of machining systems throughout the engineering industries (Ayres, 1988). However, as in the first Industrial Revolution, the realisation of these new potential productivity gains was a prolonged process, requiring as it did not merely the diffusion of discrete individual innovations, but also the reorganisation of production systems to accommodate unit drive or batch drive, new factory layouts based on electric power, new skills and maintenance systems.

It was a similar story for synthetic materials, including synthetic fibres and synthetic rubbers. Most of these materials were first innovated in the German chemical industry in the 1920s and 1930s and they shared a common underlying scientific base in macromolecular chemistry. In the early days they were rarely competitive with natural materials, such as rubber, wool, leather and metals. The driving motivation was often autarkic—to overcome German dependence on imported materials. As learning progressed, however, many related and induced innovations were made in extrusion machinery, injection-moulding machines and in new applications. During and after the war the scaling up of production and numerous process innovations made the new materials increasingly competitive, and in the 1950s and 1960s they were the fastest growing sector of the world chemical industry, with very high annual gains in both labour and capital productivity. The universal availability and falling cost of oil-based 'building block' chemicals also greatly facilitated the growth of productivity as the industry switched to petrochemical technology. Thus, once again it can be seen that the productivity gains in this industry were certainly associated with a cluster of radical innovations but these bore their full fruit only when a new technological system was established after a complex social learning process lasting several decades (Freeman, Clark and Soete, 1982).

Among a number of economists who have developed similar ideas about interrelated innovations in 'systems', 'trajectories' and 'paradigms' (Dosi, 1982), the ideas of Sahal (1985) and of Perez (1983, 1985, 1987) are of particular interest in relation to long-term changes in productivity.

In line with the argument advanced so far in this paper, Sahal rejects either exclusive demand-pull or technology-push theories, maintaining that 'technology both shapes its socio-economic environment and is in turn shaped by it. Neither is a sole determinant of the other, the two codetermine each other.' He stresses in particular the influence of scale and size on the evolution of technology; ultimately he argues that the process of scaling up (or of miniaturisation) reaches limits and that at this time new radical innovations are needed to open up broad 'avenues of innovation' affording new opportunities in many sectors.

Perez similarly stresses the interplay between institutional change and technological change in developing her concept of 'techno-economic paradigms'. The realm of the technically feasible is far wider than the realm of the economically profitable. The selective mechanisms of the economy and of the natural and social environment interact with new technological trajectories to shape successive 'techno-economic paradigms'. Her theory has several important distinguishing features which are particularly helpful in considering long-term trends in productivity.

In the first place her concept of a change in techno-economic paradigm is one of a change in the basic approach of designers, engineers and managers which is so pervasive that it affects almost all industries and sectors of the economy. It is a 'meta-paradigm' theory. Secondly, she argues that the *economic* motivation for such a change of paradigm lies not only in the availability of a cluster of radical innovations including organisational innovations offering numerous new potential applications; but also in the *universal* and *low cost* availability of a key factor or combination of factor inputs. She suggests that this key factor was cheap *steel* from the 1880s to the 1930s, cheap *oil* from the 1930s to the 1980s, and cheap micro-electronics (chips) at the present time. Finally, she argues that before a new techno-economic paradigm can generate a new wave of expansion, there is a crisis of 'structural adjustment' corresponding to the recession and depression phases of Schumpeter's 'long waves' of economic development. The old institutions were adapted to a now increasingly obsolete technological style. They tend to 'lock out' alternative systems. There is therefore a period of mismatch between the new technology and the old institutional framework. The need for new institutions is perhaps most obvious in education and training, although it affects almost all institutions, including the capital market, standards, proprietary aspects of technology, government regulation of various sectors of the economy, industrial relations, trade union structure and so forth.

Perez therefore offers a link between the cyclical theories of technological evolution advanced by Abernathy and Utterback (1975), Sahal (1985) and others and the theories of path-dependency, structural change and 'lock-out' of alternatives put forward by Arthur (1988), David (1985) and Dosi and Orsenigo (1988).

The link to long-term productivity trends is evident. The productivity potential of a new techno-economic paradigm is at first realised only in one or a few leading sectors. Not until these effects have been clearly demonstrated does the diffusion begin to affect the entire economy. However, since what is needed is now a new infrastructure, many institutional and organisational changes, universal availability of new skills, as well as new types of equipment and materials, there is inevitably a prolonged period of structural adaptation.

So far this chapter has drawn upon the evidence of empirical and historical studies of innovation to develop a taxonomy of innovations and to relate the characteristics of their various types to their effects on productivity. This exposition was designed to explain some of the paradoxes in the present debate on long-term productivity trends. In the final section of the chapter we consider the specific use of information and communication technology and advance the hypothesis that the paradoxical slow-down in the 1970s and 1980s may be explained in part by the change of techno-economic paradigm. The final section is based on an analysis originally put forward in a paper for the OECD 25th Anniversary Symposium (Freeman, 1986).

V. Productivity effects of innovations in information and communication technology

The new 'information technology' (IT) paradigm, based on a constellation of industries, which are among the fastest growing in all the leading industrial countries, such as computers, electronic components and telecommunications, has already resulted in a drastic fall in *costs* and a counter-inflationary trend in prices in these sectors as well as vastly improved technical performance. This technological revolution is now affecting, although very unevenly, all other sectors (Freeman and Soete, 1987), because of its actual or potential economic and technical advantages. In considering this technological revolution, we must take into account not only particular products, processes or services but also the changes in organisation and structure of both firms and industries, which accompany the introduction of IT.

In addition to fundamental changes in management structure of large firms, and in their procedures and attitudes, there are many other parallel effects of the spread of IT through the economy: the capability which it confers for more rapid changes in product and process design; the much closer integration of design, production and procurement functions within the firm; the reduced significance of economies of scale based on dedicated capital-intensive mass production techniques; the reduction in numbers and weight of mechanical components in many products; the much more integrated networks of component suppliers and assemblers of final products and the related capital-saving potential; the growth of new 'product services' to supply manufacturing firms with the new software, design, technical information and consultancy which they increasingly require; and the extremely rapid growth of many small new innovative enterprises to supply these services and new types of hardware and components. According to some estimates, if software is included with R&D expenditures in electronics and telecommunications, then this accounts for nearly half of all contemporary R&D activity.

The skill profile associated with the new techno-economic paradigm appears to change from the concentration on middle-range craft and supervisory skills to increasingly high and low-range qualifications, and from narrow specialisation to broader multipurpose basic skills for information handling. Diversity and flexibility at all levels substitute for homogeneity and dedicated systems. Software design and maintenance become key skills everywhere.

The transformation of the profile of capital equipment is no less radical. Computers are increasingly associated with all types of productive equipment as in computer numeric control (CNC) machine tools, robotics and process control instruments as well as with design through computer-aided design (CAD), and with administrative functions through data processing systems, all linked by data transmission equipment. According to some estimates, computer-based capital equipment already accounts for between a quarter and a half of all new fixed investment in plant and equipment in the United States and other leading industrial countries.

The deep structural problems generated by this change of paradigm are now evident in all parts of the world. Among the manifestations are the acute and persistent shortage of the high-level skills associated with the new paradigm, even in countries with high levels of general unemployment. In the early 1980s studies in many different OECD countries unanimously reported persistent skill shortages in software design and development, systems analysis and computer engineering. If anything these problems have become more acute with manufacturing firms in both Japan and Britain complaining of 'poaching' by the service industries.

As a result there is a growing search for new social and political solutions in such areas as flexible working time, re-education and retraining systems, regional policies based on creating conditions for information technology (rather than tax incentives to capital-intensive mass production industries), new financial systems, possible decentralisation of management and government, and access to data banks at all levels. So far, however, there still seem to be partial and relatively minor changes. If the Keynesian revolution and the profound transformation of social institutions in the Second World War and its aftermath were required to unleash the post-war wave of growth, then social innovations on a much more significant scale are likely to be needed now. This applies especially to the international dimension of world economic development and the telecommunications network.

In describing the advantages of a new techno-economic paradigm, we have stressed the ability to bring about a 'quantum jump' in productivity. However, the *actual* rates of productivity increase have declined since the 1960s in most industrial countries. How is this apparent paradox to be explained? There are of course many factors to be taken into account, such as macro-economic policies, the exhaustion of 'catching up gains' in the 1960s and 1970s, demographic changes and so forth. Varying levels of capacity utilisation are particularly important for short and medium-term changes, although for *long-term* trends in the entire world economy, technical change is clearly a major factor. Why then the *slowdown* of the 1970s and 1980s?

First of all, it is essential to keep in mind that the new paradigm has been diffusing in a world still dominated by the older energy-intensive mass production paradigm. The symptoms of diminishing returns to the massive investment in this older paradigm were evident in declining capital productivity in most industrial sectors in almost all OECD countries since the late 1960s. However, they have also become apparent in the declining rate of increase in labour productivity.

Secondly, in assessing the growing impact of the new techno-economic paradigm, it is necessary to take into account all that has been said above about the problems of structural adjustment, before a 'good match' is achieved between the new paradign and the institutional framework. This process is very uneven between different countries and different industrial sectors. Therefore in examining these phenomena it is essential to move to a disaggregated level of analysis, since what we are discussing is the extremely uneven diffusion of a new technological paradigm from a few leading sectors to the economy as a whole.

The TEMPO project at SPRU attempted to study the long-term changes in labour and capital productivity in the principal sectors of the British economy (the forty industries distinguished in the Cambridge growth model) from 1948 to 1984. The account which follows is based on the five volumes of that analysis and the full summary (Freeman and Soete, 1987). In our view, although there are important national variations, the broad picture which is described below is characteristic of all the major OECD industrial economies.

When we analyse changes in labour productivity and in capital productivity over the past twenty years at a sufficiently disaggregated level, then we find the following picture:

1. The sectors with the highest rates of growth in labour productivity are the electronic industries, and especially the computer industry and the electronic component industry. These are the industries which make the greatest use of their own technology for design, production, stock control, marketing and management. They are also the only industrial sectors which show a substantial rise in *capital* productivity. They are the sectors which demonstrated the advantages of the new technologies for everyone else and may be described as the 'carrier' and 'motive' branches of the new paradigm. Baily and Chakrabarty (1988) have estimated that no less than half of the total growth of US manufacturing productivity in the 1980s is due to the computer industry alone.

2. In those sectors which have been heavily penetrated by micro-electronics, both in their product and process technology, there is also evidence of a considerable rise in labour productivity and even some advance in capital productivity in the most recent period. This applies, for example, to the scientific instruments, the telecommunications and the watch industries. These sectors have now virtually become a part of the electronics industry.

3. In sectors where microelectronics has been used on an increasing scale over the past ten years, although older technologies still predominate in product and process technology, there is a very uneven picture. Some firms have achieved very high productivity increases, some have stagnated, and others actually show a decline in productivity. This is the case, for example, in the printing, machine-building and clothing industries. This uneven picture is completely consistent with Solter's (1960) vision of the spread of new technologies within established industries through new capital investment. In many cases information technology is introduced in a piecemeal fashion in one department or for one activity and not as part of an integrated system. For example, one or a few CNC machine tools are introduced or a few robots or word processors. These are small 'islands' of automation. This is not yet computer-integrated manufacturing or office systems and does not yet achieve anything approaching the full *potential* productivity gains. There may even be a temporary fall in productivity because of the lack of the necessary skills in design, software, production engineering, maintenance, and management generally. Problems of institutional and social adaptation are extremely important, and flexibility in this social response is very varied between countries, as well as between enterprises.

4. Sectors producing standardised homogeneous commodities on a flow production basis in rather large plants have made considerable use of

information technology in their process control systems and in various management applications. They were indeed among the earliest users of computers for these purposes. This applies for example to the petrochemical, oil, steel and cement industries. This has helped them to achieve considerable improvements in their use of energy and materials, although gains in labour productivity have often been less than in the 1950s and 1960s, and capital productivity usually shows a marked decline. To understand this phenomenon it is essential to recognise that these industries are amongst those most heavily affected by the shift from an energy and materials–intensive mass production technological paradigm to an information-intensive paradigm. At the height of the consumer durables and vehicles consumption boom of the 1950s and 1960s, they were achieving strong labour productivity gains based on big plant economies of scale. However, with the change in technological paradigm, the slowdown in the world economy and the rise in energy prices in the 1970s, they often faced problems of surplus capacity and high unit costs based on below–capacity production levels. Nevertheless, see (8) below for those cases in which surplus capacity has been eliminated.

5. Service sectors which are completely based on information technology —software services, data banks, computerised information services, design services, etc.—are among the fastest growing and (for individual firms) the most profitable activities in the leading industrial countries. However, although their growth potential is enormous, they so far account for only a small proportion of total service output and employment and they suffer from acute skill shortages.

6. Some other service sectors have been considerably affected by information technology, such as banking, insurance and distribution. In these sectors, although the diffusion of new technology is extremely uneven, both by firm and by country, there is evidence of significant gains in labour productivity although measurement problems are acute. This phenomenon is rather important because hitherto it has often been observed that the service sector of the economy was not capable of achieving the type of labour productivity gains achieved in manufacturing. Information technology now offers the *potential* (and in some cases already the reality) of achieving such gains outside manufacturing. However, the progress of technology depends heavily on organisational, institutional and structural changes. The institutional factors, for example, are extremely important in explaining the very slow rate of change in Japanese retail distribution.

7. In most service sectors, information technology has diffused to only a small extent, and these are still characterised by very low labour productivity gains, or none at all. The capacity to design, use and maintain software systems is largely lacking and although the stagnation in labour productivity in these sectors may be attributed to

the *lack* of information technology, it certainly cannot be attributed to the impact of information technology. These account by far for the larger part of the tertiary sector.

8. Finally, in many industrialised economies there are sectors which have shown labour productivity gains over the past ten years, which are owing far more to structural rationalisation than to the direct impact of new technology. Examples are in the textile industries and also some of those sectors discussed in (4) above, where plant closures and rationalisation have been implemented as in the UK steel industry and European petrochemicals. Since in any industry there is always a 'tail' of low productivity plants, a significant rise in *average* labour productivity can always be achieved simply as a result of scrapping the older generation of plant, even without any further technical improvements in the more recent plants, which can now work closer to full capacity. This may be described as the *Verdun* effect in contrast to the *Verdoorn* effect of the high boom period.

Summing up this discussion, it is not difficult to see that the slowdown in *average* labour productivity gains over the 1970s and 1980s, which has been a world-wide phenomenon by comparison with the 1950s and 1960s, is precisely the aggregate outcome of a structural crisis of adaptation or change of techno-economic paradigm, which has accentuated the uneven development in different sectors of the economy.

On the one hand, the previously dominant energy-intensive mass production paradigm or 'technical regime' was reaching limits of productivity and profitability gains, due to a combination of exhaustion of economies of scale, erosion of profit margins through 'swarming', market saturation in some sectors, diminishing returns to technical activities (Wolf's Law) and cost pressures on input prices. On the other hand, the new paradigm, which offers the *possibility* of renewal of productivity gains and increased profitability, has so far deeply affected only a few leading edge industries and services.

The full realisation of the productivity gains which can be achieved as a result of information technology depends on the diffusion of the new paradigm throughout the economy. This in turn will be possible only as a result of many social and institutional changes, which will involve interrelated organisational and technical innovations, as well as a large increase in new skills and a transformation of the existing capital stock. The recent book of the MIT Commission on Industrial Productivity (Dertouzos, Lester and Solow, 1989) provides rather strong confirmation of this view in relation to the US economy in the 1980s.

VI. Conclusion

The hypothesis which has been advanced in this chapter to explain part of the productivity paradox of the 1970s and 1980s would require a large amount of long-term statistical analysis in many countries to verify thoroughly. However, the work of historians as well as the analysis of contemporary trends lends it some plausibility. For example, Landes (1970) commenting on the slowdown in British productivity growth in the 1870s and 1880s says:

We may note simply that such calculations as we have of her rates of industrial growth and increase in productivity—and they are confirmed by the major industrial time series—show a distinct falling-off after the mid-century decades of high prosperity. They do not turn up again until after 1900. From 1870 on, with the exception of a branch like steel, which was transformed by a series of fundamental advances in technique, British industry had exhausted the gains implicit in the original cluster of innovations that had constituted the Industrial Revolution. More precisely, it had exhausted the big gains. The established industries did not stand still. Change was built into the system, and innovation was if anything more frequent than ever. But the marginal product of improvement diminished as the cost of equipment went up and the physical advantage over existing techniques fell. (p. 235)

The recognition of diminishing returns in the old steam-powered factory systems was also apparent in the debates of the 1880s about the subcontracting arrangements, which were characteristic of both American and British Industry. There was a search going on for managerial and organisational innovations simultaneously with the efforts to improve technology by process innovations, and by the introduction of electricity. However, as in the 1970s, the realisation of these potential gains depended on a paradigm change with a new infrastructure. Abramowitz (1986) has pointed in the same direction in his analysis of 'catching up'. Technological leadership and even catching up depend on being able to run in new directions (Perez and Soete, 1988).

Bibliography

Abernathy, W.J. and Utterback, J.M. (1975), 'A dynamic model of process and product innovation', *Omega*, Vol. 3, No. 6.

Abramowitz, M. (1986), 'Catching up, forging ahead and falling behind', *Journal of Economic History*, Vol. 46, No. 2, pp. 385–406.

Arrow, K. (1962), 'The economic implications of learning by doing', *Review of Economic Studies*, Vol. 29, No. 80 (June), pp. 155–73.

Arthur, B. (1988), 'Competing technologies: an overview', in G. Dosi *et al.*, (eds), *Technical Change and Economic Theory*, Chapter 26, Pinter Publishers, London.

Ayres, R. (1988), 'Technological transformations and long waves', IIASA, Laxenburg.

Baily, M. and Chakrabarty, A.K. (1988), 'Innovations and the productivity crisis', Brookings Institution, Washington.

Clark, N. and Juma, C. (1988), 'Evolutionary theories in "economic thought"', in G. Dosi *et al.* (eds), *Technical Change and Economic Theory*, Chapter 9, Pinter Publishers, London.

David, P.A. (1985), 'Clio and the economics of QWERTY', *American Economic Review*, Vol. 75, No. 2, pp. 332–7.

Dertouzos, M.L., Lester, R.K. and Solow, R.M. (1989), *Made in America: Regaining the Productive Edge*, MIT Press, Cambridge, Mass. (Report of the MIT Commission on Industrial Productivity).

Devine, W. (1983), 'From shafts of wires: historical perspectives on electrification', *Journal of Economic History*, Vol. 43, No. 2, pp. 347–72.

Dosi, G. (1982), 'Technological paradigms and technological trajectories', *Research Policy*, Vol. 11, No. 3 (June), pp. 147–62.

Dosi, G. and Orsenigo, L. (1988), 'Coordination and transformation', in G. Dosi *et al.* (eds), *Technical Change and Economic Theory*, Chapter 2, Pinter Publishers, London.

Dosi, G., Freeman, C., Nelson, R., Silverberg, G. and Soete, L. (1988) (eds), *Technical Change and Economic Theory*, Pinter Publishers, London.

Enos, J. (1962), *Petroleum Progress and Profits: A History of Process Innovation*, MIT Press, Cambridge, Mass.

Fels, R. (1964) (ed.), abridged edition of Schumpeter's (1939) *Business Cycles*, McGraw Hill, New York.

Freeman, C. (1979), 'The determinants of innovation', *Futures*, Vol. 11 (June), pp. 206–15.

Freeman, C. (1986), 'The challenge of new technologies', OECD 25th Anniversary Symposium, OECD, Paris.

Freeman, C., Clark, J. and Soete, L. (1982), *Unemployment and Technical Innovation: A Study of Long Waves in Economic Development*, Pinter Publishers, London.

Freeman, C. and Soete, L. (1987) (eds), *Technical Change and Full Employment*, Blackwell, Oxford.

Gilfillan, S. (1934), *The Sociology of Invention*, Chicago.

Gille, B. (1978). *Histoire des Techniques*, Encyclopédie de la Pléiade, Tours.

Gold, B. (1981), 'Technological diffusion in industry: research needs and shortcomings', *Journal of Industrial Economics*, March, pp. 247–69.

Hollander, S. (1965), *The Sources of Increased Efficiency: A Study of Du Pont Rayon Plants*, MIT Press, Cambridge, Mass.

Hughes, T.F. (1982), *Networks of Power 1880–1930*, Johns Hopkins University Press, Baltimore.

Jewkes, J., Sawers, D. and Stillerman, J. (1958), *The Sources of Invention*, Macmillan, London.

Keirstead, B. (1948), *The Theory of Economic Change*, Macmillan, Toronto.

Kuhn, T. (1961), *The Structure of Scientific Revolutions*, Chicago University Press, Chicago.

Landes, D.S. (1970), *The Unbound Prometheus*, Cambridge University Press, Cambridge.

Lundvall, B.-A. (1988), 'Innovation as an inter-active process: user-producer relations', in G. Dosi *et al.* (eds), *Technical Change and Economic Theory*, Chapter 17, Pinter Publishers, London.

Mensch, G. (1975), *Das Technologische Patt: Innovationen Uberwinden die Depression*, Umschau, Frankfurt, English Edition (1979), *Stalemate in Technology*, Ballinger, New York.

Nelson, R. and Winter, S. (1977), 'In search of a useful theory of innovation', *Research Policy*, Vol. 6, No. 1, pp. 36–75.

Nelson, R. and Winter, S. (1982), *An Evolutionary Theory of Economic Change*, Harvard University Press.

Pavitt, K. (1984), 'Sectoral patterns of technical change: towards a taxonomy and a theory', *Research Policy*, Vol. 13, No. 6, pp. 343–73.

Pavitt, K. (1986), 'Technology, innovation and strategic management', in J. McGee and H. Thomas (eds), *Strategic Management Research*, Chapter 26, John Wiley, Chichester.

Perez, C. (1983), 'Structural change and the assimilation of new technologies in the economic and social system', *Futures*, Vol. 15, No. 4, pp. 357–75.

Perez, C. (1985), 'Micro-electronics, long waves and world structural change', *World Development*, Vol. 13, No. 3, pp. 441–63.

Perez, C. (1987), 'Las neuvas technologías: una visión de conjunto', in C. Omanarie (ed.), *La Tercera Revolución Industrial*, RIAL, Buenos Aires, Grupo Editor Latinamericano.

Perez, C. and Soete, L. (1988), 'Catching up in technology: entry barriers and windows', in G. Dosi *et al.* (eds), *Technical Change and Economic Theory*, Chapter 21, Pinter Publishers, London.

Phillips, A. (1971), *Technology and Market Structure*, Lexington Books, Lexington.

Rogers, E. (1962), *Diffusion of Innovations*, Free Press, New York.

Rolt, L.T.C. (1970), *Victorian Engineering*, Penguin, Harmondsworth.

Rosenberg, N. (1976), *Perspectives on Technology*, Cambridge University Press, Cambridge.

Rosenberg, N. (1982), *Inside the Black Box*, Cambridge University Press, Cambridge.

Ruttan, V. (1959), 'Usher and Schumpeter on invention, innovation and technological change', *Quarterly Journal of Economics* (November), pp. 596–606.

Sahal, D. (1985), 'Technological guideposts and innovation avenues', *Research Policy*, Vol. 14, No. 2, pp. 61–82.

Schumpeter, J.A. (1912), *The Theory of Economic Development*, Duncker & Humboldt, Leipzig, English trans. Harrand, 1934.

Schumpeter, J.A. (1928), 'The instability of capitalism', *Economic Journal*, pp. 361–86.

Schumpeter, J.A. (1939), *Business Cycles: A Theoretical, Historical and Statistical Analysis*, 2 volumes, McGraw Hill, New York.

Schumpeter, J.A. (1943), *Capitalism, Socialism and Democracy*, Allen & Unwin, London.

Shionoya, Y. (1986), 'The science and ideology of Schumpeter', *Revista Internazionale di Scienze Economiche e Commerciale*, Vol. 33, No. 8, pp. 729–62.

Townsend, J. (1976), *Innovation in Coal-Mining Machinery: the Anderton Shearer-Loader*, SPRU Occasional Paper No. 3, University of Sussex.

Von Hippel, E. (1976), 'The dominant role of users in the scientific instrument innovation process', *Research Policy*, Vol. 15, No. 3, pp. 212–39.

5 Networks of innovators:
a synthesis of research issues*

This chapter will first of all summarise some of the key findings of earlier empirical research in the 1960s on the role of external sources of scientific, technical and market information in successful innovation by business firms. This already demonstrated unambiguously the vital importance of external information networks and collaboration both with them and with users during the development of new products and processes. Moreover, the dilemmas of co-operative research in competitive industries were recognised and studied long ago (e.g. Solo, 1954; Woodward, 1965; Johnson, 1973). What then is new about the present wave of interest in 'networks of innovators'? Are there new forms of organisation or new technologies or new policies which justify renewed research efforts since they go beyond those developments already analysed in earlier empirical and theoretical work?

Section 2 reviews the evidence of new developments in the 1980s in industrial networks, regional networks and government-sponsored innovative activities. It shows that there has indeed been a major upsurge of formal and semi-formal flexible networks in the 1980s including some new types. It also shows that some older forms of research co-operation have been modified and transformed. The papers at Montreal largely concentrated on the role of regional supplier networks, which are a good example of such 'new wine in old bottles'. This chapter attempts to locate the regional network discussion within a wider context of new developments in networking.

Section 3 discusses the causes of these new developments and whether they are likely to remain a characteristic of national and international innovation systems for a long time to come, or prove to be a temporary upsurge to be overtaken later by a wave of take-overs and vertical integration.

---

*This chapter was presented as a paper at the International Workshop on Networks of Innovators, Montreal, May 1990 and was later published in *Research Policy*, Vol. 20, No.6, 1991.

Finally, Section 4 sums up some of the other key issues which require further research and debate, and the implications for social science theory.

Section 1.   Empirical research on the sources of innovative success

Until the 1960s, most studies of innovation were anecdotal and biographical or purely technical. Although economists had always recognised the great importance of innovation for productivity growth and for the competitive performance of firms, industries and nations, they made very few empirical studies of innovative activities or the diffusion of innovations. Even those economists, such as Schumpeter, who put innovation at the centre of his entire theory of economic growth and development, did not study the specific features of actual innovations in any depth. He attributed innovative success to a general quality of 'entrepreneurship' although he recognised that with the growth of large monopolistic firms the nature of this activity had radically changed (Schumpeter, 1928). However, although he identified the growth of professional in-house R&D as a fundamental change in the organisation of large-scale industry, he did not examine the interaction between the R&D function and other established functions within the firm, still less with external networks. Moreover, his approach to entrepreneurship as an exceptional heroic act of will disposed him to view the launch of new products as a way of imposing the creative ideas of the entrepreneur on passive or unreceptive users. Thus it remained as a task for his successors to put flesh and blood on the bare bones of his concept of entrepreneurship and innovation, and to modify it in the light of the new findings of empirical research.

Geographers and sociologists did rather better than economists in the 1950s, especially in diffusion studies, but it was not until the 1960s that a more systematic, empirical approach to innovation studies took off among economists. In the 1960s and early 1970s most, if not all, of the work was concentrated on the study of specific individual innovations. It aimed to identify those characteristics of each innovation which led to commercial as well as technical success, as well as recognising that an element of technical and commercial uncertainty is inherent in this activity.

The most effective way to identify those factors which are important for success is by paired comparisons between those innovations which succeed with those which fail. This was the main feature of one of the most comprehensive empirical studies of innovations which was representative of a whole generation of research: Project SAPPHO (Rothwell et al., 1972). This project measured about a hundred characteristics of about forty pairs of innovations. Only about a dozen of the many possible hypotheses systematically discriminated between success and failure. The most important of these were the following:

1. *User needs and networks*
   Successful innovators were characterised by determined attempts to develop an understanding of the special needs and circumstances of potential future users of the new process or product. Failures were characterised by neglect or ignorance of these needs. Numerous studies since SAPPHO have confirmed the vital importance of these user-producer linkages, notably the work of Lundvall (1985, 1988) and his colleagues.

2. *Coupling of development, production and marketing activities*
   Successful innovators developed techniques to integrate these activities at an early stage of development. Failures were characterised by the lack of adequate internal communications within the innovating organisation and lack of integration of these functions. Again this result has been abundantly confirmed by later research, particularly in the case of Japanese techniques for managing innovation (Aoki, 1986; Baba, 1985; Takeuchi and Nonaka, 1986; Imai, 1985). These integrating activities may be regarded as 'internal networks' within the firms.

3. *Linkage with external sources of scientific and technical information and advice*
   Successful innovators, although typically having their own in-house R&D, also made considerable use of other sources of technology. Failures were characterised by the lack of communication with external technology networks, whether national or international.

4. *Concentration of high quality R&D resources on the innovative project*
   Whereas size of firm did not discriminate between success and failure, the size of R&D project did so. Moreover, the innovations which failed not only had lower resources than those which succeeded but also suffered from failures in development leading to lower quality products. Both quantity and quality of R&D work thus complemented external networks.

5. *High status, wide experience and seniority of the 'business innovator'*
   The term 'business innovator' was used in the project to describe that person who was mainly responsible within the firm for the organisation and management of the innovative attempt. He thus corresponded most closely to the Schumpeterian 'entrepreneur'. Contrary to the original expectations of the SAPPHO researchers, this individual was generally older in the innovations which succeeded than in those which failed. This result was interpreted as indicating that particularly in large organisations, innovation could not succeed without the strong commitment of top management to the project and that the role of network co-ordination was very important, both within the firm and outside it.

6. *Basic research*

The performance of in-house oriented basic research was associated with success, particularly in the chemical industry. This performance was important mainly because of the linkages it facilitated with external networks especially universities.

The original SAPPHO Project was concentrated on only two branches of manufacturing industry: chemicals and scientific instruments. However, later research in several other industries and countries not only confirmed the main results but also showed that they applied to other sectors such as machinery and electronics (e.g. Maidique and Zirger, 1984; Mueser, 1985; Lundvall, 1985) Furthermore, almost all these and other studies confirmed the central importance of external collaboration with users and external sources of technical expertise.

These empirical studies of innovation demonstrated the importance both of formal and informal networks, even if the expression 'network' was less frequently used. Although they were rarely systematically measured, the general impression from case studies is that informal networks were the most important. Multiple sources of information and pluralistic patterns of collaboration were the rule rather than the exception. Thus the in-house competence of the R&D department was complemented by occasional or regular links with universities, government laboratories, consultants, research associations and other firms. Already in the 1950s, Carter and Williams (1957, 1959) had shown that these multiple links were characteristic of the 'progressive' firm.

However, although informal networks predominated, formal R&D collaboration agreements between firms were certainly not something which suddenly began in the 1980s. The largest single R&D project before the Manhattan Project was a joint R&D effort by five large oil companies and two plant contractors to develop a fluid bed catalytic cracking process for the oil industry in the 1930s (Enos, 1962). Both this and many other agreements, especially in the oil, chemical and electrical industries, provided for patent-sharing, cross-licensing and exchange of technical know-how between firms over quite long periods.

There were many other examples of collaborative research programmes and networks during the Second World War, some of them led by government. The American synthetic rubber research programme (1942–56) is one which has been hotly debated by historians and economists for a long time (Solo, 1954; Morris, 1989). Whereas the degree of success of this programme is still a matter of intense controversy, there is no disagreement that the British wartime radar programme, comprising a network of innovators from industry, universities and the armed forces around a core R&D programme at the Government Telecommunications Research Establishment, was an outstanding success (Postan, Hay and Scott, 1964). However, these programmes, although sometimes continued into the Cold War period, were essentially transitory arrangements. There were also other more durable forms of continuing co-operation.

Co-operative research associations (RAs) were established in the United Kingdom shortly after the First World War, and in France, Germany and other countries soon afterwards. They were seen as a means of sharing the costs of acquiring technical information and of testing facilities, pilot plant and prototype development. They were thus thought to be mainly a device for overcoming market failure in industries where the threshold costs of R&D and other scientific and technical services were too high for small firms. In practice, however, many large firms joined RAs in some industries, particularly to take advantage of their information, abstracting and translation services. However, the most sensitive strategically important areas of R&D remained in-house in the large firms for competitive reasons (Johnson, 1973).

The expectation had been that RAs would serve to provide technical support for firms who were lacking their own R&D, and that once they had developed their indigenous technical capability they might no longer wish to use the services of the RAs for these competitive reasons. However, the Federation of British Industries (FBI) (1961) survey of R&D showed that the RAs were actually used intensively by firms who had their own R&D. The RAs were thus an important ancillary and complementary source of scientific and technical information rather than a substitute for indigenous innovative activity.

Essentially the same point can be made about licensing and technical know-how agreements. These grew very rapidly after the Second World War and made a very big contribution to the international transfer of technology. Again, the expectation had been that licensing payments would flow mainly from firms who had no R&D to those who had strong R&D. However, the first Netherlands Survey of R&D in the late 1950s and the UK FBI Survey in 1961 both showed that licensing transactions were mainly between firms who already had R&D resources. Moreover, since that time empirical research has demonstrated that the successful exploitation of imported technology is strongly related to the capacity to adapt and improve this technology through indigenous R&D. Again, Japan is an excellent example (Freeman, 1987). It is not just a question of acquiring a lot of information; often there is an overload of information. The problem of innovation is to process and convert information from diverse sources into useful knowledge about designing, making and selling new products and processes. Networks were shown to be essential both in the acquisition and in the processing of information inputs.

Nor, of course, are regional and contractor networks a new phenomenon. Piore and Sabel (1984) have argued that the externalities generated by regional networks of firms have been historically important since the early days of the Industrial Revolution and they give many examples, both from Europe and North America. Although there are certainly critics who would disagree with their assessment of mass production, there are few who would disagree with this emphasis on the value of regional networks. Alfred Marshall (1890) already pointed to the vital role of externalities in 'industrial districts' where, as Dominique Foray (1990) reminded the Montreal Workshop in the title of his paper, 'The secrets of industry are in the air'. Perez and Soete (1988) have also presented similar convincing arguments on the role of externalities for innovation networks in developing countries.

Thus, both empirical and theoretical research has long since demonstrated the importance for successful innovation of both external and internal networks of information and collaboration. Furthermore, it has shown that external networks were just as important for firms who had their own R&D as for those who had none.

What, then, is new about innovation networks in the 1980s and 1990s? Section 2 attempts to answer this question.

Section 2. The growth of networks of innovators in the 1980s and changes in their mode of operation

First, it is necessary both to define 'networks of innovators' a little more precisely and to distinguish between various types of network. One of the most interesting recent papers in this field (Imai and Baba, 1989) defines innovation networks as follows:

Network organisation is a basic institutional arrangement to cope with systemic innovation. Networks can be viewed as an inter-penetrated form of market and organisation. Empirically they are loosely coupled organisations having a core with both weak and strong ties among constituent members . . .. We emphasise the importance of co-operative relationships among firms as a key linkage mechanism of network configurations. They include joint ventures, licensing arrangements, management contracts, sub-contracting, production sharing and R&D collaboration.'

As DeBresson (1990) shows in his introductory paper there are many other definitions of networks, but the definition given by Imai and Baba captures most of the points which are important in considering networks of innovators. Enlarging upon and subdividing the types which they distinguish, Table 5.1 shows the categories of network which are relevant from the standpoint of innovation.

Following Camagni (1990), this approach does not classify regional (or national) networks as a separate category, but rather treats regional (or national) elements as constituting a 'milieu' which may affect any or all of the above, especially Category (6).

Table 5.1 Categories of network relevant to innovation

---

(1) Joint ventures and research corporations
(2) Joint R&D agreements
(3) Technology exchange agreements
(4) Direct investment (minority holdings) motivated by technology factors
(5) Licensing and second sourcing agreements
(6) Subcontracting, production-sharing and supplier networks
(7) Research associations
(8) Government-sponsored joint research programmes
(9) Computerised data banks and value-added networks for technical and scientific interchange
(10) Other networks, including informal networks

A network may be defined as a closed set of selected and explicit linkages with preferential partners in a firm's space of complementary assets and market relationships, having as a major goal the reduction of static and dynamic uncertainty.

Network relations of a mainly informal and tacit nature, exist also within the local environment, linking through open chains, firms and other local actors ... our proposal is to use the term 'network' (*réseau*) only in the case of explicit linkages among selected partners and to refer to the former as 'milieu relationships'. (Camagni, 1990, p.4)

Before considering each of the main forms of co-operation in somewhat greater detail it is essential to make two observations. First, none of these categories is mutually exclusive; as has already been observed, most large firms participate in several of these modes of networking and many participate in all. Even quite small firms may take part simultaneously in most of these forms of co-operation, as was shown in the paper by Acs (1990) on small firms in Maryland.

Moreover, large firms may have many agreements in each category. The Arpo Database at Milan Polytechnic indicates that almost all of the top twenty information technology (IT) firms in the United States, European Community and Japan made more than fifty co-operative agreements of various kinds in the 1980s and some made more than a hundred (Cainarca *et al.*, 1989). Kodama (1990) points out that the leading Japanese electronic firms are members not just of one or two engineering research associations but sometimes of a dozen or more at the same time. Participation in joint programmes and agreements at least for firms in this industry has become quite a normal way of life.

Second, informal networks (Category 10) are extremely important but very hard to classify and measure. However, just because of this difficulty it is essential to notice that they have a role somewhat analogous to 'tacit knowledge' within firms. It is now very generally recognised that in the technology accumulation within firms and other organisations, tacit knowledge is often more important than codified formal specifications, blueprints, etc. (Pavitt, 1986). Because tacit knowledge is so much more difficult to communicate, the movement of people, in addition to documents and drawings, is usually essential for effective technology transfer. Similarly with networks; behind every formal network and often giving it the breath of life are usually one or more informal networks.

Few of the Montreal papers dealt with informal networks, although they often touched upon them indirectly. However, the paper by Eriksson and Håkansson (1990) did highlight their importance, and the Uppsala group have demonstrated this in much of their other work over the past ten years (see e.g. Johanson and Mattson, 1987).

More specifically in relation to innovation networks, Eric von Hippel (1987, 1988) has analysed informal know-how 'trading' in various US industries, particularly the steel industry. In addition to demonstrating its importance empirically he has provided an economic explanation for its varying intensity in different branches of industry, and its relationship with formal co-operative R&D and formal licensing arrangements.

Personal relationships of trust and confidence (and sometimes of fear and obligation) are important at both the formal and informal level, as many of the Montreal Workshop papers confirm. For this reason cultural factors such as language, educational background, national loyalties, shared ideologies and experiences and even common leisure interests continue to play an important role in networking. An appreciation of these sociological factors in both formal and informal networks is a necessary complement to narrower 'economic' explanations, and helps greatly to understand the importance of regional networks, geographical proximity and 'national systems of innovation' (Lundvall, 1988, 1990).

With these definitions and qualifications in mind, let us consider the changes in networking in the 1980s, both in terms of quantitative indicators and qualitative changes. Many researchers have attempted to keep track of the new developments (e.g. Cainarca et al. 1989; Camagni and Gambarotto, 1988; Mowery, 1988; OECD, 1986) but one of the most useful sources is the MERIT Data Bank, originally set up by the TNO in the Netherlands and now at the University of Limburg (Hagedoorn, 1990; Hagedoorn and Schakenraad, 1990). It is based on public announcements of new agreements and has some bias towards European and North American sources. For obvious reasons it does not cover Category (10) of Table 5.1 and its systematic coverage is confined to Categories (1) to (6). Nevertheless, it provides a clear-cut confirmation of an extremely rapid growth of inter-firm innovative networks in biotechnology, materials technology and information technology in the 1980s (Figure 5.1) (Hagedoorn and Schakenraad, 1990).

When the MERIT data is broken down by type of agreement, it shows some variation by nature of technology, although in all these categories R&D co-operation agreements account for a quarter or more of the total (Table 5.2) with joint ventures also very important. Several earlier studies (e.g. OECD, 1986; Mowery, 1988, 1989; and Hladik, 1985) had shown that R&D-motivated joint ventures were growing rapidly in the 1970s and 1980s. Mowery in particular demonstrated their growing importance in international collaboration between US and foreign manufacturing firms.

The MERIT data bank confirmed Mowery's assessment and also showed that joint ventures and other forms of research co-operation had grown rapidly between European and Japanese firms. In fact, the so-called 'Triad' (United States, Europe and Japan) accounted for over 90 per cent of all the agreements recorded and only the Asian newly industrialising countries (NICs) entered the picture in large numbers from outside the Triad.

As Table 5.2 indicates, direct investment was particularly important in biotechnology. This is primarily owing to the special type of symbiotic relationships between large (mainly chemical) firms and the new (biotechnology-based) small firms, which have characterised the early developments in this technology. Minority equity stakes provide a special form of co-operation in these circumstances.

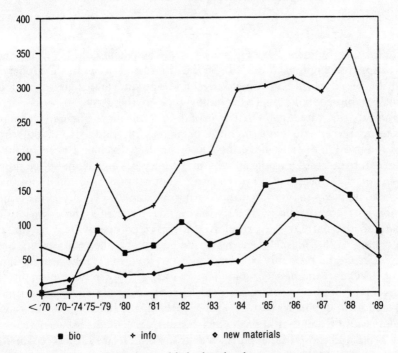

Figure 5.1 Growth of newly established technology co-operation agreements in biotechnology, information technologies and new materials
(*Source:* MERIT–CATI data bank (Hagedoorn and Schakenraad, 1990).

Table 5.2 Modes of technology co-operation in biotechnology, information technologies and new materials, numbers and per cent

	Biotechnology	Information technologies	New materials
Joint ventures	164	458	177
research corporations	13.5%	16.9%	25.7%
Joint R&D	362	749	173
	29.8%	27.6%	25.1%
Technology exchange	84	328	54
agreements	6.9%	12.1%	7.8%
Direct investment	234	357	65
	19.3%	13.1%	9.4%
Customer–supplier	186	245	42
relations	15.3%	9.0%	6.1%
One-directional	183	581	177
technology flows	15.1%	21.4%	25.7%
Total	1213	2718	688
	100.0%	100.0%	100.0%

Source: MERIT–CATI data bank (Hagedoorn and Schakenraad, 1990).

What are described by Hagedoorn and Schakenraad (1990) as 'one-directional technology flows' are on the other hand rather more important for the more mature information technology and materials technology than for biotechnology. Their importance in these two areas is partly owing to the rapid growth of second sourcing agreements. Ordinary licensing agreements have of course been growing rapidly for a long time and the growth of cross-licensing and technology exchange agreements is of greater interest from the standpoint of networking. It should be noted however that classification of an agreement as 'uni-directional' does not necessarily mean that co-operation is unimportant, especially in the wider context of a multiplicity of networking arrangements and a variety of strategic alternatives. Nevertheless, if forms of co-operation were ranked according to the degree of intensity and equality in the relationship, then the order would probably be from highest to lowest: (1) joint ventures; (2) joint R&D agreements; (3) technology exchange; (4) direct investment; (5) Customer–supplier contracts; (6) licensing and second sourcing (Hagedoorn, 1990). Moreover, the MERIT Data Bank almost certainly understates the number of one-way licensing agreements between firms in the Triad and those in the Third World since these are far less frequently the subject of public announcements.

So far, we have indicated a few of the more important sources which confirm a very rapid growth of various types of R&D co-operation in the

1980s, especially in the newer generic technologies (Categories 1 to 5 in Table 5.1). When it comes to Category 6, far more important than the sheer quantitative increase in the number of agreements has been the qualitative change in the content of the relationships. Although this is difficult to demonstrate statistically, the evidence from numerous case studies and from the papers at the Montreal Workshop is strong. So too is the evidence from the analytical studies of new developments in management technologies and productivity trends, such as the Report of the MIT Commission on Industrial Productivity (Dertouzos et al., 1989).

What all these studies show is that much new wine is being poured into old bottles in subcontractor and supplier networks. The clearest case is undoubtedly that of Japan. Attempts are being made almost everywhere to imitate some features of the Japanese model and it is also being spread by direct Japanese investment, so we shall examine briefly the major changes there. Considerable attention has been paid to the Japanese automobile industry and to the workings of the JIT system or Toyota–Ohno system in that industry. But perhaps still more interesting is the example of the Japanese electronics industry, which has grown even faster in the past three decades.

A recent study of networks supporting small and medium-sized enterprises (SMEs) in this industry (van Kooij, 1990) shows that whereas in the 1950s, subcontracting firms were viewed in a somewhat condescending way as low cost suppliers who could absorb some of the shocks of business fluctuations, this attitude changed profoundly over the next three decades, partly because of the shortage of capacity and skills. This analysis is also confirmed by the Japanese economist, Mari Sako (1989) in her studies of the Japanese electronics industry and the historical development of sub-contracting in Japan.

Modification or innovation of a part or component of a product or process by one subcontractor inevitably affected the manufacturing of the whole. Especially in electronics, innovation among subcontractors is subject to the constraint of compatibility with the customer's (or parent company's) technology. Therefore the subcontractor must supply a product according to detailed specifications which can be modified only within certain limits. To a degree this compels parent companies to offer advice and supply the necessary technology to subcontractors so as to increase their economic and engineering capabilities. This results in a higher dependency on upgraded subcontractors because of their specialised technology and equipment instead of the traditional low cost approach.

As Figure 5.2 shows, technological specialisation was given as the main reason for the use of subcontracting by large enterprises in the Japanese electronics industry and the proportion was highest in the firms concerned with mechatronics. Cost and scale of inventories was trivial in comparison. This is particularly interesting in view of the great emphasis placed on inventory control in the JIT system in the automobile industry.

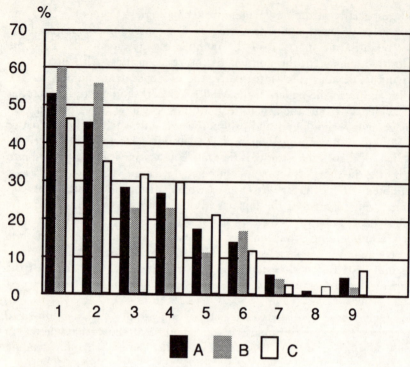

Legends

A = All manufacturing enterprises
B = Parent companies which have introduced mechatronic equipment
C = Parent companies which have not introduced mechatronic equipment

1 = Subcontracting enterprises have specialised technology and equipment
2 = Parent company's production capacity is insufficient
3 = Production lot is small and outside orders are more efficient
4 = Reduction of personnel costs and the unit price of products
5 = Use of subcontractors enables more flexibility toward fluctuations in lot size
6 = Enables saving of capital for plant and equipment investment, etc
7 = Strong capital and personal ties with subcontractors
8 = Parent company does not have to hold excess inventories
9 = Others

Note
Total exceeds 100 due to some respondents giving more than one response.
Cited from Sato (1984), p.12

Figure 5.2 Reasons for large enterprises to use subcontractors
Source: Small and Medium Enterprise Agency, *Shitauka Kigyo Jittai Chosa* (Survey of the State of Subcontracting Enterprises), December 1981; and Van Kooij, 1990.

As the technical competence of subcontractors improved, a more equal relationship between large and small enterprises began to develop in many cases. Instead of the rigid hierarchy within groups with great prestigious firms at the top and small weak ones at the bottom, the parent firm *vis-à-vis* its *Kogaisha* ('children' or 'daughter' companies) transformed its position into a nucleus within an industrial combine.

To accomplish this gradual transformation, parent companies undertook a series of activities, of which the main aim was the improvement of the flow of information from 'parent to child' and back, and among the 'children' themselves. This was achieved by assigning the function of liaison to a special department within the parent company.

To illustrate this, van Kooij gives examples from Toshiba TV and VCR manufacture, from Mitsubishi's R&D meetings and Hitachi's project groups. In these cases the object of the association was research co-operation and improvement of managerial and technological competence, even though the leadership of the large enterprise continued to prevail. New small high-technology firms, on the other hand, combined in a more independent way, forming networks of co-operation for new product and process development and research interchange. Van Kooij's account suggests that technological requirements played a big part in transforming the Japanese subcontractor networks.

The new developments described by Saxenian (1990) in her paper on technological co-operation in Silicon Valley in California show some striking resemblances to these Japanese developments, particularly her example of the upgrading of the PCB manufacturers. However, the co-operating firms in her investigation more often had the characteristics of the relatively small number of new high-tech firms of the Japanese electronics industry as portrayed by van Kooij. In both cases technological competence and specialisation were the basis for rather equal and trusting relationships between firms who needed each other's special capabilities in new product and systems development.

Imai (1989) has argued that the evolution of Japanese corporate and industrial networks has gone so far as to constitute a new type of production system. He traces the qualitative changes in the forms of networking from the old pre-war *Zaibatsu* networks, based on ownership and control, to the fuzzier and more flexible type of networking, based on information exchange between more equal partners, who may or may not be affiliated to the same business groups.

In research associations (Category 7 in Table 5.1), an analogous process of qualitative change can be seen in Japan. As we have seen in Section 1, these were originally established over half a century ago in Europe, mainly with the object of strengthening the technical capability of small firms who lacked R&D. When the Japanese imitated these European developments much later, they also had it in mind to assist small firms. The law passed in 1961 which set up the engineering research associations

(ERAs) envisaged co-operation between government laboratories (especially MITI's Mechanical Engineering Laboratory) and various makers of parts and components, especially in the automobile industry. The first four ERAs were in filters, suspensions, indicators and engine parts and shared the MITI laboratory facilities (Levy and Samuels, 1989).

As Japanese industry advanced technologically, there was some doubt in the late 1960s about whether the ERA type of organisation would be needed any longer, and after the first twelve had been set up in 1961–5 no more were created in 1965–70. However, this was followed by a veritable 'boom' in creating ERAs, especially in the early 1980s (twenty-five between 1981 and 1983). However, as Levy and Samuels (1989, p. 32) point out: 'both their raison d'être and nature of their participants were transformed'. The new ERAs were mainly in electronics, information technology, materials technology and biotechnology and their objects had shifted to broad areas of advanced technology. Large firms came into the ERAs and thirty firms accounted for nearly one-third of the memberships by 1985, with Hitachi participating in eighteen ERAs and Toshiba in sixteen. Government support doubled between 1977 and 1982 although funding is shared with industry, and industrial associations often collaborate with MITI in administering the projects.

The total amount of Japanese government support for industrial R&D is of course far less than in the United States or many European countries. However, the mode of support is particularly interesting. Much of the support comes through special loans or through tax benefits and these are strongly geared towards collaborative networking projects. By the late 1980s, four-fifths of all government R&D loans were going to joint projects which included not only the ERAs but also many other types of 'centres', 'consortia', 'fora' etc.

The apparent success of many of these collaborative projects and programmes led to widespread imitation of this technique of organisation and funding, both in Europe and the United States. The British Alvey Programme (1983–7) was established as a direct result of a study of Japanese initiatives in fifth generation computing and similar programmes were started in several other European countries and in the United States (Arnold and Guy, 1986). They were all based on the principle of the ERAs: temporary coalitions of large (and some small) firms with the participation of universities and government laboratories in many cases and joint funding by industry and government.

So prevalent did this new mode of funding become in the 1980s that by the end of the decade about two-thirds of the European Community R&D budget was disbursed in this form for the support of the new generic technologies. Lynn Mytelka (1987) and Margaret Sharp (1991) have shown the very important role of ESPRIT in the development of new strategic alliances and networks in the European electronic industries.

Finally, there remains to consider the ninth category (Table 5.1) of research collaboration: computer networking. Unfortunately, very little research has been done on this aspect of innovative networking, perhaps because it is the most recent type. However, Bar and Borrus (1989) give an informative account of the use of various forms of computer networking by innovative US firms, particularly Hewlett Packard. It also plays a very important part alongside other networks in the Japanese system and is specifically mentioned by van Kooij (1990) in relation to the Toshiba VCR network. Thomas and Miles (1989) have given a general account of the rapid growth of telematic services in the United Kingdom in the 1980s and of their relevance to innovation and diffusion of innovations. Jagger and Miles (1991) show that scientific data and economic information were the main growth areas in the 1980s. Nevertheless, in-depth case studies of the experience of data banks and value-added networks are still few and far between.

To sum up this somewhat extended discussion of the changing patterns of collaboration in innovative networks in the 1980s, there have indeed been some major changes both quantitatively and qualitatively. In quantitative terms there is abundant evidence of a strong upsurge of various forms of research collaboration, especially in the new generic technologies (Categories (1) to (5) in Table 5.1) using extensive international collaboration as well as national and regional networks. There is also ample evidence of a qualitative change in the nature of the older networking relationships which have existed for a long time: subcontracting networks (6), research associations (7), government R&D projects and programmes (8). Finally, computerised data banks and value-added networks (9) provide entirely new possibilities for networking which, however, have been very little researched.

In Section 3, we turn to consider the causes of these changes in networking systems and their implications for theory and research in the 1990s.

Section 3. Causes of the changes in networking for innovation

Section 2 has brought together and summarised some of the available evidence relating to the growth of innovation networks and the qualitative changes in their mode of operation in the 1980s. This section discusses the underlying causes of these changes and their implications for theory.

When Hagedoorn and Schakenraad (1990) analysed the motives for firms to enter into co-operative agreements with each other, they found that strategic motives relating to technological competence and market positioning predominated. Simple lack of financial resources to fund design and development accounted for only a very small number of cases, mainly in new biotechnology firms. Even here, of course, whereas the small new firms were motivated by the need to finance R&D, their larger partners were often primarily motivated by long-term strategic considerations.

Especially in information and materials technology agreements, technological complementarity and reduction of lead times were very frequently diagnosed as the dominant motives for R&D co-operation. They were also important for joint ventures although in this case the strongest single motive related to market expansion and strategic positioning in new markets. In general, Hagedoorn and Schakenraad found that in contrast to much of the previous literature, considerations of cost-sharing and cost-minimising appeared to play a smaller role in comparison with the strategic objectives of new technology and markets.

Most of the papers at the Montreal Workshop also testify to the importance of technological complementarities, shortening lead times and strategic objectives. Saxenian (1990), in particular, in her paper on innovation networks in Silicon Valley brought out these factors very strongly in relation to the development of new computer systems. She argues that firms would have simply been unable to compete if they had not been willing to enter into a variety of forms of technological co-operation. Because of the extremely rapid pace of technical change and the broad range of specialised technological capabilities needed for system development, there was simply no time to go it alone. The work of Camagni and Gambarotto (1988) and Cainarca et al. (1989) again brings out these points, and Mowery (1989) concludes that:

Technological developments in a number of industries also have increased the importance of access to new or unfamiliar technologies.... Collaboration can provide more rapid access to technological capabilities that are not well developed within a firm and whose development may require a large investment and considerable time. (p.25)

Taken together with the quantitative evidence from the MERIT Data Bank, it is abundantly clear that the main source of change underlying the new developments in networking for innovation lies in the rapid development and diffusion of new generic technologies and especially information technology. Imai and Baba (1989) sum it up as follows:

Information Technology exerts a strong impact on the entire range of existing products and services. Eventually it renovates the total system. The dominant mode of innovation is systemic.... The interactive process of information creation and learning is crucial for systemic innovation. Interaction includes three dimensions: between users and suppliers, between R&D, marketing and manufacturing and between physical products, software and services.

Table 5.3 illustrates this point in the transport sector. The change in the patterns of innovation from the energy-intensive products and systems of the 1950s and 1960s to the computerised control systems of the 1970s and 1980s is very striking. Systemic innovations, such as containerisation, were of course also very important in the early post-war period, and so was the energy-saving achieved by scaling up in many cases. However, the technical complexity of containerisation was not great and intensive technical collaboration between firms was not the main requirement for its successful development. Nevertheless, in the systemic innovations of the 1970s and 1980s not only were innovation networks necessary for the development of the original electronic equipment (circuits, hardware, peripherals, instruments, etc.), but even more so for the new applications, especially with the users in relation to customised software.

We therefore have to consider some of the specific features of information technology which have led to the more technology-intensive and more numerous innovation networks of the 1980s. Here the theory of techno-economic paradigm change developed by Carlota Perez (1983, 1985) offers the most convincing explanation. Whereas other writers (e.g.

Table 5.3   Innovations in the transport sector 1940s to 1980s

---

(1) *System innovations and economies of scale to take advantage of low cost oil-intensive technology (1940s to 1960s)*
>   Containerisation
>   Unitisation
>   Roll-on, roll-off
>   Oil and gas pipelines
>   Dieselisation of railways
>
>   Scaling up size of trucks (to 38 tons)
>   Scaling up size of aircraft (from DC3 to 747)
>   Scaling up size of tankers (from 20,000 dwt to 500,000 dwt)
>   Scaling up of port facilities to handle large tankers, roll-on, roll-off, containerisation and unitisation

(2) *Information and control innovations to take advantage of increasingly low cost electronics and computing (1960s to 1980s)*
>   Radar and computer-controlled airport traffic
>   Computerised airline booking systems
>   Aircraft instrument landing systems and flight control systems
>   Computerisation of railway marshalling yards
>   Computerisation of railway signalling systems
>   Computerisation of road haulage and delivery systems
>   Unmanned trains
>   Tachograph
>   Computerisation of travel agencies
>   Computerisation of road traffic control systems

Source: I.M. Brodie, 'Transport', Working Paper, TEMPO Sector Study, SPRU (mimeo) March 1984.

Dosi, 1982) used the expression 'change of technological paradigm' to describe fundamental changes in the technology of a particular industrial sector, she pointed to the fact that some changes of paradigm are so pervasive, because they offer such a wide range of technical and economic advantages, that they affect the behaviour of the entire system, changing the 'common-sense' rules of behaviour for engineers, managers and designers in many sectors or in all, as well as their intersectoral relationships and technological complementarities.

Clearly, information technology is such a case. Not only has it found applications in every manufacturing and service sector, often changing profoundly both products and processes, but it also affects every function within each firm: design (CAD); manufacture (robotics, instrumentation, flexible manufacturing systems (FMS), control systems, CIM, etc.); marketing (computer-based inventory and distribution systems) accounts and administration (management information systems, etc.). Finally, it affects through its convergence with the telecommunications system, the network of communications within the firm and between the firm and its supplier networks, technology networks, customer networks, etc. In this last area it provides entirely new possibilities for rapid interchange of information, data, drawings, advice, specifications, etc. between geographically dispersed sites via fax, VANs electronic mail, tele-conferencing, distance learning, etc. It is hardly surprising therefore that taking into account both the pervasiveness of IT and its systemic characteristics, most of the new developments in networking in the 1980s have been associated in one way or another with the diffusion of this technology. Not only is the IT industry itself characterised by intensive technological networking for the development of its own products (through complementarities in materials, components, circuits, sub-assemblies, instruments, final products, software, peripherals, etc.), but also its diffusion throughout the economy to new sectors of application depends on the development of new networks in every sector (banks, machine-tool makers, travel agents, consultants, airlines, law firms, accountants, hospitals, chemical engineers, etc.). Finally, it provides the technical means for improving communication networks everywhere and for making them feasible in areas where they could hardly have been introduced before. It is a networking technology *par excellence*.

The world-wide diffusion of this new techno-economic paradigm has led not only to intensified technical collaboration within supplier networks and between users and producers of IT products and systems, it has also engendered a fierce competitive struggle between the suppliers of these products and systems. Characteristic of periods of change of techno-economic paradigm is the rise of new firms competent in the new technologies and the strategic repositioning of many established firms as they try to cope with the rapid structural and technical change affecting their markets and their very existence.

If we take into account also the international aspects of production, marketing and technology development, then clearly a period of great turmoil could have been expected in the 1980s as a result of the many new strategic alliances and networks. This is indeed the picture which emerges from the MERIT Data Bank and other similar sources and studies. The need for firms in the 'Triad' countries to gain access to partners in each of the three main areas (European Community, Japan, United States) was obviously one of the main driving-forces. Hagedoorn and Schakenraad (1990) have suggested that the apparent downturn in numbers of new networking agreements in the late 1980s (Figure 5.1) may have been due to the fact that much of the strategic repositioning for the single European market had already been completed. By the same token a new wave of agreements affecting the East European countries may be anticipated in the 1990s.

Even though the Japanese market is far more homogeneous and smaller than either the US or the EC market, nevertheless strategic factors have certainly influenced the networks of European and US firms in their desire to gain access to Japanese technology and markets. Within Japan, as we have seen, a growth in the technology intensity of supplier networks, and government-sponsored programmes have been major features of internal development in the 1970s and 1980s. The desire of the Japanese government to promote the transition to an 'information society' as rapidly as possible has been a factor in the acceleration of this process (Freeman, 1987). One of the participants in the Montreal Workshop aptly described the Japanese economy as 'nothing but networks of innovators' (Walter Stohr). The desire to emulate Japanese achievements in technology has been another factor in the international acceleration of innovation networking in the 1980s and of qualitative change in the supplier networks of industries.

However, it would be quite wrong to interpret the new developments in the networking as primarily a Japanese phenomenon or exclusively a phenomenon associated with information technology. The empirical evidence is perfectly clear that similar developments affect all the leading industrial countries and indeed 'globalisation' is an important aspect of the growth of new types of network. Moreover, even if information technology is the driving-force behind most of the new agreements and networks, a similar process affects other rapidly developing generic technologies, such as materials technology and biotechnology (Figure 5.1, Table 5.2).

Again, as we have emphasised in Section 1, networking for innovation is in itself an old phenomenon and networks of suppliers are as old as industrialised economies. Ann Markusen's (1990) Montreal paper gave a clear reminder that many aspects of the most recent wave of networking agreements were already clearly evident in the networking of the US military–industrial complex from the Second World War onwards. Particularly interesting is her point that short product life, reduced lead times, high technical performance standards, higher quality of components and materials, accelerated development and diffusion of new techniques such as NC and CAD through supplier networks etc. were all major features of the US 'networks for innovation' in weapon systems well before the 1980s.

Despite these very important qualifications, the evidence reviewed in Section 2 and the analysis in this section show clearly that information technology has led to the widespread diffusion of modes of networking which were previously far less common. Whether this is a temporary phenomenon, to be superseded by a new wave of vertical integration and industrial concentration is a fundamental issue for research to which we turn in the final section.

Section 4. Conclusions

This final section will briefly indicate a few major problems which emerge from this analysis for further research and debate and which have important policy implications.

First, as Section 3 has indicated, it is important to keep track of the trends in networking in the 1990s. According to one view the upsurge of new networking arrangements is a transitory phenomenon of adaptation to the diffusion of new generic technologies. As firms become more familiar with these technologies they will wish to shift the strategically sensitive areas under their direct and immediate control, i.e. to internalise some of the networks which are now the subject of co-operative arrangements. According to this view, the rise of many new high-tech small firms in such areas as CAD, software, instruments, personal computers, bio-technology etc., which was characteristic of the 1970s and 1980s, will be followed by a new wave of rationalisation and industrial reconcentration in the 1990s and first decade of the twenty-first century.

A few of today's small and medium-sized firms will become giants of the next century through growth. However, some key small firms are already being taken over by larger ones (e.g. Genentech by Hoffmann Laroche, or Apollo by Hewlett-Packard) and even quite large firms like Nixdorf or Plessey have been swallowed up by even larger firms like Siemens and GEC. Examples were given at the Montreal Workshop of small firm networks which have already been displaced by networks under the control of a large firm. Albert Bressand (1989) suggests that a number of service networks are electronic cartels in the making, particularly airline reservation systems.

This process of renewed concentration in the ICT industries may be compared with similar waves of concentration in the evolution of the automobile industry after the First World War or the electrical industry in the 1890s (Table 5.4). In the early formative period of any major new technology system, almost by definition there are no dominant designs or standards and a state of organisational flux exists. Innovator–entrepreneurial firms flourish and since there are no standard components, labour-intensive techniques are characteristic. As the technology matures, however, economies of scale become more and more important and standardisation takes place. The pattern of innovation tends to change in ways which Utterback and Abernathy (1975) have indicated and the number of firms falls dramatically, as has occurred successively in the electrical, auto and computer industries. This whole long cycle of development may be plausibly related to Schumpeter's long wave theory, as in the work of Carlota Perez (1983).

An alternative (and not necessarily contradictory) view is that networking between autonomous firms will grow still more important and will become the usual way of conducting product and process development. Even if some small firms are swallowed up, many more new ones will be born and will develop such specialised competences that they will be able to enter new networks on equal terms with large established organisations. As we have seen in Section 1, networking of various kinds was indeed quite a normal feature of the industrial and regional landscape long before the advent of modern information and communication technology (ICT). However, it is often maintained not only that ICT itself greatly facilitates various forms of networking but also that it has inherent characteristics, such as rapid change in design, customisation and flexibility, which together with its systemic nature and the variety and complexity of its applications, will lead to a permanent shift of industrial structure and behaviour, and will assign to networking a greatly enhanced role in the future, extending well beyond the 1990s.

Clearly, here is a rich area for theoretical and empirical research in the 1990s. Longitudinal case studies on the evolution of networks could be particularly valuable. However, it is also essential to continue the type of data collection on networks of all kinds represented by the MERIT data bank, so that we can keep track of the main trends in network formation and decay.

Longitudinal case studies would enable us to gain a better understanding of such complex issues as power relationships within networks. Some authors (e.g. Saxenian, 1990) have stressed the rather equal relationships within networks of innovators, whereas others have pointed to a tendency for the strongest firms to exploit their position at the core of the networks.

Clearly this debate about the future of networking and of industrial concentration is closely related to the debate in theoretical economics about markets, hierarchies and transaction costs (Williamson, 1975, 1985). It is notable that many papers and books about networks carry a main title or a subtitle such as 'Beyond markets and hierarchies' (Fransman, 1990) or 'Transcending markets and hierarchies' (Imai and Baba, 1989). Several of the papers at the Montreal Workshop also showed this dissatisfaction with

Table 5.4 Long waves in the development of new technologies

Major features of successive techno-economic paradigms	Formative stage of new technology system	Rapid growth of techno-economic paradigm. Structural crisis of adjustment	Consolidation in new dominant technological regime
Electric power Steel Heavy industry	1840s–1870s	1880s–1890s	1900s–1930s
Automobile and IC engine Oil Assembly Line	1880s–1910s	1920s–1930s	1940s–1980
Computers Chips Telecoms	1940s–1960s	1970s–1980s	?
SMEs	Inventor–entrepreneur Innovator–entrepreneur Spin-offs	Many new SMEs in supply networks and services	Many mergers and take-overs, deaths. A few grow big. Some niches survive
Large firms	Diversification into new technologies by a few large firms	Large firms come to dominate supply of key products and materials	Oligopolistic global industries
Technology	Radical innovations Establishment of scientific principles	Scaling up for main products and systems. Intense science–technology interaction	Established systems. Mainly in-house R&D. Mainly incremental innovations
Factor intensity	Mainly labour-intensive	Becoming capital-intensive	Predominantly capital-intensive

Management	Flux. Organic. Few management principles	Emergence of new models of management and new conventional wisdom	Established textbook management style and practice
Standards and design	Hardly any established standards or designs	*De facto* standards of strong suppliers sometimes conflicting	Increasingly *de jure* standards and international standards
Infrastructure	Not yet in place. Competing ideas for what is needed	Heavy investment in new infrastructure with robust designs	Consolidation of global infrastructures
Political institutions and social institutions	Informal. Rapidly evolving. Partnerships' mobility	Lobbies and professional associations emerge. Formal networks. Early lock-in.	Political–industrial complex inertia and rigidity. Lock–in.

the market/hierarchy dichtomy (e.g. Foray, 1990; Storper and Harrison, 1990), and urged that networking should not be explained primarily in terms of 'costs', whether transaction or others, but should rather be examined in terms of strategic behaviour, appropriability, technological complementarity and other complementary assets (Teece, 1986, 1989) and sociological factors such as interpersonal relationships of trust and confidence, and professional ethics of co-operation.

It is not without interest that the idea of networks as a 'third form' intermediate between markets and hierarchies was originally suggested by Williamson himself in a footnote about the Japanese *zaibatsu*. However, Goto (1982) points out that he regarded this as a 'culturally specific' Japanese phenomenon. Goto himself argues that although networking modes of organisation have been especially important in Japan, they have a much wider economic significance:

In the case of the post-war Japanese economy, with its high overall rate of growth and rapid changes in its inter-industry structure, associated with a high rate of technical change, there was a favourable situation for the group mode of transaction to be relatively more efficient than the market mode or integral organisation mode of the carrying out of transactions.

It is notable that Japanese economists and historians have particularly stressed the importance of alternatives to markets and hierarchies and their growing importance with the rise of information technology (see e.g. Imai and Baba, 1989, 1990). However, many European and American economists have also stressed the importance of either displacing Williamson's theory or developing it further.

A second major set of issues relates to the geography of networking at the regional, national and international levels. Here the study of informal as well as formal networks is particularly important, as well as the trends of innovation networks and strategies within multinational companies (MNCs). Studies of regional and national systems of innovation could throw a great deal of light on the persistence (or otherwise) of geographically circumscribed networks and the reasons for their rise (and decline). Patel and Pavitt (1991) have maintained that innovation activities are an important case of 'non-globalisation', and *Business Week* (1990) runs a special feature on the 'stateless' corporation. The statistics of R&D performance by MNCs outside their main base are still very inadequate, but this does seem to be increasing from a very low base. However, purely quantitative analysis is inadequate here. The nature of R&D and other technical activities performed in each location are clearly of great importance in relation to the MNCs', own networks and their external linkages, agreements and strategies.

This whole area of research has very direct relevance to policy-making at the regional, national and international levels, as shown particularly by

DeBresson (1989). It is one where the contribution of economists is vital but which cannot be left to economists because of the many subtle sociological and political questions about both informal and formal networks. As in most of the major issues a network approach by social scientists themselves is essential. The Montreal Workshop showed that such an approach, particularly between geographers, economists and organisational theorists can be very fruitful.

Bibliography

Acs, Z.J.L. (1990), 'High technology networks in Maryland', Paper for Montreal Workshop.

Aoki, M. (1986), 'Horizontal versus vertical information: structure of the firm', *American Economic Review*, Vol. 76, No. 5, pp. 971–83.

Arnold, E. and Guy, K. (1986), *Parallel Convergence: National Strategies in Information Technology*, Frances Pinter, London.

Baba, Y. (1985), 'Japanese colour TV firms: decision-making from the 1950s to the 1980s', DPhil Dissertation, University of Sussex.

Bar, F. and Borrus, M. (1989), 'From public access to private connections: network strategies and competitive advantage'. Report to OECD Conference on Information Networks and Competitive Advantage, Paris, October (Berkeley Roundtable).

Bressand, A. and Kalypso, N. (1989) (eds), *Strategic Trends in Services: an Inquiry into The Global Service Economy*, Harper & Row, New York.

Cainarca, G.C., Colombo, M.G. and Mariotti, S. (1989), 'Accordi tra imprese nel sistema industriale dell'informazione e della comunicazione', in G.C. Cainarca et al., *Tecnologie dell'informazione e accordi tra imprese*, Milan.

Camagni, R.P. (1990), 'Local milieu, uncertainty and innovation networks', Paper for Montreal Workshop.

Camagni, R. and Gambarotto, F. (1988), 'Gli accordi di cooperazione e le nuove forme di sviluppo esterno alle imprese', *Economia e Politica Industriale*, No. 58.

Carter, C.F. and Williams, B.R. (1957), *Industry and Technical Progress*, Oxford University Press, Oxford.

Carter, C.F. and Williams, B.R. (1959), 'The characteristics of technically progressive firms', *Journal of Industrial Economics*, Vol. 7, No. 2, pp. 87–104.

Contractor, F.J. and Lorange, P. (1988), *Cooperative Strategies in International Business*, Lexington Books, Lexington, Mass.

DeBresson, C. (1989), 'Breeding innovation clusters: a source of dynamic development', *World Development*, Vol. 17, No. 1, pp. 1–16.

DeBresson, C. (1990), 'Introductory Paper' at Montreal Workshop on Networks of Innovators, pp. 361–86.

Dertouzos, M., Lester, R. and Solow, R. (eds), (1989), *Made in America* (Report of the MIT Commission on Industrial Productivity), MIT Press, Cambridge, Mass.

Dosi, G., Freeman, C., Nelson, R., Silverberg, G., Soete, L. (eds) (1988), *Technical Change and Economic Theory*, Pinter Publishers, London.

Enos, J.L. (1962), *Petroleum Progress and Profits*, MIT Press, Cambridge, Mass.

Eriksson, A. and Håkansson, H. (1990), 'Getting innovations out of supplier networks', Paper at the Montreal Workshop.

Federation of British Industries (FBI) (1961), *Industrial Research in Manufacturing Industry*, FBI and NIESR, London.

Foray, D. (1990), 'The secrets of the industry are in the air', Paper at the Montreal Workshop.

Fransman, M. (1990), *The Market and Beyond: Information Technology, Cooperation and Competition in the Japanese System*, Cambridge University Press, Cambridge.

Freeman, C. (1987), *Technology Policy and Economic Performance: Lessons from Japan*, Pinter Publishers, London.

Goto, A. (1982), 'Business groups in a market economy', *European Economic Review*, pp. 53–70.

Grubler, A. (1990), *The Rise & Fall of Infrastructures*, Physica-Verlag, Heidelberg.

Hagedoorn, J. (1990), 'Organisational modes of inter-firm cooperation and technology transfer', *Technovation*, Vol. 10, No. 1, pp. 17–30.

Hagedoorn, J. and Schakenraad, J. (1990), 'Strategic partnering and technological cooperation', Chapter 1 in C. Freeman and L. Soete (eds) *New Explorations in the Economics of Technical Change*, Pinter Publishers, London.

Håkansson, H. and Johanson, J. (1988), 'Formal and informal cooperation strategies in international industrial networks', in F.J. Contractor and P. Lorange (eds), *Cooperative Strategies in International Business*, Lexington Books, Lexington, Mass.

Hladik, K.J. (1985), *International Joint Ventures*, Lexington Books, Lexington, Mass.

Imai, K. (1989), 'Evolution of Japan's corporate and industrial networks', Chapter 6 in B. Carlsson (ed.), *Industrial Dynamics*, Kluwer, Dordrecht.

Imai, K. *et al.* (1985), 'Managing the new product development process: how Japanese companies learn and unlearn', in K.B. Clark *et al.* (eds), *The Uneasy Alliance: Managing the Productivity-Technology Dilemma*, Harvard Business School Press, Boston.

Imai, K. and Baba, Y. (1989), 'Systemic innovation and cross-border networks: transcending markets and hierarchies to create a new techno-economic system', OECD, Conference on Science, Technology and Economic Growth, June, Paris.

Imai, K. and Itami, H. (1984), 'Interpretation of organisation and market', *International Journal of Industrial Organisation*, pp. 285–310.

Jagger, N. and Miles, I. (1991), 'New telematic services in Europe', in C. Freeman, M. Sharp, W. Walker (eds), *Technology and the Future of Europe*, Pinter Publishers, London, pp. 155–168.

Johanson, J. and Mattson, L-G. (1987), 'Inter-organisational relations in industrial systems: a network approach compared with the transaction cost appraisal', *International Studies of Management and Organisation*, Vol. XVII, No. 1, pp. 34–48.

Johnson, P.S. (1973), *Cooperation Research in Industry: An Economic Study*, Wiley, New York.

Kodama, F. (1990), 'Rivals' participation in collective research: economic and technological rationale', NISTEP Conference, 2–4 February, Tokyo.

Levy, J.D. and Samuel, R.J. (1989), 'Institutions and innovation: research collaboration as technology strategy in Japan (mimeo) Centre for International Studies, MIT.

Lundvall, B-A. (1985), *Product Innovation and User–Producer Interaction*, Aalborg University Press, Aalborg.

Lundvall, B-A. (1988), 'Innovation as an inter-active process: from user–producer interaction to the national system of innovation', Chapter 17 in G. Dosi *et al.* (eds), *Technical Change and Economic Theory*, Pinter Publishers, London.

Lundvall, B-A. (1990), 'From technology as a productive factor to innovation as an inter-active process', Paper at the Montreal Workshop.

Maidique, M.A. and Zirger, B.I. (1984), 'The new product learning cycle', *Research Policy*, Vol. 14, pp. 299–313.

Markusen, A. (1990), 'The military industrial divide: cold war transformation of the economy and the rise of new industrial complexes', Paper at the Montreal Workshop.

Marshall, A. (1890), *Principles of Economics*, Chapter 10, Macmillan, London.

Morris, P.J.T. (1989), *The American Synthetic Rubber Research Programme*, University of Pennsylvania Press.

Mowery, D.C. (ed.) (1988), *International Collaborative Ventures*, Ballinger, Cambridge.

Mowery, D.C. (1989), 'Collaborative ventures between US and foreign manufacturing firms', *Research Policy*, Vol. 18, No. 1, pp. 19–33.

Mueser, R. (1985), 'Identifying technical innovations', *IEEE Transactions in Engineering Management*, EN–32 (4), pp. 158–76.

Mytalka, L. and Delapierre, M. (1987), 'The alliance strategies of European firms in the IT industry and the role of ESPRIT', *Journal of Common Market Studies*, Vol. 26, No. 2, December.

Organisation of Economic Co-operation and Development (1986), *Technological Agreements Between Firms*, OECD, Paris.

Patel, P. and Pavitt, K. (1991), 'Large firms in the production of the world's technology: an important case of non-globalisation', *Journal of International Business Studies*, Vol. 22, No. 1, pp. 1–21.

Pavitt, K. (1986), 'International patterns of technological accumulation', in N. Hood (ed.), *Strategies in Global Competition*, Wiley, New York.

Perez, C. (1983), 'Structural changes and the assimilation of new technologies in the economic and social system', *Futures*, Vol. 15, No. 5, pp. 357–75.

Perez, C. (1985), 'Micro-electronics, long waves and world structural change: new perspectives for developing countries', *World Development*, Vol. 13, No. 3, pp. 441–63.

Perez, C. and Soete, L. (1988), 'Catching up in technology entry barriers and windows of opportunity', in G. Dosi *et al.* (eds), *Technical Change and Economic Theory*, Pinter Publishers, London.

Piore, M.J. and Sabel, C.F. (1984), *The Second Industrial Divide*, Basic Books, New York.

Postan, M.M., Hay, D. and Scott, J.D. (1964), *Design and Development of Weapons in the Official History of the Second World War*, HMSO, London.

Rothwell, R. *et al.* (1972), 'SAPPHO updated', *Research Policy*, Vol. 3, No. 3, pp. 259–91.

Sako, M. (1989), 'Neither markets nor hierarchies: a comparative study of the printed circuit board industry in Britain and Japan' (mimeo), Industrial Relations Department, London School of Economics.

Saxenian, A.L. (1990), 'The origins and dynamics of production networks in Silicon Valley', Paper at the Montreal Workshop.

Schumpeter, J.A. (1928), 'The instability of capitalism', *Economic Journal,* pp. 361–86.

Sharp, M. (1991), 'The single market and European technology policies', in C. Freeman, M. Sharp, W. Walker (eds), *Technology and the Future of Europe*, Pinter Publishers, London, pp. 59–76.

Solo, R. (1954), 'Research and development in the synthetic rubber industry', *Quarterly Journal of Economics*, Vol. 68, pp. 61–82.

Storper, M. and Harrison, B. (1990), 'Flexibility, hierarchy and regional development: the changing structure of international production systems and their forms of governance in the 1990s', Paper at the Montreal workshop.

Takeuchi, H. and Nonaka, I. (1986), 'The new product development game', *Harvard Business Review*, January–February, pp. 137–45.

Teece, D.J. (1986), 'Profiting from technological innovation: implications for integration, collaboration, licensing and public policy', *Research Policy*, Vol. 15, No. 6, pp. 285–305.

Teece, D.J. (1989), 'Technological development and the organisation of industry', OECD Conference on Science, Technology and Economic Growth, June, OECD, Paris.

Thomas, G. and Miles, I. (1989), *Telematics in Transition; The Development of New Inter-active Services in the UK*, Longman, London.

Utterback, J.M. and Abernathy, W.J. (1975), 'A dynamic model of product and process innovation', *Omega*, Vol. 3, No. 6, pp. 639–56.

Van Kooij, E.H. (1990), *Technology Transfer in the Japanese Electronics Industry*, Economic Research Institute for Small and Medium-sized Business, Zootemeer, The Netherlands.

Von Hippel, E. (1987), 'Cooperation between rivals: informal know-how trading', *Research Policy*, Vol. 16, No. 5, pp. 291–302.

Von Hippel, E. (1988), *The Sources of Innovation*, Oxford.

Von Hippel, E. (1989), 'Cooperation between rivals: informal know-how trading', Chapter 7 in B. Carlsson (ed.), *Industrial Dynamics*, Kluwen, Dordrecht.

Williamson, O.E. (1975), *Markets and Hierarchies: Analysis and Industry Implications*, Free Press, New York.

Williamson, O.E. (1985), *The Economic Institutions of Capitalism*, Free Press, New York.

Woodward, E. (1965), *Structure of Industrial Research Associations*, OECD, Paris.

6 Innovation, changes of techno-economic paradigm and biological analogies in economics*

Introduction

The shift from mechanistic models to an evolutionary approach in economics is long overdue. Despite the advocacy of Marshall (1925) and of Schumpeter (1939, 1943) it has been a long time coming. However, there were many indications in the 1980s that the pace is accelerating. The work of Nelson and Winter (1982) and the joint work of many authors edited by Dosi *et al.* (1988), together with the establishment of new journals (for example, *The Journal of Evolutionary Economics*) and the 'Schumpeter Society', exemplify this change.

To capture the interactive nature of the technology–economy relationship, analogies with biological evolution are now often invoked. These imply a selection from a range of 'mutations' in technology and/or in the innovating organisations. By what processes do some organisational and technical innovations survive and prosper while others founder and die? This chapter attempts to explore some aspects of this interaction between the selection environment and innovations and to discuss the advantages and limitations of biological analogies. Section 2 explores the nature of the 'selection environment' for innovations, including the natural environment, the built environment and the institutional environment. It concludes that despite the positive stimulus to be derived from biological analogies, there is no real substitute for the development of models and theories which take into account those specific features of social development and technical change which are uniquely human and which indeed vary with each successive technological revolution. The final section of the chapter (Section 3) discusses one such attempt to open up a

---

*An earlier version of this chapter was originally prepared for the Labour Institute for Economic Research (Finland) and published in Finnish in *TTT Katsaus*, No. 4, 1989. Second version published in *Revue économique*, Vol. 42, No. 2 (March 1991), pp. 211–32.

new perspective on the evolutionary aspects of technical and organi-sational innovation—the idea of successive 'techno-economic paradigms' introduced by Carlota Perez (1983).

'Selection' works at many different levels—that of the R&D project and programme in the R&D system, the individual innovation within the firm, the firm itself (this is the level of most biological analogies in economic theory), the industrial branch or region, the nation, and the social system itself. The last two points in particular remind us that one of the fundamental differences between biological evolution and human social evolution is that not only the natural environment but also the institutional environment are themselves changing rapidly as they interact with new technology.

Nevertheless, the emphasis on 'selection' in terms of some criteria of viability and comparative advantage seems apt in the real life selection processes which do indeed operate at all these different levels. From the astronomically huge numbers of possible mutations only a few survive, so that there are clearly powerful focussing systems. Freedom of choice is constrained on all sides and each step is path-dependent. Within the science system the 'internalist' criteria of experimental validation and logical coherence *do* play a part. At the technical level the hard test of 'does it work' is obviously fundamental in addition to many other criteria of 'satisfactory' performance which are more open to subjective inter-pretation and manipulation. Pilot plant work and prototype testing are selection procedures of a fairly rigorous kind. Market demand, profitability, market size and cost considerations are clearly of paramount importance in a capitalist economy when it comes to selling such new products and services, however optimistic early estimates may have been. In fact the capacity to generate a wide variety of potential new products, services and organisations and to confront them on a trial and error basis with these various selection processes over a prolonged period is probably the strongest single evolutionary advantage of capitalist institutions themselves. Schumpeter thought that the bureaucratisation of R&D and the concentration of industry would lead in the end to the death of entrepreneurship, the loss of technical dynamism, and to socialism. Although he may well have underestimated the continuing technical dynamism of capitalism, he was probably not mistaken in believing that the innovation capacity of a social system would be decisive for its long-term survival and growth.

At all these levels and in their interplay, evolutionary selection is at work, and at all these levels the biological metaphor can be a useful stimulus to new thinking. Lorenz (1984) defended himself against the accusation of anthropomorphism when he compared jealousy in the behaviour of geese to that of human beings by claiming that logically there is no such thing as a 'false' analogy. He was right to emphasise that analogies (observed similarities) between animal and human behaviour can be a fertile source of new ideas and explanations in both natural and social science, since they can lead to the observation of what is *different* about humans, as well as what is the same. However, it is important not to be carried away by evolutionary analogies and to mistake the analogy for the reality, as often occurs with computer simulation models which have a similar heuristic value. At the very least any good biological model would have to be Lamarckian and not neo-Darwinian. Moreover, the 'mutations', whether in technologies or in the behaviour of firms or other institutions, are often purposively introduced, even though they may follow from the screening and testing of a number of alternative combinations, some of which are random, or nearly so.

It would be as dangerous for economics to take over wholesale the models of biology as it was to make too much of equilibrium models derived from physics (Allen, 1988).

The role of the selection environment

In contemporary societies, the interactions between human needs, the economy, entrepreneurship and the internal dynamics of the science-technology system generate an increasingly wide range of technological and organisational possibilities. But this certainly does not mean unconstrained freedom to use new (or old) technology in any way we wish, either for individuals or for society as a whole. The social environment acts not only as a stimulus to the capacity and range of technology and the deployment of alternative new combinations. It also constrains, frustrates and prevents in various ways the deployment of new technologies. Furthermore, the environment may at one stage act as a containing and restraining influence, whereas at a different stage it may provide a powerful stimulus.

The element of *timing* was already stressed by Schumpeter (1939):

> One essential peculiarity of the working of the capitalist system is that it imposes sequences and rules of timing. Its effectiveness entirely rests on this and on the promptness with which it punishes infringements of those sequences and rules. (p. 412)

However, it is not only the economic and institutional environment which 'imposes sequences' and 'punishes'. Catastrophic events in the natural environment can at any time introduce a new set of penalties, constraints and priorities. In order to analyse the changing influence of the selection environment, it is necessary to distinguish between the natural environment, the built environment and the institutional environment. Within the institutional environment it is also necessary to distinguish different types and levels of selection.

(i) *The natural environment*

At a time of mounting concern about the 'greenhouse effect', 'acid rain' and destruction of the tropical rainforest, it is hardly necessary to stress the continuing importance of interactions between technology and the natural environment. Even when there were fewer human beings and the mode of production was predominantly agricultural these interactions were important. The possibilities for hunting, gathering, growing crops, herding animals and extracting minerals have always been constrained by climatic and geological factors. Although agricultural and mining technologies have vastly enlarged the possibilities for the scope, volume and quality of production, they have not removed and cannot altogether remove these constraints. Social conflicts rather then geological factors or environmental hazards provoked the oil crises of 1973 and 1979. However, the depletion of fossil fuels, the hazards of nuclear power and the polluting effects of many processes using oil and coal have led to increasing pressures for the development and improvement of new and old energy technologies (such as solar, wind and water power) which use renewable sources of energy. Similar considerations, although at the moment a little less pressing, apply to materials, transport and construction.

The sheer scale of human populations and economic activities means that whatever the forms of social organisation, interactions between the natural environment and human technology will be increasingly important. Scientific breakthroughs and advances in biotechnology and space technology may open up entirely new possibilities for energy and food production and thereby relax some of the constraints. However, the use of pollution abatement technologies, changes in energy, transport and agricultural systems and even scientific research all depend on massive new investment. Catastrophic environmental degradation could destroy the human species as well as many others even though the role of human foresight, knowledge and capacity for adaptive response clearly distinguish the human from other animal species. Successful action depends on a combination of advances in scientific understanding, appropriate political programmes, social reforms and other institutional changes, as well as on the scale and direction of new investment. Organisational and social innovations would always have to accompany any technical innovations and some would have to come first.

Nevertheless, even with a timely response, in a very real sense the environment itself will 'select' which technologies (if any) are effective in coping with such problems as the greenhouse effect. Human beings are 'free' to develop a range of possible social and technical innovations which they hope will dampen the effects sufficiently for them to survive. The more they understand about the scientific and social problems, the more likely they are to improvise effective strategies after a learning period. However, there is also obviously a very strong selection process at work and the freedom to choose between alternatives is highly constrained: it is the 'freedom of necessity', about which Bernal wrote in 1949. Although some changes in the natural environment are the direct result of human activity (whether intended or not) and may be responsive to purposive social control, however puny and misdirected such efforts may now appear, others confront us as purely external forces. The analogy with biological evolutionary processes is therefore valuable in so far as it shows the great danger of separating economics completely from ecology. However, it would be misleading if it led to neglect of the ways in which the human species can itself purposively modify the environment.

(ii) *The built environment*

Contemporary human societies are influenced and limited in their choice and exploration of new technologies not only by the natural environment. The capital stock of the human race in cities, villages, power-stations, transport facilities, factories, farms and other forms of fixed capital is now so great that it shows some characteristics of the natural environment and indeed in some ways is part of it. The built environment now predominates in its influence on the evolution of some animals and plant species.

However, it both stimulates, channels and constrains human technological developments in a number of ways which have little to do with the natural environment. Obviously the prior existence of long-lived physical assets may often be a constraint on investment in new equipment, not just in purely physical terms but even more so in cost, profitability and social acceptability. At other times the depreciation and deterioration of these assets may stimulate new investment and technical changes. Theories of replacement cycles for physical assets have been important in business cycle theory and were a major element in Kondratieff's (1926) theory in which he postulated that cycles of infrastructural investment lasted about half a century. Kuznets suggested a similar though shorter cycle for the construction industry. At all times considerations of location, scale, durability and cost of physical equipment powerfully affect decisions about new investment embodying new technologies, especially infrastructural investment. Grubler (1990) has recently demonstrated anew the very great importance of technical change interacting with waves of new infrastructural investment in transport systems.

In the long run all fixed assets can be changed or replaced, but in the short run most of them are 'clay' rather than 'putty', acting at times as a powerful constraint on the rapid diffusion of new technologies. This could be seen very clearly in the energy crises of the 1970s. After the first OPEC shock in 1973 desperate efforts were made to save oil; however, to the extent that they were successful, it was more from social restrictions on consumption rather than changes in technology. A few power-stations were equipped to switch rapidly from oil to coal and in many countries it was possible to make minor energy-saving 'retro-fitting' applications to existing capital stock. A persistent energy-saving trend could set in only with new less energy-intensive generations of capital equipment in factories, vehicles and buildings, and with subsidies for the installation of such equipment. The strength of such trends varies between countries, depending on social policies and priorities and scale of investment as well as on R&D technology policies. However, in all countries the speed of the change in technology was constrained by the heritage of a large existing investment in old plant and infrastructure. For this reason, among many others, any large-scale transition to the use of biotechnology outside a few industries and services is likely to be a matter of decades rather than of years. For this reason, too, it is important to make an early start in dealing with severe long-term environmental hazards.

(iii) *The institutional environment*

The nature and timing of those technical and organisational innovations which will be generated, adopted and improved or discarded will be influenced not only by the natural and built environment but also, of course, by the institutional environment, including previous accumulated experience in science and technology. Capitalist institutions have so far proved the most effective in human history in stimulating a flow of technical and organisational innovations and diffusing them through the production system. No one paid a stronger tribute than Marx to this technical dynamism of capitalism. Nevertheless, this does not mean of course that *any* innovation is promoted and diffused under capitalism. On the contrary, the economy and the web of established technologies are highly selective. It is well established that most attempted innovations fail. A very high proportion fail in the development stage before they are ever launched, but after market launch there are still many failures. In particular for the more radical innovations, there is not only a high rate of failure, but even for those which ultimately succeed there is usually a prolonged gestation period often lasting decades with many setbacks (Jewkes *et al.*, 1958).

Although other factors, such as war or the threat of war, have certainly had a very powerful influence in some countries and some periods, there can be little doubt that under capitalism it has been economic criteria of potential market demand, cost and profitability which have predominated in the selection process. This does not mean that it is possible to make accurate *ex ante* estimates of costs and rate of return on any innovation, especially the more radical ones. On the contrary, all the evidence continues to point in the opposite direction. Nor does it mean that there are no other influences at work, such as safety or political power struggles in firms or governments. Still less does it mean that market demand is the only influence on innovation since by definition there is no previous experience of market demand for truly radical innovations (Mowery and Rosenberg, 1979). However, in the long run the need for profitable accumulation asserts itself as the predominant influence on the success or failure of new products and processes.

We have argued in Section 1 that biological analogies can be fruitful in highlighting aspects of this selection process provided that the differences as well as the similarities between social and biological evolution are also stressed. One of these differences relates to the interaction of the 'selection environment' with the 'mutations' which emerge and survive. Another relates to the purposive nature of that interaction with human individuals and social institutions deliberately cultivating and *designing* certain types of 'mutation'. Marx expressed this difference well in his comment that what distinguishes the worst of architects from the best of bees is that the architect erects first of all in the imagination what is subsequently constructed in reality. This simply does not occur with the 'blind watchmaker' or neo-Darwinian biological evolution, although of course it is a feature of some theories of creative evolution.

Finally, the institutional selection environment for innovations operates at several different levels. The realm of the scientifically conceivable is far wider than the realm of the technically feasible, which is in turn far wider than the realm of the economically profitable (Perez, 1985). The realm of the economically profitable is in turn wider than the socially acceptable and the criteria of acceptability are themselves evolving. We shall briefly consider the various levels of selection.

(A) SCIENCE AND TECHNOLOGY IN THE INSTITUTIONAL ENVIRONMENT

It would, of course, be a mistake to think of technology as simply drawing upon a 'genetic pool' of random mutations from science or of the economy as drawing upon a similar genetic pool of mutations from technology. The 'linear model' of innovation has been criticised *ad nauseam*, and rightly so. Virtually all case studies of innovation and most histories of technology point to the strength of the interaction between technology and science as well as between the economy and technology. The internalist–externalist debate in the history of science has receded with the growing awareness of these interdependencies. The importance of the social context is increasingly recognised as well as the fact that autonomous developments in technology sometimes lead science. Some historians of technology, such as Hughes (1983, 1988), who studied in depth the development of specific technologies, became impatient with the pretensions of particular disciplines, whether economists or historians of science, to reduce a complex interactive system to the narrow perspective of one discipline:

Interaction suggests that hard analytical categories, such as technology, science, politics, economics and the social should be used sparingly if their use leads to difficulty in comprehending interconnection. A system or networks approach may help historians present the history of technology in accordance with the interactive mode. Inventors, engineers, managers and financiers who have taken a lead in creating and presiding over technological systems show a way of grasping the seamless web. (1988, p. 12)

The emphasis on interactive systems and networks is shared by most European historians of technology such as Gille (1978), Callon (1986), Bijker (1987) and the group at Edinburgh working on information and communication technology with their emphasis on the 'social shaping of technology' (Molina, 1989). The growing use of such expressions as 'socio-technical system' or 'techno-economic paradigm' is another indication of the general recognition of the importance of these interdependencies.

When all this has been said, however, there is still an *internal* selection at work within science and technology. Campbell (1960), in his paper 'Blind variation and selective survival as a general strategy in knowledge processes', has argued that the mental scanning of a vast range of random possibilities explains the greater part of original innovative ideas. Yet even from this extreme position, the Popper-Lakatos (1970) criteria of falsifiability and continual experimental validation in fundamental science are still an even more important internal selection process. However they may originate, some of the results of fundamental research *do* create an entirely new range of possibilities for technology. The 'genetic pool' is enlarged both by experience with technologies *and* by internal developments in science itself, *and* by their interaction. Clearly this is another extremely important difference from the genetic pool of neo-Darwinian biology. This has very important implications for technology policy, which have been strongly emphasised by Nelson (1988). The closer the interaction between science and technology, the more important it becomes for industrial R&D laboratories to find ways to gain selective early access to the results of fundamental research, especially in universities. Thus the national institutional environment could be an important stimulus to the evolutionary process or, in other institutional situations, could retard it.

(B) TECHNOLOGY AND THE ECONOMY

It is at the stage of innovation and diffusion of innovation by firms that biological analogies have been most widely used in economics. Some analysts have concentrated on the evolution of the artefacts or innovations themselves (see, for example, Clark and Juma (1987) and their comments on Marx's account of the hundreds of specialised types of hammer which evolved during the Industrial Revolution; or see also the comments of Lorenz (1984) on the 'irrational' persistence of some design features through radical changes in technology—Marx's 'locomotives with horses' legs'). In this approach the birth, survival or death of firms is secondary to the technological evolution itself. Faber and Proops (1988) suggest that inventions represent the *genotypes* of technological evolution, whereas innovations are the *phenotypes*.

However, most evolutionary economists have concentrated on the *firm* as the dominant analogy with the biological 'survival of the fittest'. In this approach the survival and development of *innovations*, whether technical or organisational, is taken usually as dependent on the survival and growth of innovating *firms*. This illustrates once again some of the profound differences between natural and social evolution. Businaro (1983) made a thorough and consistent attempt to explore the scope and limits of reductionism to the firm level. The behaviour of the system cannot be reduced simply to the behaviour of individual firms since technology has a continuity which outlives any particular firm and transcends their failures. Nor can the growth and survival (or death) of firms be really likened to the life cycle of biological organisms. Edith Penrose (1952) made perhaps the most devastating critique of biological analogies in her attack on the analogy between the growth of animals (or plants) and the growth of firms and other attempts to give explanations of human affairs that do not depend on human motives. Nevertheless there is *some* merit in the biological analogy both at the level of technology and at the level of the firm.

For reasons of space it is not possible to pursue the analysis of firm behaviour here, but it is essential to insist on one key point: the role of profitability. Even though there may be enclaves where 'non-market' selection persists for long periods in a capitalist economy and even though unprofitable individual products like Concorde may survive for a long time through political subsidies, selection according to profitability clearly predominates. Future civil supersonic aircraft are likely to be more profitable than Concorde.

Political and social influences may very well determine the innovations which are selected for further development. Nevertheless, after market launch and during diffusion it is *economic* selection with all its constraints and stimuli, interacting with the strategies and decisions of firms, which will largely determine the growth, survival or disappearance of innovating firms as well as the improvements of the technology. Schumpeter and Marx were surely not mistaken in identifying profits as having a very important effect on 'bandwagons' and 'swarming' behaviour during early phases of diffusion, and the erosion of profits at a later stage leading to bankruptcies, rationalisation and concentration. And it is mainly the firms which invest in the capital stock embodying successive generations of new technology.

(C) THE ECONOMY AND THE WIDER SOCIAL SYSTEM

This point is particularly relevant in connection with the discussion on the transition to the assembly line and other types of mass and flow production in large firms. Some historians (for example, Piore and Sabel, 1984) have suggested that the decline of flexible small firm production systems was as much a matter of political and social power of large corporations as of economic advantages. There was, in their view, a real choice for society in quality of work and the human advantage of different types of work organisation. Some regions in Europe chose a different path. According to some accounts, even the economic advantages favoured small firms. However, most of the evidence on scale economies suggests that it was the enormous strength of the capitalist profitability selection pressures which, so far from favouring small firms, was the main force driving concentration. Klein (1977) points out that there were indeed several technical alternatives still in competition for the US passenger car market at the end of the nineteenth century—electric cars, steam cars and the internal combustion engine. There were also at that time many small producing firms using a variety of manufacturing techniques. However, the Ford assembly line and the internal combustion engine showed such decisive *economic* as well as technical advantages (Klein, 1977, pp. 98–9) by the First World War that the competitive process led inexorably to a strong concentration of production and ownership in large-scale plants. Analogous developments took place in other industries. Some of these were closely linked to the motor vehicle industry, such as tyres, rubber and oil. Others were indirectly affected, such as consumer durables or service industries, like tourism and retail distribution.

But in all these cases the relative profitability of large-scale flow production or assembly line methods and of mass markets was the driving-force in competitive selection, rather than the preferences of individuals or groups for particular styles of work organisation or size of firm. In fact, Ford found it very hard to retain his labour force in the early days of the assembly line because of the speed-up and monotony involved. However, the productivity and profitability potential was so great that he could double wages to attract and retain the type of labour he wanted. It was this which drove the diffusion of the organisational as well as the technical innovations.

This is not to say that different social institutions could not override the profitability imperatives of capitalist competition nor, for example, that strong trade unions or social legislation cannot mitigate them. However, it would have required either a very different social regulatory framework or a different social system to override the pressures to adopt the assembly line in early twentieth-century United States. A similar resurgence of the competitive strength of large firms is taking place today (see, for example, Harrison, 1989). Scale economies in design, development and world-wide marketing still influence profitability. After a period of proliferation of small innovative firms in computing software and biotechnology, a new phase of concentration is setting in with many take-overs, especially in Europe. Nevertheless, the Piore–Sabel debate, in both its historical and contemporary context, does highlight an extremely important issue in relation to social 'shaping' of technology: How much freedom do we really have to modify and adapt a major wave of technical and organisational innovations if they offer decisive economic advantages to competitive firms in a capitalist economy?

(D) ORGANISATIONAL INNOVATIONS

It is true that some organisational innovations can and do proceed with little *direct* relationship to technical innovations. There are many examples of such innovations in service industries over the past half-century, such as self-service and supermarkets in retail distribution, containerisation in transport, or packaged holidays in tourism. Although changes in physical layout played some part in these innovations, and preceding technical innovations in refrigeration, vehicles and communications play an important role, they followed their own trajectory. As Schumpeter indicated, they can be treated in much the same way as a stream of technical innovations and are part of the general profit-driven dynamic of capitalism. They were related, however, to the wider social and technical trends of mass production, standardisation of consumer products, mass markets, car ownership and cheap energy. Thus they were far more influenced by the dominant contextual web of technical and economic development and the dominant style of management (the techno-economic paradigm), than by specific technical innovations in each particular sector. It is essential to look, therefore, not just at individual innovations but also at the entire system. The main purpose of the last section of this paper is to examine these systemic aspects of innovation.

Some other organisational innovations were much more directly induced by technical innovations. Almost any major process or product innovation will lead to some corresponding organisational change in the company, for example changes in training systems, maintenance procedures, technical services, and so forth. Joan Woodward (1968) argued on the basis of a thorough empirical survey that a firm's technology largely determined its organisation and management structure. However, a big organisational innovation in the production system itself may also reciprocally affect technical innovations. Burton Klein (1977) describes the technical changes which followed the introduction of the assembly line by Ford:

Once the organisational change was made, the automobile firms found many opportunities for developing more efficient machines by making them more automatic. For example, replacement of the vertical turret lathe by a more automatic horizontal lathe doubled output per worker. (p. 91)

There is an interplay between technical and organisational innovation both inside and outside the innovating firms. This can ultimately lead to the organisation of completely new service industries as, for example, roadside garages to cope with maintenance and repair of motor vehicles or the wide range of contemporary computer-based consultancy services and data banks. However, response is not instantaneous. There are great disparities in the trajectories of innovations in different sectors and industries, and in a complex institutional environment there will be many cases of time lags and adjustment problems as well as bottlenecks in various parts of the system. Both Rosenberg (1976) and Hughes (1983) have emphasised these features of innovation very strongly in their histories of technology. The problems of mismatch between technology, firm-level organisation and other institutions are likely to be most severe when a radically new innovation or combination of innovations confronts an institutional environment which has been developed to accommodate a very different system of technology. Some matching of institutions and technology may take place locally through organisational innovations at the level of the firm or group of firms. However, the bigger changes in technology may lead to a wider institutional change affecting the legal and political system, as well as the educational system, technical standards, tax and incentive systems, and so forth. This is, of course, a reciprocal influence.

This leads directly to the topic discussed in the final section of this chapter: the interdependence of technological, economic and organisational developments throughout the system and the way in which radically new technologies are able to enter and pervade the system, despite their initial disadvantages.

Changes of techno-economic paradigm

So long as the emphasis is entirely on the individual firm, innovation or product, economic theory has not quite broken away from the mechanistic models which it too uncritically adopted from physics and mathematics. Diffusion research on the evolutionary development and selective improvement of *individual* products or processes is of course relevant to analysis and forecasting of specific innovations within the broad spectrum of new technologies. However, if we are considering clusters of related innovations with the potential to affect a very broad range of products and processes and even the economy as a whole, such as electricity, steam power, mass production or computerisation, then a different approach is needed. The concern here is with the complementarities and externalities of families of interrelated technical, organisational and social innovations and with the rigidities of the built and institutional environments and established technological systems. In Schumpeter's analysis, it is these successive technological revolutions which underlie the Kondratieff cycles, or long waves of economic development, although he did not explore the interdependencies in each wave.

An important first step is the identification of the characteristics of those major changes in technology which have such widespread consequences that they merit some such description as 'technological revolution', or 'change in techno-economic paradigm', or 'change in technological regime'. Any such taxonomy or classification system, must of course do some violence to the infinite complexity of the real processes of technical and economic change. Nevertheless, a taxonomy is essential both for analytical purposes and as a tool for empirical research (Freeman and Perez, 1986). It is useful to distinguish between four categories of innovations and their diffusion: incremental innovations, radical innovations, new technology systems and changes of techno-economic paradigm.

Incremental innovations occur more or less continually, although at differing rates in different industries, but they are concerned only with improvements in the existing array of products, processes, organisations and systems of production. They are therefore closely linked to the development of market demand and the experiences of users. For this reason user–producer and learning-by-doing relationships are extraordinarily important for this type of innovation (Lundvall, 1988). Incremental innovations account for the vast majority of patents and award schemes in firms. They are reflected in the official measures of economic growth by changes in the coefficients in the existing input–output matrix. Although their combined effect is extremely important in the growth of productivity, no single one has dramatic effects or induces structural change in the economy.

Radical innovations are discontinuous events and they have been the main concern of most diffusion studies, frequently showing the typical sigmoid pattern identified in the standard diffusion models and in product cycle theory. They could not arise from the incremental improvement of an existing product, process or system. For example, nylon could not emerge from the improvement of natural materials, nor could the railway emerge from putting several stage coaches together, as Schumpeter observed. They require both organisational and technical change, and just because they do not readily fit into the existing built and institutional environments they lead to structural changes in the economy.

New technological systems are 'constellations' (Keirstead, 1948) of innovations which are technically and economically interrelated. Obvious examples are the clusters of innovations in synthetic materials, petrochemicals and plastics machinery introduced in the 1930s, 1940s and 1950s. Another example is the cluster innovations of electrically driven household consumer durables. Nelson and Winter's (1982) 'natural trajectories' help to explain the technical interrelatedness of these clusters of radical and incremental innovations, but economic interdependencies and organisational innovations are also important as, for example, in the habituation to consumer credit systems in the purchase of consumer durables or the externalities in skills, such as software skills, which become available as a technology matures. The same process of consolidation of a system, which is increasingly hospitable, explains why innovations which would have been considered very radical in the early phases of a technological trajectory, may become increasingly 'incremental' as time goes by (Perez, 1988).

Changes of techno-economic paradigm correspond to the 'creative gales of destruction' which are at the heart of Schumpeter's long wave theory. The introduction of electric power or steam power are examples of such profound transformations. A change of this kind carries with it many clusters of radical and incremental innovations and may embody a number of new technology systems. A vital characteristic of this fourth type of technical change is that it has *pervasive* effects throughout the economy, i.e. it not only leads to the emergence of a new range of products, services, systems and industries in its own right; it also affects directly or indirectly almost every other branch of the economy as in the example of mass production. The expression 'techno-economic' rather than 'technological paradigm' emphasises that the changes are interactive, including organisational as well as technical changes which go beyond specific product or process technologies. They affect the input cost structure and conditions of production and distribution throughout the system. This fourth category would correspond to Nelson and Winter's concept of 'general natural trajectories', and once established as the dominant influence on engineers, designers and managers becomes a 'technological regime' for several decades. In this perspective Schumpeter's long cycles may be seen as a succession of techno-economic paradigms. These long cycles may also indirectly affect such phenomena as art and literature (Korpinen, 1987), but that is beyond the scope of this chapter.

We now turn to an elaboration of the main characteristics of techno-economic paradigms and their patterns of evolutionary diffusion through long waves of economic development. A new techno-economic paradigm develops initially within the old. This already presupposes a socio-economic system which tolerates or even encourages variety and experiment. However, the new technology becomes established as a dominant technological regime only after a long period of gestation and competition with the previously dominant technologies. It has to prove its potential and actual profitability first in one or a few industries, and its full success occurs only after a crisis of structural adjustment entailing deep social and institutional changes and the replacement of the leading motive branches of the economy. The reasons for the mismatch arise from the different rates of change in various parts of the system as well as from inertia in the built environment and social institutions.

Clearly one major characteristic of the diffusion pattern of a new techno-economic paradigm is its spread from the initial industries or areas of profitable application to a much wider range of industries and services and the economy as a whole. A paradigm change is a radical transformation of the prevailing engineering and managerial *common sense* for best productivity and most profitable practice, which is applicable to almost any industry. However, its spread to other areas is usually heavily dependent on organisational and social changes. Examples are to be found today in the rapid growth of new types of software and consultancy firms, data banks and value-added networks, and the difficulties of diffusion of computer systems in some of the older service and manufacturing industries.

The organising principle of each successive paradigm and the justification for the expression 'techno-economic paradigm' is to be found not only in a new range of products and systems but also in the dynamics of the relative *cost* structure of all possible inputs to production. Perez (1983) argues that in each new paradigm a particular input or set of inputs, which may be described as the key factor of that paradigm, fulfils the following conditions:

1. clearly perceived low and rapidly falling relative cost;
2. apparently almost unlimited availability of supply over long periods;
3. clear potential for the use or incorporation of the new key factor or factors in many products and processes throughout the economic system either directly or (more commonly) through a set of related technical and organisational innovations, which both reduce the cost and change the quality of capital equipment, labour inputs, and other inputs to the systems.

This combination of characteristics holds today for microelectronics and telecommunications. It held until recently for oil, which underlay the post-war boom (the fourth Kondratieff upswing). Before that, the role of key factor was played by low-cost steel in the *belle époque* before the First World War (Freeman, 1990), by low-cost coal and steam-powered transport in the Victorian boom of the nineteenth century.

Clearly, every one of these inputs identified as key factors in each period existed (and was in use) long before the new paradigm was fully developed. From a purely technical point of view, the explosive surge of interrelated innovations in a technological revolution could probably have occurred earlier. However, as Perez (1988) pointed out, there are strong economic factors that first of all delay but later stimulate diffusion and improvement innovations. The massive externalities created to favour the diffusion and generalisation of an existing paradigm act as a powerful deterrent to change for a prolonged period. Arthur (1988) has demonstrated just how powerful these containment mechanisms are, and David (1985) has shown how they can be influenced by technical standards. The existing stock and availability of skills, capital equipment, components, markets and enabling institutions is an extremely powerful combination favouring the already established techno-economic paradigm. The frustrations and difficulties of the early diffusion of computer-related innovations were often described in the 1950s and 1960s and similarly with electric power in the 1860s, 1870s and 1880s.

Clearly, this approach implies a framework for evolutionary development which stresses the systems context rather than just the individual product or firm. Clearly, too it differs radically from the dominant conceptualisation both in most evolutionary theory with its emphasis on the innovating firm or product and with neo-classical economic theory, although it has points of contact such as the persistent search for least-cost combinations of factor inputs. Most formulations of neo-classical theory put the main emphasis on varying combinations of labour and capital and on substitution between them, and implicitly or explicitly assume reversibility and responsiveness even to small changes in these relative factor prices in either direction. This method stresses the system's response to *major* changes in the price of *new* inputs, and *new* technologies which exploit their potential to reduce costs of both labour and capital as a result of new total factor input combinations and organisation–managerial innovations. Once the new technology is widely adopted, the change is irreversible. Brian Arthur's (1988) work on path dependence shows very clearly why this is so.

At the level of the firm, the new ideal information-intensive organisation now emerging increasingly links design, management, production and marketing into one integrated system—a process which may be described as 'systemation'—and goes far beyond the earlier concepts of mechanisation and automatisation. Antonelli (1989) has described the combination of organisational innovations as the emergence of the 'network firm'. Firms organised on this new basis can produce a flexible and rapidly changing mix of products and services, taking advantage of varying international prices of inputs and demand changes. However, collaborative arrangements *between* firms, networking arrangements and strategic alliances are also increasingly characteristic of the industrial environment both nationally and internationally. Like the multinational corporation, these new networks can take advantage of the growing externalities provided by the global telecommunications infrastructure, which will ultimately bring down to extremely low levels the costs of transmitting very large quantities of information all over the world. These developments are already transforming international monetary and investment flows, as well as design and R&D information flows.

The transformation of the profile of capital equipment is no less radical although heavily constrained by the factors relating to the built environment discussed in Section 2 and by the problems of organisational change in the education and training systems for software skills. Computers are increasingly associated with all types of productive equipment as in CNC machine tools, robotics and process control instruments as well as with the design process through CAD, and with administrative functions through data processing systems, all linked by data transmission equipment. According to some estimates, computer-based capital equipment already accounts for nearly half of all new fixed investment in plant and equipment in the United States.

A special supplement to *The Economist* (30 May 1987) entitled 'Factory of the future' outlined the complete reorganisation of the production system which is now taking place and is far more important than any particular discrete piece of equipment, even though the associated investment may take place incrementally and entail much trial and error:

For the first time in three-quarters of a century the factory is being reinvented from scratch. Long, narrow production lines with men crawling all over them—a feature of manufacturing everywhere since the early days of the car-making dynasties—are being ripped apart and replaced with clusters of all-purpose machines huddled in cells run by computers and served by nimble-fingered robots. The whole shape of the industrial landscape is changing in the process. . . . In short nothing less than a whole new style of manufacturing is in the process of being defined.

It is because of this 'new style of manufacturing' that evolutionary models can no longer concentrate, as in the 1970s and 1980s, on discrete product innovations of firms but must take full account of system changes as well. For this reason there is now a proliferation of studies on the diffusion of 'computer-integrated manufacturing', 'flexible manufacturing systems', 'computer-aided design', and so forth (e.g. Antonelli, 1989).

However, just as the natural environment constrains the range and effectiveness of alternative solutions to environmental hazards and crises, so too the built and institutional environments constrain the feasible range of adaptations of the new techno-economic paradigm. There is some freedom to redefine what is socially acceptable in work intensity, work environment, labour relations, and so forth, and the Japanese 'just-in-time' method is not an immutable or unique solution to the new range of organisational and managerial problems. The scope for alternatives depends on the depth of understanding of the nature of the paradigm change, the power of the competitive and 'locking-in' processes, and the forms of international competition in the world economy as well as on social and political programmes and conflicts.

Finally, it is clear that the capacity to make innovations will vary at different times at the national level. Periods of paradigm change are also periods of great but uneven opportunity (Perez and Soete, 1988). For a variety of reasons it seems probable that Japanese institutional innovations in management systems, including the management of R&D, government policies for technology and the organisation of large firms will temporarily provide a particularly favourable environment for the new technologies (Freeman, 1987). Clearly there is competition between the Japanese national economy and others, but here too the cruder forms of biological evolutionary analogy break down. There is a selective process at work but this does not necessarily lead to war or to the disappearance of the alternatives. There is also scope for mutual learning and co-operation in the regulation of the international system. This depends on further institutional and political innovations, but it is certainly a possible path, just as at other levels the survival and adaptation of firms and individuals is possible through learning and mutual aid. 'Creative destruction' does not necessarily mean the disappearance of firms as both Penrose (1952) and Pavitt (1984, 1986) have pointed out.

As Silverberg (1988) puts it in his discussion of evolutionary models:

We are not always free to do what we want because the rest of the system may react in a very conservative identity-preserving way, or in counter-intuitively disastrous ones. On the other hand, very astutely applied change by an appropriately situated agent such as governments, social movements, etc. may be able to trigger a complete and self-propagating reorganisation of the system to an unequivocally more favourable state, which may not be attainable by the agents acting routinely on their own. (p. 555).

The experience of China since 1949 and the Soviet Union since 1917 could be interpreted as examples of overestimation by both governments and social movements of the degrees of freedom in attempting to reshape both the technology and the economy. They were also examples of underestimation of the enormous conformist pressures of the capitalist world market. This is certainly not to say that all such attempts are doomed to failure, only that the freedom to reshape technology and society depends on depth of understanding. It also depends critically on an experimental willingness to reassess experience and to learn in an open-minded way from both social and technical innovations. In other words, *glasnost* is an absolutely essential condition for attempts at *perestroika*. Human beings will continue to strive for socially desirable reforms or ideal visions of society, and human motivation certainly cannot be excluded from evolutionary models of social change even if what people actually achieve turns out to be very different from their ideals. Nevertheless, to avoid dogmatic Utopianism a constant process of debate and social learning is essential. Civil liberty is not a luxury; it is a necessity for an innovative society.

Conclusions

In the resurgence of evolutionary economics, analogies with biological theories have had a very important stimulating role. This chapter has argued that the analogies should be pursued not only to indicate similarities but also to highlight differences between evolution in the natural world and the evolution of human social systems. It has pointed to four main differences:

1. The greater complexity and various levels of the selection environment in social evoluton comprising not only the natural environment but also a built environment and a complex institutional environment. It is not only a question of the selective adaptation of individual tools, products or firms but also of wider forms of social organisation, of production, an interconnected web of technologies and a variety of social institutions. The *systems* level is very important in any analysis (Clark, 1990).

2. The teleological aspect of human evolutionary processes. Some biological theories also postulate an element of design in natural evolution and it is also possible to overestimate the degrees of freedom which human beings enjoy in both technical and organisational design. Nevertheless, there is a real difference, perhaps best illustrated by the fact that human beings now confront the possibility of eliminating some hereditary diseases through advances in scientific understanding and medical technology. This is a degree of purposive intervention which is now reaching the level of the natural genes themselves.

3. As this example also illustrates, social learning processes, knowledge accumulation and diffusion of knowledge have features which are unique to human societies. Any satisfactory evolutionary theory must pay special attention to those human institutions which play a central role in those processes (see, for example, Clark, 1989).

4. The above-mentioned three features of social evolution mean that 'technology both shapes its socio-economic environment and is in turn shaped by it. Neither is a sole determinant of the other. The two co-determine each other' (Sahal, 1985). In the complex process of 'co-determination' this chapter has emphasised a unique feature of techno-economic evolution—the succession of techno-economic paradigms involving a complex process of matching and mutual adjustment between pervasive new technologies, the built environment and the organisational/institutional framework within which these technologies develop.

Again, of course, it is possible to stretch the biological metaphor and to make analogies with theories of 'punctuated evolution'. But in the end, social scientists have really no alternative than to go beyond analogies and develop their own evolutionary models.

Bibliography

Allen, P. (1988), 'Evolution, innovation and economics', in G. Dosi *et al.* (eds), *Technical Change and Economic Theory*, Pinter, London.

Antonelli, C. (1989), *New Information Technology and Industrial Change: The Italian Case*, Kluwer, Boston.

Arthur, B. (1988), 'Competing technologies: an overview', in G. Dosi *et al.* (eds), *Technical Change and Economic Theory*, Pinter, London.

Bernal, J.D. (1949), *The Freedom of Necessity*, Routledge and Kegan Paul, London.

Buker, W., Hughes, T. and Pinch, T. (1987), *The Social Construction of Technical Systems*, Unit Press, Cambridge.

Businaro, U. (1983), 'Applying the biological metaphor to technological innovation', *Futures*, Vol. 15, No. 6, pp. 464–77.

Callon, M., Law, I. and Rip, A. (1986) (eds), *Mapping the Dynamics of Science and Technology*, Macmillan, London.

Campbell, D.T. (1960), 'Blind variation and selective survival as a general strategy in knowledge processes', in M.C. Yovits and S. Cameron (eds), *Self-Organising Systems*, Pergamon Press, New York.

Clark, N. (1989), 'Organisation and information in the evolution of economic systems', Paper given at the Workshop on Evolutionary Economics, University of Manchester, mimeo, July.

Clark, N. (1990), 'Evolution, complex systems and technological change', *Review of Political Economy*, Vol. 2, No. 1, pp. 26–42.

Clark, N. and Juma, C. (1987), *Long-Run Economics: An Evolutionary Approach to Economic Growth*, Pinter, London.

David, P.A. (1985), 'Clio and the economics of QWERTY', *American Economic Review*, Vol. 76, No. 2, pp. 332–7.

Dosi, G. (1982), 'Technological paradigms and technological trajectories', *Research Policy*, Vol. 11, No. 2, pp. 147–62.

Dosi, G., Freeman, C., Nelson, R., Silverberg, G. and Soete, L. (1988) (eds), *Technical Change and Economic Theory*, Pinter, London.

Elliott, B. (ed.) (1987), *Technology and Social Process*, Edinburgh University Press.

Faber, M. and Proops, J.L.R. (1988), 'Evolution in biology, physics and economics: a conceptual analysis', University of Keele, Department of Economics and Management Science.

Freeman, C. (1987), *Technology Policy and Economic Performance*, Pinter, London.

Freeman, C. (1990), 'The third Kondratieff wave: age of steel, electrification and imperialism', in Kihlström *et al.* (eds), *Festschrift in honour of Lars Herlitz*, Gothenburg.

Freeman, C. and Perez, C. (1986), 'The diffusion of technical innovations and changes of techno-economic paradigm', Venice Conference.

Gille, C. (1978), *Histoire des Techniques*, Gallimard, La Pléiade, Paris.

Grubler, A. (1990), 'The rise and fall of infrastructures', Physica Verlag, Heidelberg.

Harrison, B. (1989), 'The big firms are coming out of the corner', Paper given at the Conference on Industrial Transformation, UN Centre for Regional Development, Nagoya, mimeo, September.

Hughes, T. (1983), *Networks of Power: Electrification in Western Society 1880–1930*, Johns Hopkins University Press, Baltimore.

Hughes, T.P. (1988), 'The seamless web: technology, science, etc.', in B. Elliott (ed.), *Technology and Social Process*, Edinburgh University Press.

Jewkes, J., Sawyers, D. and Stillerman, J. (1958), *The Sources of Invention*, Macmillan, London.

Keirstead, B.G. (1948), *The Theory of Economic Change*, Macmillan, Toronto.

Klein, B. (1977), *Dynamic Economics*, Harvard University Press, Cambridge.

Korpinen, P. (1987), 'Long cycles in fine arts: towards a new theory of style', CRPEE Workshop, University of Montpellier, July.

Lakatos, I. and Musgrave, A. (1970), *Criticism and the Growth of Knowledge*, Cambridge University Press, Cambridge.

Lorenz, K. (1984), 'Analogy as a source of knowledge', *Science*, 19 July, pp. 229–35.

Lundvall, B.-A. (1988), 'Innovation as an interactive process', in G. Dosi *et al.* (eds), *Technical Change and Economic Theory*, Pinter, London.

Marshall, A. (1925), 'Mechanical and biological analogies in economics', in A.C. Pigou (ed.), *Memories of Alfred Marshall*, Macmillan, London.

Molina, A.H. (1989), *Transputers and Parallel Computers: Building Technological Capabilities Through Socio-Technical Constituencies*, PICT Policy Research Paper No. 7, Research Centre of Social Sciences, Edinburgh.

Mowery, D. and Rosenberg, N. (1979), 'The influence of market demand on innovation', *Research Policy*, Vol. 8, No. 2, pp. 102–53.

Nelson, R. (1988), 'Institutions supporting technical change in the United States', in G. Dosi *et al.* (eds), *Technical Change and Economic Theory*, Pinter, London.

Nelson, R. and Winter, S.G. (1982), *An Evolutionary Theory of Technical Change*, Harvard University Press, Cambridge.

Pavitt, K. (1984), 'Sectoral patterns of technical change: towards a taxonomy and a theory', *Research Policy*, Vol. 13, No. 6, pp. 343–73.

Pavitt, K. (1986), 'Chips and trajectories', Chapter 1 in R. Macleod (ed.), *Technology and the Human Prospect*, Pinter, London.

Penrose, E. (1952), 'Biological analogies in the theory of the firm', *American Economic Review*, Vol. 42, pp. 804–19.

Perez, C. (1983), 'Structural change and the assimilation of new technologies in the economic and social system', *Futures* Vol. 15, No. 5, pp. 357–75.

Perez, C. (1985), 'Micro-electronics, long waves and world structural change', *World Development*, Vol. 13, No. 3, pp. 441–63.

Perez, C. (1988), 'New technologies and development', in C. Freeman and B.-A. Lundvall (eds), *Small Countries Confronting the Technological Revolution*, Pinter, London.

Perez, C. and Soete, L. (1988), 'Catching up in technology', in G. Dosi *et al.* (eds), *Technical Change and Economic Theory*, Pinter, London.

Piore, M. and Sabel, C. (1984), *The New Industrial Divide*, Basic Books, New York.

Rosenberg, N. (1976), *Perspectives on Technology*, Cambridge University Press, Cambridge.

Rosenberg, N. (1982), *Inside the Black Box*, Cambridge University Press, Cambridge.

Sahal, D. (1985), 'Technological guideposts and innovation avenues', *Research Policy*, Vol. 14, No. 2, pp. 61–82.

Schumpeter, J.A. (1939), *Business Cycles*: 2 vols, McGraw Hill, New York.

Schumpeter, J.A. (1943), *Capitalism, Socialism and Democracy*, Allen & Unwin, London.

Silverberg, G. (1988), 'Modelling economic dynamics and technical change: mathematical approaches to self-organisation and evolution', in G. Dosi *et al.* (eds), *Technical Change and Economic Theory*, Pinter, London.

Woodward, J. (1968), *Management and Technology*, HMSO, London.

Part III
Values, Economic Growth and the Environment

7 The luxury of despair: a reply to Robert Heilbroner's *Human Prospect**

Heilbroner's *Human Prospect* is a well-written and powerful advocacy of the case for extreme pessimism in relation to the human race. Even though its message is in many essential respects the same as in *The Limits to Growth*, it is important because it includes dimensions which were lacking in the MIT models, and especially the political and social framework which was so largely absent from that work. For this reason it represents a major contribution to the international debate which has been the positive achievement of the Club of Rome and the MIT models.

Since much of what I have to say is critical of Heilbroner's thesis, I should emphasise at the outset that there is also much in his analysis which I admire, and with which I agree. In particular I accept his view that the issue of relationships between rich and poor nations, and the problem of income redistribution within nations are likely to be at the centre of the world political stage over the next century. However, I am not so pessimistic as he is about the utter hopelessness of a quest for paths by which inequalities between nations and within nations might be reduced. Nor do I share his view that human ideas, ideals and foresight have so little influence on the course of events. Indeed, it is a consciousness of the extent to which ideas *do* influence the course of events which led us to participate in this debate.

The responsibility of intelligentsia

Heilbroner starts his book by asking the question 'Is there hope for mankind?' and up to the last section, it was certainly my impression that he was going to follow through the logic of his argument quite ruthlessly, and finish by answering his own question with a clear and unequivocal 'No'.

*I should like to give my grateful thanks to my colleagues at SPRU who provided helpful comments in the preparation of this chapter. It was originally published in *Futures*, Vol. 6, No. 6, December 1974.

However, he formally disclaims the Doomsday label. In the final section of his book, apparently himself slightly appalled at the utterly dark and dismal prospect which he has conjured up earlier in the first four sections, he has a curiously lame backtracking conclusion:

Let me therefore put these last words somewhat more 'positively' offsetting to some degree the bleakness of our prospect, without violating the facts or spirit of our inquiry. Here I must begin by stressing for one last time an essential fact. The human prospect is not an irrevocable death sentence. It is not apocalypse or Doomsday toward which we are headed, although the risk of enormous catastrophes exists.[1]

If most of his readers have nevertheless concluded that he has been arguing that catastrophes 'of fearful dimensions' are virtually inevitable, he has only himself to blame. For he has emphasised that imaginative anticipation or well-meaning exhortations and warnings have little or no effect and that it is catastrophes which bring about the major changes in behaviour essential for human survival. He has also argued forcefully that the Malthusian checks which will be effective are not those of foresight and planning, but those of famine and war; that there is an 'ultimate certitude' about global environmental pollution; that authoritarian regimes are virtually inevitable, even in some curious way desirable, and that whether they are capitalist or socialist they are going to become embroiled in wars of redistribution arising from dwindling physical resources, which will make it impossible to sustain manufacturing industry and urban life. Finally, he has argued that there are fundamental traits in the human character, as well as acute social problems and physical shortages, which will favour authoritarian forms of government indefinitely.

Nevertheless, one must accept his technical disclaimer, however unconvincingly it reads, and describe his prospect not as a model of doom but as a prospect of despair. Whereas some of the MIT modellers made it clear that their model was not a prediction, but a warning of what might happen if present trends continued, Heilbroner makes no such distinction, and from his final section it seems that he does not intend his piece as a warning of what might be avoided, rather a statement of what is largely inevitable to which we must all succumb and adapt. This is apparent from the extraordinary section in which he discusses the responsibility of the intelligentsia:

It is their task not only to prepare their fellow citizens for the sacrifices that will be required of them but to take the lead in seeking to redefine the legitimate boundaries of power and the permissible sanctuaries of freedom for a future in which the exercise of power must inevitably increase and many present areas of freedom, especially in economic life, be curtailed.[2]

This must be taken in the context of his prediction of the universal spread of authoritarian regimes, his despairing comments on the decline of intellectual freedom, and the abandonment of the industrial mode of production.

Certainly, I would accept (and who could not?) that individually and collectively we are often impelled to change our behaviour by 'catastrophes'; but I believe too that foresight, imagination and understanding can enable us both individually and collectively to avoid some catastrophes which might otherwise engulf us. We do not need a famine every other year to be reminded of the importance of the harvest. On a global scale it is just conceivable that intelligent policies could enable us to augment it sufficiently to avert the worst disasters. However, as we shall see, a curious feature of Heilbroner's variant of pessimistic determinism is that, like the Malthusians before him, he regards an increase of food production as a 'danger'.

This perverse doctrine may have all the greater impact by virtue of Heilbroner's reputation, at any rate on this side of the Atlantic, as one of the outstanding radical critics among American social scientists. As he himself remarks, his piece is likely to give aid and comfort to those whom he has always regarded as his enemies, and I agree with him. According to his own account, intellectual honesty compelled him to come to conclusions which he himself found unpalatable and unwelcome. I agree that there is no point in wishful thinking or self-deception about issues which are clearly so important for all of us. Equally, it would be dangerous if a social doctrine based on fundamental intellectual fallacies, however sincerely conceived, were to gain wide acceptance. This would be particularly true if such a fashion were to give a cloak of respectability to economic and social policies which would otherwise be abhorrent. It is my belief that this is what occurred with the doctrines of Malthus in the first half of the nineteenth century, and the neo-Malthusian doctrines of our day could have similar consequences.

Malthus once again

I am aware of course that some of those who find the MIT doom models a plausible scenario resent the epithet 'Malthusian' or 'neo-Malthusian'. It may be that Heilbroner too dislikes being described as a Malthusian, although this seems highly improbable. In his opening section he places the issue of population and resources right at the forefront, and in considering what he regards as the sombre prospect of world population growth, he writes:

These Malthusian checks will exert even stronger braking effects as burgeoning populations in the poor nations press ever harder against food supplies that cannot keep abreast of successive doublings. At the same time the fact that population control in these countries is likely to be achieved in the next generations mainly by premature deaths rather than by the general adoption of contraception or a rapid spontaneous decline in fertility brings an added 'danger' to the demographic outlook. This is the danger that the Malthusian check will be offset by large increases in food production that will enable additional hundreds of millions to reach child-bearing age.[3]

The implications of this statement seem to me to come perilously close to the type of advice which was given to the British government at the time of the Irish famine: let the 'Malthusian checks' take their course, otherwise the problem will get worse. This is the straight anti-'humanitarian' message of Forrester; and it is indeed as unpalatable to me as it is totally unacceptable to the affected populations in the Third World.

Again, in his concluding section Heilbroner returns to this theme:

Therefore the outlook is for convulsive change—change forced upon us by external events rather than by conscious choice, by catastrophe rather than by calculation. As with Malthus's much derided but all too prescient forecasts, nature will provide the checks, if foresight and 'morality' do not. One such check could be the outbreak of wars arising from the explosive tensions of the coming period, which might reduce the growth rates of the surviving nation-states and thereby defer the danger of industrial asphyxiation for a period.[4]

It is not merely in the repeated invocation of Malthusian terminology, but also in the central intellectual assumptions that Heilbroner's *Human Prospect* is essentially and obviously a neo-Malthusian prospect.

The fact that a doctrine was misused or is used to justify reactionary social policies would not of course be sufficient to refute it. What matters is whether the Malthusian analysis represents such a true picture of the behaviour of human social systems that it can be reliably used to forecast future trends. The predictive power of the theory is the main point at issue. Heilbroner is asking us to believe in a scenario for the Third World of which the central feature is four successive doublings of populations over very short periods. This tendency he believes is so powerful, and so unlikely to be affected by acts of individual and collective foresight that only the sterner checks of famine and war on a hitherto unimaginable scale are likely to redress it.

Although it is true that he does consider the possibility that population growth rates in the Third World *could* slow down well before 2070, the main thrust of his argument is based on the view that they are unlikely to do so, except as a result of famine, disease and war. He recognises that population growth in Europe, North America, the Soviet Union and Japan is likely to be much slower, and the figures he estimates for these areas is well under 2,000 million by 2070, whereas he plays with the figures of 40,000 million for the Third World by 2070 or 20,000 million by 2050. In other words he is arguing that the countries of the Third World will be unable to accomplish in the twenty-first century what the richer countries have accomplished in the nineteenth and twentieth centuries. Why should this be so impossible?

Population trends in the Third World

Heilbroner's arithmetic is correct. Four successive doublings, each over a 25-year period would indeed bring the population of the Third World from 2,500 million in 1970 to 40,000 million in 2070. However, a similar projection made for Britain in 1801 would have predicted a population of 168 million a century later in 1901, and a projection for Europe (including the Soviet Union) in 1850 would have given a 1950 population of over 4,000 million, compared with the actual 1950 population of 576 million. There are several reasons for supposing that Heilbroner's projections are similarly overestimating the probable future trend.

In the original version of his essay, as it appeared in the *New York Review of Books*, he ignored the small but definite indications of a fall in birth-rate and major changes of attitude in the two most populous countries in the world: India and China. He mentioned only Taiwan and South Korea as countries where there had been 'limited success' in introducing birth control programmes and concluded: 'Thus in the underdeveloped world as a whole, population growth proceeds unhindered along its fatal course.'[5] Evidently, it has been pointed out to him that he might be making a serious error at least in relation to mainland China. There are very few changes in the paperback book version compared with the original in the *New York Review of Books*. Although all of them are extremely revealing, the new paragraph on China is the most interesting of all:

In fact, the only underdeveloped nation for which some cautious optimism may be voiced seems to be mainland China, where population-control programs, reportedly aimed at a zero growth rate by the year 2000, have been introduced with all the persuasive capability of a totalitarian, educational and propaganda system.[6]

Leaving aside his introduction of the expression 'totalitarian' to describe this aspect of Chinese policy, this seems to call for some revision of the rest of his argument, since China accounts for a quarter of the entire world population, and a third of that in the developing countries. But no such revision has been made.

However, it is not only in relation to China that his argument can be faulted; he ignores much other evidence on population trends both in Asia and in Latin America. The World Bank report on the MIT models pointed out that of sixty-six countries for which reasonably reliable data were available, fifty-six showed falling fertility rates.[7] His statement that 'in those Latin American countries where growth rates are highest, population control programmes are not as yet even advocated',[8] is only a half-truth. In Mexico, which has a very high growth rate, and which is the second most populous country in Latin America, not only are such programmes widely 'advocated', but also the government has at last begun to take the issue seriously. Birth-rates are already falling in several other Central American countries with very different social systems, such as Costa Rica, Cuba and Puerto Rico. The birth-rate has been falling slowly for some time under a variety of different regimes in Chile, and it has been relatively low for some time in Uruguay.[9]

One of the most significant developments in the past twenty years has been the breakup of the previously monolithic opposition to birth control from two of the strongest ideologies in the world: Roman Catholicism and official Marxism. Indeed, one interesting feature of the widespread trend to falling birth-rates is that these are reducing simultaneously in countries with differing socio-cultural backgrounds, and very diverse political systems. This trend provides no evidence for Heilbroner's suggestion that only 'authoritarian' regimes are likely to be competent in stabilising population growth rates. The birth-rate is falling rapidly in Hong Kong and Singapore as well as in China and Taiwan. Is this really due to 'totalitarian' pressures? So far as Europe is concerned, fertility rates are falling below replacement level in a range of countries, with a variety of political regimes. Ironically, in some cases 'authoritarian' regimes are attempting (with little success) to increase the birth-rate.

In considering the position in the Third World from 1970 to 2070, by comparison with Europe from 1870 to 1970, it is of course perfectly legitimate to point out that the fall in death rates in Third World countries has sometimes been much more rapid, and the population 'explosion' is consequently more severe. But equally, there is now a variety of much more efficient forms of birth control, far more widely available, whose use is persistently advocated by many private organisations as well as national and international agencies. Malthusians and neo-Malthusians are entitled to take some of the credit for the very widespread international public concern with population growth rates and for the change in attitudes. But if they do so, then they are hardly entitled also to claim that persuasion, imagination, individual and collective choice and planning have little or no role in human affairs. Presumably still less would they wish to claim that this persuasion has come most effectively from 'totalitarian' or 'authoritarian' sources.

It is true that such factors are probably less important than a general rise in living standards. The possibilities of achieving a stable world population depend largely upon social mechanisms which are the very opposite of the 'Malthusian check' which Heilbroner describes with such gloomy enthusiasm.

This is of course only one side of the picture. The other important aspect of the problem is the possibility of increasing agricultural productivity and here the Malthusians have a slightly stronger case.

It would be foolish to be complacent about ensuring an adequate food supply for a rapidly growing population, especially in view of the present low level of stocks, the possibility of adverse climatic changes, and the difficulties experienced in many parts of the world in achieving sustained increases in yields. Nevertheless, the evidence is fairly strong that on a world scale supply has been constrained less by purely physical factors than by low effective demand because of the poverty of most consumers. The potentialities for increasing output are considerable throughout the Third World as well as in countries such as Canada, the United States and Australia. Even with existing technology it would be physically possible to feed the size of world population which Heilbroner envisages. Plant and animal geneticists, entomologists, ecologists and agronomists are working hard and with considerable success throughout the world to make available to cultivators new varieties and new techniques which would facilitate sustained agricultural improvements.

Surely, in these circumstances, the responsibility of social scientists is to help their colleagues in the natural sciences and the affected populations to devise social arrangements which will make these techniques more rapidly effective, and will ensure conditions for their application which reduce inequalities of wealth and income, and which do not cause social and environmental disruption. It is more difficult to do this than to make models of doom, but it might be much more useful. Even if the target of increasing world food production steadily by 3 or 4 per cent per annum, and distributing it more equitably, is difficult to achieve, it is also not beyond our capabilities.

The conflict over resources

The distinctive feature of Heilbroner's version of neo-Malthusian ideology, in common with the MIT modellers, is singling out the problem of industrial materials and the associated pollution as the most intractable global problem and the main cause of the wars of redistribution which he foresees. Heilbroner differs from them and from most other doom modellers in assigning a *qualitatively* different significance to the problem of industrial materials and the associated pollution:

Here we come to a crucial stage of our inquiry. For unlike the threats posed by population growth or war, there is a certitude about the problem of environmental deterioration that places it in a different category from the dangers we have previously examined. Nuclear attacks may be indefinitely avoided; population growth may be stabilised; but ultimately there is a limit to the ability of the earth to support or tolerate the process of industrial activity, and there is reason to believe that we are now moving toward that limit very rapidly.[10]

He then goes on to project a growth rate of 7 per cent per annum for industrial output and consumption of materials. This of course shows that 'a volume of resource extraction 32 times larger than today's' would be needed in fifty years' time and 'looking ahead over the ten doublings of a century, the amount of annual resource requirements would have increased by over a thousand times'. He then asks: 'Do we have the resources to permit us to attain—or sustain—such gargantuan increases in output?'

The answer to his question may be 'No', but neither is there any need for us to attempt it. The basis for his 7 per cent projection is unclear; but if we take it to apply to the world as a whole, and we take his upper population estimate of 42,000 million, then this would imply an annual per capita consumption about ten times as high as the present per capita consumption in the United States. If we take a lower population estimate—say 21,000 million—then per capita consumption of materials would be about twenty times as high as the present US level. This goes beyond even the wildest fantasies of a submarine and a helicopter in everyone's back garden.

Doom models are often based on the implicit assumption that the North American use of energy and materials represents the pattern of the future towards which all nations must converge if they aspire to raise their living standards. This assumption is fallacious. A number of European countries already have what many would regard as a much higher quality of life than that of the United States, with a lower materials intensity and a lower energy intensity. The rest of the world is not obliged to follow the United States in its profligate use of oil and other natural resources, or in its pattern of conspicuous waste of packaging materials and advertising. Nor is it obliged to follow the European or Japanese pattern. It is even unlikely that the Americans themselves will continue to expand their per capita consumption of materials for another century at the rate of 7 per cent per annum. This implies that the so-called 'post-industrial society' not only has not arrived but will never arrive. One does not have to believe in the post-industrial society to recognise that the scenario of an indefinite 7 per cent increase in consumption of industrial materials is absurd. Almost all economists and sociologists are agreed that services are likely to grow much more than manufacturing in industrial societies over the next century. It is also quite obvious that many such service activities have a much lower materials intensity than manufacturing. A possible exception is the capital investment in construction required for some services, but there are scarcely any of those concerned with potential materials shortages who are predicting a shortage of *construction* materials.

Like all the Malthusian scenarios, these projections of materials' scarcity ignore one of the most important and characteristic features of human societies, especially industrialised societies: their capacity for technical and social change and substitution. If the world were confronted with critical shortages of particular industrial and construction materials, then all kinds of substitution mechanisms would come into play. One of them, as Heilbroner himself says, would be the recycling of industrial materials, which is already important for ferrous and non-ferrous metals, as well as for rubber and paper. Another would be the design and use of more durable products and greater economy in the use of materials. A third would be the invention and development of new materials and combinations of materials which are in more abundant supply. To be sure, all of these require deliberate research, investment and economic policies but most of those who have gone deeply into the question of physical availability of materials, since the MIT models brought this question to the forefront, are agreed that sheer physical shortage of materials is rather unlikely to bring the world to a grinding halt.

Politically induced shortages are quite another matter. Although there are passages where Heilbroner himself appears to recognise the implausibility of his scenario in relation to future materials shortages, this does not stop him making it the foundation of his long-term projections, or assuming without any justification that there will be a world of *falling* physical output due to physical shortage of materials. Indeed, he goes even further and assumes a post-industrial society which is apparently a non-industrial society, since he talks of 'dismantling' the industrial mode of production.

It is perhaps legitimate to talk about a post-industrial society in the same sense as one can speak of a post-agricultural society. Although agricultural productivity has risen so much over the past century that it is no longer necessary for more than a small fraction of the employed population to work in agriculture in Europe and North America, this is still an activity which is absolutely critical for human survival. Industrial productivity too has been rising so fast that manufacturing employment may also need only to be a small fraction of the total. This creates quite new possibilities both for employment and for leisure, but it does not mean that industry will cease to be an essential activity for the survival of the vast majority of human beings on this planet.

What has been said does not at all exclude the possibility of serious political and social conflict, including violent conflict, over such questions as access to reserves, or sources of particular critical materials, or over the terms of trade between primary commodities and manufactures. These conflicts have been with us for a long time and may well become more acute, but they do not justify the view of an inexorable worsening of the human situation as a result of acute physical shortages. Nor can we exclude the possibility that nationalistic ideologies will exploit the supposed future physical shortages of materials to provide a spurious justification for aggressive, pre-emptive, militaristic behaviour. Indeed, we know only too well that the Nazi movement used the false geopolitical scenario of resource shortages and unequal access to materials, as well as the false Malthusian population scenario of *Volk ohne Raum*, as one of the main strands in the ideological preparations for the Second World War. One of the most 'mischievious' consequences of Heilbroner's perspective may well be to provide future militaristic nationalist movements with an equally spurious, though superficially plausible, ideological smokescreen for their otherwise utterly unjustifiable and repugnant behaviour. We already know that the question of military intervention was seriously considered in the recent oil crisis, and with the experience of Suez, it would be foolish to ignore the possibility of military responses to resource problems, whether from parliamentary regimes or more authoritarian ones.

The uncertainty of environmental collapse

During the course of his exposition Heilbroner gradually moves over from warnings of the huge *increases* in materials requirements, to assuming a *decline* in physical output. Like the MIT doom modellers, he seems determined to have a black scenario. The massive increase brings the environmental disruption of the planet, and the decline justifies his scenario of the war of all against all for scarce resources. The MIT modellers at least discussed the possibility that the growth curve could asymptote gradually towards limits or that there could be non-catastrophic 'hunting behaviour' as limits were approached. One reason that the MIT global modellers regarded catastrophic outcomes as more probable, although not quite inevitable, was that they assumed an inevitable association between industrial production and environmental pollution. Heilbroner takes over this crucial but unjustified assumption. Hence apparently his use of the word 'certitude' with respect to environmental catastrophe. This is all the more strange, as in his own review of *The Limits to Growth*, he pointed out the fallacy in the MIT argument:

A very important conclusion follows. As the MIT models themselves show, it is not 'growth' that is the mortal enemy, but pollution. The programme of the ecologically-minded scientist, therefore, should not be aimed against growth, but only against pollution-generating growth. Any technological change that will increase output without further damaging the air or water or soil, or any technological change that will enable us to increase output by shifting from a less to a more abundant resource (again without an increase in pollution), represents perfectly safe growth, and should be welcomed with open arms.[11]

There is nothing 'certain' or 'inevitable' about pollution. As a result of a quite small effort in the industrialised countries, important though still inadequate results have already been achieved in relation to both air and water pollution and in the conservation of amenity. It is essential to press on with far greater vigour to ensure that environmental standards for industry are steadily improved throughout the world and that large areas of wilderness and parklands are conserved. This is a very difficult objective, especially in the United States, but it is not an impossible one.

At the time of the Stockholm Conference it was widely believed that the Third World would not take environmental problems seriously. However, the experience of the United Nations Environmental Programme since Stockholm belies this pessimistic view. The peculiarly narrow and backward-looking view of the authoritarian Brazilian regime is now increasingly seen to be the exception and not the rule. The UNEP was the first UN agency in which China participated, and many Third World countries are now actively involved. Not only are most Third World governments ready to take environmental questions seriously, but the Science Councils and other scientific organisations in those countries are also taking up these issues with enthusiasm, in seeking solutions to the local environmental problems which they confront. This constructive approach to the use of science and technology is in striking contrast to the fashionable malaise which attributes the ills of civilisation to science.

I was particularly encouraged to see that one of the passages which Heilbroner has substantially revised for the paperback edition concerns science: he now fully recognises that it is not 'science' but social systems and human behaviour which are the problems.

Political prospects and 'authoritarianism'

The most persuasive part of Heilbroner's *Human Prospect* is his discussion of political and social systems. However ill-conceived his uncritical adoption of neo-Malthusian ideas in relation to population and resources, there is nevertheless a ring of truth in some of his observations about current and future political systems. As Harold Laski never tired of pointing out, daily experience confirms the validity of one of the few major generalisations in political science: Lord Acton's dictum that 'power corrupts and absolute power corrupts absolutely'. Every newspaper also furnishes new evidence of the continuing realism of Machiavelli's cynical analysis of the behaviour of sovereign nation-states. No one who has lived through the wars in Korea and Vietnam, the Sino-Soviet conflict, the Arab–Israeli wars, Ulster and Watergate, can possible be complacent about the difficulties of averting corruption in government, brutality and torture in the treatment of political opponents, wars, terrorism, assassination and civil wars in the conduct of nation-states and political movements. Heilbroner apparently shared with me the hope of a fusion of the striving for social justice and civil liberty, a hope which was so cruelly crushed alike in Chile and

Czechoslovakia. In all of this it is difficult to deny that Heilbroner has genuine grounds for pessimism, which stands in no need of an additional Malthusian booster-injection to put us in a black mood.

However, sobering though these conditions are, they are not essentially new. What *is* new since the Second World War, as he rightly points out, is the enormous increase in the destructive power of modern weapons. Does this render our situation entirely without hope? I do not believe so, although I do agree with him that it does mean a gloomy prospect unless or until a more effective international security system is established. To this extent his warnings (and those of many others) are fully justified. However, the logical conclusion from these considerations is to place even greater emphasis on the importance of international institutions, and the importance of devising 'positive-sum games' for the resolution of international conflicts. It is also to press forward with world-wide efforts to reduce poverty as a major source of violent conflicts. In both these directions, although it must be conceded that the picture is black, it is not hopeless and indeed I should maintain that the US–Soviet and US–Chinese *détente* render the situation slightly more hopeful than it was, say, in 1938 or in 1950.

The gist of Heilbroner's argument is that international conflicts are likely to become more acute because of the struggle for control over resources, which will be reinforced by a strong trend towards authoritarian regimes in capitalist and socialist countries alike. Although I concede that there are good reasons for alarm on both these counts, once the neo-Malthusian prop is knocked away, then these tendencies appear a little less dangerous and all-pervasive, and by no means as inevitable future trends. I would maintain that post-war developments in both parts of Germany and in the Soviet Union give substantial grounds for hope, by comparison with the 1930s or the 1940s. Material prosperity has been an important factor in these more hopeful developments. Even if we grant for the sake of argument the Machiavellian view that politics is mainly a matter of the expedient and cynical pursuit of self-interest by individuals, groups and nation-states, then this does not at all rule out effective international agreements based on mutual toleration and even civil liberty. Nor indeed does a more generous view of human behaviour. Only if we follow Koestler and the more pessimistic theologians in postulating a fundamental 'design-fault' in human beings must we give way to complete despair.

Like some faint-hearted liberals in the 1930s, Heilbroner is inclined to write off the purely practical advantages of democracy far too quickly, and to concede far too much to the supposed psychological advantages and other attractions of militaristic and authoritarian regimes. Even before Watergate the supporters of parliamentary democracy were very well aware of its many failings as a system of government. The only thing they maintained pretty strongly, following the principle of a well-known upholder of parliament, was that the other systems were much worse. Heilbroner has said nothing to persuade me to revise this view, and many Greek, Spanish and Portuguese people, after considerable practical experience, appear to share my scepticism.

Of course, one must have some regard to the historical circumstances in developing countries such as China and to the desirable diversity of socio-political systems, but there are several fundamental reasons for believing that capitalist or socialist democracies are *more* likely to provide effective solutions to contemporary social, economic and political problems than supposedly more 'natural' and efficient authoritarian regimes. The first reason is that nobody yet knows all the answers to these problems and consequently any social system which permits an open debate on alternative solutions and proceeds to some extent by trial and error, is inherently far more likely to find and implement practical solutions. The second reason is closely related to the first: very few of the contemporary problems of agriculture, industry, the environment and society can be solved without science. In the long run science flourishes only in an environment which permits, even encourages, an iconoclastic critical approach to established orthodoxy. Even if Heilbroner were right in his vision of an unending series of wars and conflicts, this would confer a very great evolutionary survival advantage on those nation-states which are capable of fostering and using science. Their incapacity to tolerate the unorthodox, whether in art or in science or in politics, is one of the many Achilles' heels of the authoritarian regimes.

Another is the powerful tendency of such regimes to foster extreme inequalities in distribution of wealth, power and privilege. Once the constraint of open criticism is removed, then the Actonian mechanism comes fully into play. Indeed it is hard to understand why one who is rightly so concerned about problems of the environment, population, industrial working conditions and the danger of nuclear war, should accept so easily some supposed advantages of authoritarian regimes. The concentration of political power, the removal of the constraints of public debate and criticism, the suppression and victimisation of unwelcome critics, and many other similar characteristics of authoritarian regimes are far more likely to exacerbate these problems than to diminish or resolve them.

The human determinants

The conclusion, therefore, which I draw from the admittedly discouraging political and social prospects confronting us, is the very opposite of that which he draws. Whereas he speaks of the responsibility of intellectuals to prepare the population for the reduction of freedoms, I would maintain that the responsibility of intellectuals now more than ever is to uphold those freedoms, which we know from very hard-won experience are vital to prevent the arbitrary abuse of power. It is important of course to retain a sense of history and the diversity of cultures, to distinguish those freedoms which really are fundamental to the future of human civilisation, from the 'freedom' of large corporations to pollute the environment or manipulate the political process. If this is what Heilbroner means when he speaks of curtailing 'many present areas of freedom, especially in economic life', then I would be happy to concur. I would indeed maintain, like him, that this is the logic of the democratic process.

I do not at all underrate the dangers of authoritarian regimes and attempted military solutions. Just as Orwell's *1984* was an invaluable reminder of these dangers, so too the work of the doom modellers may often provide us with useful warnings. Both the 'dystopias' of science fiction and the models of doom have their essential place in that imaginary visualisation of future possibilities which helps us to try and avoid such outcomes. To this extent I have no quarrel with them. As part of a range of forecasting techniques they are unexceptionable, and I accept Jantsch's observation that good forecasting and planning probably requires the combination and confrontation of extrapolative techniques with goal-setting techniques.[12] My objection is to an *exclusive* preoccupation with models of gloom and doom and the tendency to assign to them a deterministic quality which is unwarranted. I object to this both on scientific grounds and on ethical and political grounds. Human beings are not moved only by fear but also by hope. All of us need to be to some degree both pessimists and optimists. We both need and deserve models of hope as well as models of doom.

Certainly, there are grounds for Heilbroner's mood of black pessimism. Many artists obviously share his mood. There are tragedies and problems in the world sufficient to daunt the bravest spirit and the most ardent reformers. Nevertheless, whatever faults Heilbroner may ascribe to the human spirit, he himself invokes the image of Atlas and he surely cannot deny that there is a certain magnificent indestructibility about human hopes and aspirations and especially about the aspirations for liberty, social justice and material progress. These hopes are themselves a part of our future and help to determine its features. If today we are not already living in a wholly totalitarian world or a Nazi-occupied poverty-stricken Europe, it is because men and women had the courage to hope and struggle against the odds of what at one time appeared almost inevitable.

Even in the most heart-breaking circumstances humans have found the courage to confirm the truth of Schiller's ode to hope. Condorcet wrote his glowing Utopian vision of the human future in the shadow of the guillotine; Gabriel Peri in the shadow of the Nazi execution squad. Hope was never entirely extinguished even in the ghettos of Warsaw or in the Gulag Archipelago. If a young girl in hiding in a cupboard in Amsterdam in 1944 or Dr Edith Bone imprisoned in Hungary by those whom she had supposed to be her friends, could nevertheless find the courage to hope, then can we as comfortably placed intellectuals in New York or in London in 1974 abdicate responsibility for models of hope and for the effort to sustain the uncertain, painful and desperately difficult progress to a better future?

Notes

1. R.L. Heilbroner, 'The human prospect', *New York Review of Books* 24 January, 1974, pp. 21–34. Further references are to this original version unless explicitly stated otherwise.
2. Ibid.
3. Ibid. p. 23.
4. Ibid., p. 33.
5. Ibid., p. 22.
6. R.L. Heilbroner, *op. cit.*, W.W. Norton edition, p. 33.
7. World Bank (International Bank for Reconstruction and Development), *Report on the Limits to Growth*, 1972, p. 5.
8. R.L. Heilbroner, *op. cit.*, p. 22.
9. *World Bank Atlas*, International Bank for Reconstruction and Development, 1973, and *op. cit.*
10. R.L. Heilbroner, *op. cit.*, p. 24.
11. R.L. Heilbroner, 'Growth and survival', *Foreign Affairs*, Vol. 51, No. 1, October 1972, pp. 139–153.
12. E. Jantsch, *Technological Planning and Social Futures*, Cassell, London, 1972.

8 Prometheus unbound*

A recent article by Nicholas Greenwood Onuf,[1] entitled 'Prometheus prostrate', relates the contemporary debate on long waves (Kondratiev cycles) to the earlier one on *Limits to Growth*[2] in the world economy. Both these debates represented a serious effort to understand and interpret long-term trends in global economic development, and both preoccupied many of those interested in problems of long-term forecasting and 'futurology' more generally.

Onuf points out that 'the long waves literature fails generally to place itself in the decade long debate on growth', and comments: 'This is all the more surprising because some of the principals figured in the [*Limits to Growth*] debate's early days'. This chapter is an attempt to take up this challenge by one of those named by Onuf, and who did indeed take part in both these debates.[3]

In particular, the chapter attempts to relate the two debates in terms of the role of *technology* in long-term growth and cycles. It starts by discussing the explicit and implicit assumptions about technology in the Massachusetts Institute of Technology (MIT) models and some of their shortcomings. It then takes up the question of the influence of technology on long waves of development and argues that changes in 'technological paradigm' are a major feature of each successive growth cycle. The MIT models made no allowance for such changes in paradigm and consequently made unrealistic assumptions about the future consumption of materials and energy. Finally, the chapter discusses the effects of paradigm change on employment and investment, and attempts to take up the central issue of Onuf's paper[4]—the social and political aspects of the microelectronic revolution.

---

*This chapter is based on a lecture given at the Conservatoire National des Arts et Métiers, Paris, 14 May 1984, and was originally published in *Futures*, Vol. 16, No. 5, October 1984.

Technology and *Limits to Growth*

Onuf[5] also himself regards technology as a crucial issue in both debates and defines the differences between the participants in terms of their theories, explicit or implicit, about the framework within which technological advances lead to economic growth. From this standpoint he identifies an important point of resemblance in form between the proponents of *Limits to Growth* and the much earlier Marxist literature emphasising the 'limits to growth' imposed by a particular social and institutional framework.

However, this superficial point of resemblance disguises a much more fundamental difference. The MIT modellers were mainly concerned with what they believed to be the *absolute* limits to growth imposed by the finite environment of this planet, rather than the limitations of any particular social system. The Marxists, on the other hand, were primarily concerned with what they believed to be the relative and transitory limitations of a particular institutional framework—capitalism—and were boundlessly optimistic about the potentialities of technical change and future growth—once these constraints were lifted. Although many economists criticised Malthus for his neglect of technical change in agriculture, as well as for his demographic theories, Marx[6] was probably his most thorough-going and devastating critic. Thus 'room to grow' means something quite different in an environmentalist context from a Marxist context.

The basic environmentalist argument that there are physical limits on this planet to the growth of population and of social artefacts is irrefutable. So too is the argument that *if* growth were to continue indefinitely on a particular materials-intensive, energy-intensive and capital-intensive path, physical limits of resource availability would sooner or later be encountered. The ecological movement of the 1970s and its reflection in the computer-based doom models of that period served a valuable purpose in drawing public attention to these ultimate limits. It was also valuable in highlighting the long-term global consequences of air and water pollution, associated with the reckless disregard of the social costs of a particular form of industrialisation. Although energy did not figure as such in the early MIT models, much the same points can be made with respect to nuclear power.

The critique of the MIT models, however, related not to these fundamental limitations of the 'room to grow', nor to the gravity of the environmental hazards associated with a particular pattern of growth, nor yet to the global nature of the problems. It related to the possibilities open to human societies to make intelligent use of technical change over the next century and so to modify the pattern of growth, that living standards could still be vastly improved throughout the world whilst the gravest environmental hazards were averted.

By and large the MIT modellers were pessimistic about the possibilities of technical change of this type. They were also pessimistic about the responsiveness of social systems to pollution hazards and to demographic problems. This led them to advocate an immediate transition to slower growth and ideally to zero growth for the world economy. They disregarded almost completely the issue of labour-displacing technical change and the employment implications of their analysis.

Moreover, Onuf[7] is only half right when he says: 'In *Limits to Growth* and the debate it inspired, growth is taken for granted. Prometheus bounds. Everyone seems to agree that technological gains cause material growth.' It is true that the MIT modellers *did* allow for some possibilities of technical change. However, in their formal modelling and in their presentation of the results of that modelling, they constrained the scope for technical change in many different ways. Prometheus bounds but only in certain limited directions and with a ball and chain around his ankles. These assumptions about technical change are often *implicit* in the specification of the equations, rather than explicit, which means that they are often disregarded in the debate.

Thus, for example, it is often overlooked that there are quite different assumptions about the long-term productivity of capital in the various subsectors of the MIT model.[8] In the industrial sector a constant capital–output ratio is assumed, whereas in the agricultural and materials sectors a constant long-term decline in the productivity of capital is assumed. The effect of these differing assumptions is that in the heartland of manufacturing industry rapid growth continues unconstrained by capital shortages, whereas in the other primary sectors it fairly soon becomes severely constrained by capital shortage.

The combined effect of these differing assumptions about the rate and direction of technical change is to make the early collapse of the economy absolutely inevitable, *either* through the effects of capital shortage in the primary sectors working their way through the system, *or* through the devastating effects of world-wide pollution.

The transition to slower growth occurred perhaps rather sooner than the MIT modellers had expected, but it occurred not so much because *physical* limits were encountered even earlier than anticipated, as because of social, political and economic changes. Hence Onuf's point about the link between the long wave debate and the 'limits to growth' debate is important. It *was* true that many participants in the 1970s' debate tended to ignore the cyclical aspects of economic growth and in particular to disregard the possibility that economic stagnation or even deep depression might occur for long periods, for reasons which had little or nothing to do with physical limits or environmental hazards. The Marxists did indeed emphasize the possibility (or even inevitability), much more than most other social theorists. Onuf's point about the Marxist contribution to the debate, and Mandel's contribution in particular, is therefore a perfectly valid one—Mandel[9] was entitled to observe that he stood on somewhat lonely ground in 1968.

Technology and long waves

When he turns to discuss the connection between technology and long waves ('regular substantial fluctuations in the growth curve of capitalism'), Onuf[10] appears to accept a Schumpeterian type of explanation. Indeed he criticises Mandel for his mis-specification of the technology which might make a major contribution to a new upswing in the world economy, arguing that the electronics revolution can fulfil this role, whereas nuclear power cannot. When there is some choice among competing technologies, Onuf argues that 'pressure will develop in favour of the cheapest among the candidates', and further comments: 'Nuclear and electronic revolutions initially competed, but the former quickly and conclusively showed itself to be uncompetitive.'

The available evidence appears to support Onuf in his contention, even though nuclear power is already an important source of electricity supply in some countries. A very substantial straw in the wind was the strategic decision of General Electric to shift the emphasis of its long-term strategy away from nuclear power and into the 'factory of the future'. However, it is not just a question of 'cheapness' and it would be a fair criticism that neither Schumpeter nor the Schumpeterians have really done enough to define their terms, so that the distinction between the Snark (a genuine technological revolution) and the Boojum (a false dawn) has not been clear.

The problem has become a little more complicated because one of the pioneers of the long wave revival, Mensch,[11] initially placed great emphasis on the appearance of many radical innovations during deep depressions. I and my colleagues[12] have argued elsewhere that such innovations could not form the basis of a major economic upswing since it takes one or more decades for the diffusion of innovations to have perceptible effects on investment and employment. Onuf also points out that for microelectronic technology to generate a world-wide economic upswing, it must have been around for some time to become such a powerful engine of growth.

However, whereas he appears to regard this as a departure from the norm, we regard this as the norm, since our view of the successive technological revolutions is that they are clusters of economically and technologically related innovations amounting to 'new technological systems'[13] which are already established in the *previous* cycle of growth. It is therefore essential to distinguish between the following.

1. *Incremental innovations.* These occur more or less continually, although at differing rates in different industries, but they are concerned only with improvements in the existing array of products and processes of production. They are reflected in the official measures of economic growth simply by changes in the coefficients in the existing input-

output matrix. Although their combined effect is extremely important in the growth of productivity, no single one has dramatic effects.

2. *Radical innovations.* Although Mensch[14] has suggested that most of these are concentrated in deep depressions, we[15] have maintained that they are more randomly distributed. They are discontinuous events and their *diffusion* (as opposed to their first introduction) may often take a cyclical form and may be associated with long cycles of the economy as a whole. A new material, such as nylon or polyethylene, is an example of such innovations.

3. *Technological revolutions.* These are the 'creative gales of destruction' which are at the heart of Schumpeter's long wave theory. The introduction of electric power or railways are examples of such profound transformations. A change of this kind would of course carry with it many clusters of radical and incremental innovations, with a tendency for *process* innovations to be concentrated rather more in the later stages of diffusion. A vital characteristic of this third type of technical change is that it must have *pervasive* effects throughout the economy, i.e. it must not only lead to the emergence of a new range of products and services in its own right, it must also affect every other branch of the economy by changing the input cost structure and conditions of production and distribution throughout the system. It is the extension of the effects of a new technological system beyond the confines of a few branches to the economy as a whole, which constitutes the basis for the major upswings of the Kondratiev cycles, and which justifies the expression 'change of paradigm' or 'change of technological regime'.

Defining a technological revolution

We may thus define the characteristics of a genuine technological revolution as:

1. *A drastic reduction in costs of many products and services.* In some areas this will be a huge reduction; in others, much less. But it provides the essential condition for Schumpeterian 'swarming', i.e. widespread perceived opportunities for new profitable investment.

2. *A dramatic improvement in the technical characteristics of many products and processes,* in reliability, accuracy, speed and other performance characteristics.

3. *Social and political acceptability.* Although economists and technologists tend to think narrowly of the first two characteristics, this third criterion is extremely important. Whereas the first two advantages are fairly quickly perceived, there may be long delays in *social* acceptance of revolutionary new technologies, especially in areas of application far removed from the initial introduction. Legislative, educational and regulatory changes may be necessary, as well as fundamental changes in

management and labour attitudes and procedures. For this reason too, the expression 'change of paradigm' best conveys the full flavour of this type of technical change. The interplay between techno-economic characteristics and the socio-institutional framework is the main theme of the final part of this article.

4. *Environmental acceptability.* Although this may be regarded as a subset of (3) above, in recent times especially, it has become important in its own right. It is of particular significance in relation to the *Limits to Growth* debate and the distinction between nuclear power and micro-electronics. It finds expression in the development of a regulatory framework of safety legislation and procedural norms which accompany the diffusion of any major technology. Particularly hazardous technologies or those which are extremely expensive to control are severely handicapped, even if they do have some economic and technical advantages.

5. *Pervasive effects throughout the economic system.* Some new technologies, for example the float-glass process, have revolutionary effects and are socially acceptable, but are confined in their range of applications to one or a very few branches of the economy. For a new technology to be capable of affecting the behaviour of the entire system, it must clearly have effects on investment decisions almost everywhere.

Using these five criteria it is quite easy to see why nuclear power does not qualify as a technological revolution, since it fails on almost every one of them. The microelectronic, computer-based information revolution, by contrast, satisfies all five criteria.

A technological revolution therefore represents a major change of paradigm, affecting almost all major managerial decisions in many branches of the economy. Several authors have used the expression 'technological trajectory' or 'technological paradigm', but probably the most thorough and systematic exposition of the idea is in the work of Carlota Perez.[16] She defines a 'techno-economic paradigm' as a new set of guiding principles, which become the managerial and engineering 'common sense' for each major phase of development.

Perez suggests that depressions represent periods of 'mismatch' between the emerging new techno-economic paradigm (already quite well advanced in a few branches of the economy during the previous long wave), and the institutional framework. The widespread profitable generalization of the new technological paradigm throughout the system is possible only after a period of change and adaptation of many social institutions to the potentialities of the new technology. The big boom periods of economic expansion occur when such a good 'match' between the new 'techno-economic paradigm' or 'style' of a long wave and the socio-institutional framework has been made.

This perspective enables us to identify some of the most critical weaknesses in the *Limits to Growth* models. They are based essentially on the extrapolation of the characteristics of one phase of growth and do not allow for the possibility of paradigm changes in the mode of growth. The characteristics of the MIT models are those of the 'fourth Kondratiev' upswing—a techno-economic paradigm based on cheap oil universally available as the foundation for energy-intensive, mass and flow production of standardised homogeneous commodities such as consumer durables, and the associated capital goods, components and services.

This techno-economic paradigm permitted the massive expansion of the world economy during and after the Second World War, following its successful development in the US automobile industry in the previous three decades and during the war itself. Although it enabled very big productivity increases in many branches of manufacturing and in agriculture, and an enormous associated proliferation of public and private service employment, it ultimately began to encounter 'limits' to further growth in the late 1960s and 1970s. This was not *just*, or even *mainly*, a question of the oil price increases, but of a combination of factors including the exhaustion of economies of scale, diminishing returns to further technical advance along existing trajectories (Wolf's Law), market saturation factors, pressures on input prices, declining capital productivity and the erosion of profit margins arising from all these factors, as well as the culmination of the competitive pressures from the Schumpeterian 'swarming' process.

The mistake of the MIT modellers (and of some Marxists) was to confuse the 'limits' of one particular development paradigm with the 'limits to growth' of the system in general. In the case of the MIT modellers, the limits were perceived as absolute limits to further economic growth. In the case of the Marxists, both in the 1930s and the 1980s, there was some tendency to see the depression as the 'final crisis' of the capitalist social system. Thus, probably not many Marxists (and not many other economists either) foresaw that the 1950s and 1960s would witness the most rapid growth and the lowest levels of unemployment in the industrialised countries in the history of capitalism.

Just because of the unexpected strength of the revival, during periods of recovery there appears to be a tendency to 'revisionism' within the Marxist stream of thought, critical of that element in Marx's analysis which points to the fundamental limitations of the capitalist system. Revisionists explain the change of paradigm as a more fundamental social adaptation of the system. From Bernstein in the 1890s to Burnham in the 1940s, they emphasise the concentration of control in the hands of efficiently managed large firms, and the ability of the state to manage the behaviour of the system as a whole. During periods of deep depression, on the other hand, the opposite tendency comes to the fore with an emphasis on the 'collapse' of the system and a permanent state of 'general crisis'.

Similarly today, with the downswing of the fourth Kondratiev long wave, there has been a pronounced increase in pessimism about the prospects for a future return to high rates of growth, and a strong tendency to view the post-war boom in retrospect as an exceptional spurt of growth, unlikely ever to be repeated. This tendency is by no means confined to Marxists. In particular there is widespread pessimism about the future prospects for employment and much discussion about the 'collapse of work'. A great deal therefore depends on the characteristics of a new technological paradigm which might conceivably lift the system into a renewed phase of prosperous growth, and the institutional changes which might be needed to make this possible. This chapter does not assume that such a development is inevitable, only that it is a possibility. Despite the pessimism, the social pressures for a renewal of growth are very strong throughout the world and there are indeed some revolutionary advances in technology, which should in principle make recovery possible.

New technological paradigms and capital investment

Onuf[17] remarks that 'Economists and technologists operating within the dominant Keynesian tradition are disposed to see the curve of *technological* growth as relatively smooth and the *rate* of such growth rather *constant*'. Although this may be true of the 'dominant Keynesian tradition', this was not always true of Keynes himself.

In his *Treatise on Money* in 1930, Keynes[18] actually *did* acknowledge the role of Schumpeterian revolutions in technology:

In the case of fixed capital, it is easy to understand why fluctuations should occur in the rate of investment. Entrepreneurs are induced to embark on the production of fixed capital or deterred from doing so by their expectations of the profits to be made. Apart from the many minor reasons why these should fluctuate in a changing world, Professor Schumpeter's explanation of the major movements may be unreservedly accepted.

This passage is remarkable for its unequivocal recognition of the role of new technology in generating new surges of investment and growth in capitalist societies. The tragedy of the Keynesian tradition was that it regressed from this standpoint to a purely abstract approach to the role of new technologies, and a one-sided emphasis on the role of demand in the short-term business cycle. For the Keynesians it became a matter of relative indifference *which* were the new technologies and fast-growing sectors of the economy and the associated problems of structural change. They also ignored the problem of long-term swings in the *direction* of technical change, and of cyclical changes in the capital–output ratio. By a kind of imperceptible process the idea of a constant capital–output ratio shifted from the status of a convenient modelling assumption to the status of a generalization about growth.

Keynes *did*, however, concern himself with the long-term tendency to a decline in the marginal efficiency of capital (productivity of capital). His pessimism about this long-term tendency led him, like Marx and other classical economists, to envisage an ultimate slowdown in growth as a whole, through a loss of incentive to new investment. Although, as we have seen, he certainly did have glimpses of the regenerative impetus provided by new waves of technical innovation, he apparently did not see such waves as counteracting more than temporarily the long-term tendency to decline in capital productivity.

From an entirely different starting-point and by a different chain of argument, Marx also came to the conclusion that the capitalist system suffered from a tendency to stagnation. In the Marxist framework, even if the new technologies did indeed provide a temporary escape route from the otherwise inexorable competitive pressures on the rate of profit, they did so only by exacerbating the fundamental long-term problem of the rising 'organic composition of capital'.

However, within the Marxist tradition, a number of economists, including Kondratiev himself, Kalecki, the Cambridge economist Maurice Dobb, and Mandel, did recognize clearly the long-term cyclical aspects of this growth. Maurice Dobb[19] in particular pointed out that the tendency to a falling rate of profit, which Marx and many other economists had identified, could be offset in several distinct ways for prolonged periods.

First, it could be offset in the way which most orthodox Marxist literature has emphasised—by a reduction in the level of real wages and by increasing work intensity. If this process were not offset by other stronger tendencies, then indeed there would have been the 'absolute immiseration' of the proletariat of which Marx spoke. That this tendency was not a purely imaginary one can be checked by many accounts of the conditions of the English working class in the first part of the nineteenth century.[20] Even though debate on this topic continues among economic historians, it is clear that pressure for a reduction of living standards was a serious phenomenon in many areas. The career of Robert Owen may be viewed as a sustained attempt to demonstrate, both in theory and in practice, that there was a real alternative to such downward pressures, in the form of better work organisation, social reforms and superior technology. However, he failed to make much impression on his fellow employers at the time, although he met with a better response from the Chartists and trade unionists.

However, the Owenite ideas of an alternative to the crude pressures on wages and work intensity were vindicated over the next century and a half. One of the reasons for the success of this alternative vision was clearly the existence of a real lower limit to the 'immiseration' tendency with its loss of working efficiency through physical exhaustion and loss of effective work incentives. The threat of serious social conflict, such as occurred in Britain in the 1830s, was clearly also an incentive to search for more constructive social alternatives to 'immiseration'.

The basis for a sustained (although cyclical) movement away from these lower limits of human misery and degradation was provided, outside the Third World countries, by successive technological revolutions. Each of these entailed both a *widening* and a *deepening* of the capital stock in the system as a whole. It seems that each technological revolution ultimately led to a rise in capital intensity and to a fall in capital productivity as the limits of each paradigm were approached. Nevertheless, in the phase of recovery and high growth after the initial teething problems were overcome and infrastructural investment was in place, each major new technology greatly augmented the productivity of both capital and labour. Rosenberg[21] has pointed out that Marx was one of the economists who most clearly recognized these changes in capital productivity over time. Technical innovation cheapened in real terms the cost of the commodities needed to sustain the physical work capacity of the labour force, and at the same time broadened the range of goods and services, customarily regarded as a necessary part of the standard of living, as well as reducing working hours.

The role of successive new techno-economic paradigms in offsetting the otherwise persistent pressures towards a declining marginal efficiency of capital was thus of the greatest historic importance. One of the most interesting results of Soete's[22] research in this context has been his finding that whereas capital productivity has been falling persistently in almost all sectors of the UK manufacturing industry since the 1960s, it has apparently been rising in the electronic computer industry and electronic components industry. It will take time before such benefits occur in other sectors, for the initial effect in the diffusion of new types of capital goods is often to make capital costs even higher. Only when the 'islands' of automation are linked together do the benefits of rising capital productivity accrue.

It is not without interest that Japan alone, among the leading industrial countries, showed small, positive gains in capital productivity in manufacturing through the 1960s and 1970s.[23] The rise in capital productivity in Japan appears to be only partly due to the more rapid diffusion of more advanced types of electronic capital goods and new information technologies, such as computer numeric control (CNC), robotics, computer-aided design (CAD) and so forth. At least in some industries it is also due to a parallel and even antecedent change in management attitudes and practices in relation to work organisation—the 'just-in-time' system of assembly and component-supply networks and its concomitant reduction of stocks and work-in-progress, and the far greater responsibility for quality, repairs and maintenance devolved to much lower levels of the work-force than has been customary in the United States and Western Europe.[24]

Further infrastructural investment and a wider availability of the requisite skills may be necessary before any widespread and sustained rise in capital productivity can be realised in Western Europe. However, in the absence of such an improvement in the productivity of capital, it would be much more difficult to achieve high levels of employment, since any sustained expansion would run into problems of capital shortage. Although parts of the Japanese management style are transferable, they are not necessarily the most desirable way to exploit the new technologies. Although greater responsibility and participation at shop-floor level is certainly desirable for many reasons, there is a range of possibilities, rather than one single model, for achieving this objective. Whether it can be achieved at all will depend, as Onuf rightly emphasises, on wider social and political developments over the next decade, as well as on management and union attitudes and policies.

New technological paradigms and labour

In the upswing phase of each long wave much new employment is associated with the expansion of the capital goods sector and the associated producer services. These services are likely to be particularly important in connection with the present technological revolution and are already one of the few growth areas for employment, even in general conditions of depression. Once an upswing is under way, a wave of new investment induces employment growth in many other areas, to replace the old obsolescent capital stock and produce a new range of goods and services.

Historically, this has led in the past to periods of very strong demand for labour with new jobs far outstripping the loss of employment through labour-saving technical change. It has been estimated that unemployment fell as low as 1 per cent in Britain before the crash of 1873.[25] The demand for labour in the industrialising countries—including the United States and Germany, which took over world technological leadership from Britain towards the end of the nineteenth century—was even stronger. Millions of immigrant workers were drawn into the labour force in both countries, both in the boom before 1914 and the upswing of the 1950s and 1960s.

In such periods of high boom, even though the growth of labour productivity may be high, output growth tends to be even higher. Contrary to what is commonly assumed, the higher levels of unemployment are usually associated with quite low growth of labour productivity. However, as limits to further growth within an established paradigm are increasingly encountered, capital productivity tends to fall and it becomes more difficult to generate new employment.

If these tendencies could be offset by the timely growth of other new branches of the economy and/or by capital-saving technical advances on a sufficient scale, then the downswing phase of the long wave might be mitigated or averted (as to some extent in Japan). Despite this, it has been argued that inertia in the institutional and social framework, reinforced by the pressure of interest groups, conspires to frustrate such a favourable course of development.

The 'good match' between technology and social institutions, which had been such a favourable feature of the earlier recovery and boom, now becomes a hindrance to further change and development (or in Marx's terminology becomes a 'fetter' on the forces of production).

In these circumstances, the rate of profit begins to decline in all but a few branches of the economy. The balance of the pattern of investment now tends to shift increasingly from the simple expansion of capacity to the rationalisation of established plants. This shift carries with it a change in the balance-of-employment effects associated with this new investment. Because of the pressure on costs, labour-saving investment becomes of paramount importance and job displacement tends to outstrip new job creation.

Thus the predominant reaction to the appearance of limits to growth within an established paradigm is not one of the rapid adoption of revolutionary new technologies and the introduction of new products. It is rather a tendency to seek protection and continuation for the established industries, products and methods, and to squeeze more out of them. This may entail using some elements of the newer technologies, though within the shell and overall framework of the old paradigm. The Kiel Institute research[26] has shown that protectionist tendencies emerged in each deep depression in response to, but not as the origin of, a slowdown in economic growth. Tendencies to seek sheltered markets in defence production, in colonies (in the 1880s and 1930s) or in areas subject to special influence (tied loans etc.) also became stronger. Xenophobic and nationalistic tendencies are a characteristic response and are clearly evident in relation to immigrants throughout Europe, as they were in comparable periods in the 1880s and 1930s.

The renewed expansion of the system on the basis of the *old* paradigm, however, runs into enormous problems—capital shortage and inflationary problems based on the declining productivity of capital and the slowdown in labour productivity growth; and institutional problems, both national and international, based on the breakdown of the 'good match' between institutions and technology which characterised the high boom period. The breakdown of the 'good match' and the emergence of an increasing degree of mismatch is especially evident in two spheres—in the relationships with the peripheral Third World countries, and in industrial relations *within* the leading industrial countries.

The issue of Third World indebtedness is beyond the scope of this chapter, and it is clearly associated with the failure to sustain the expansionary impetus in the world economy as a whole. Attempts to maintain debt and interest payments at very high rates of interest must inevitably lead, and indeed have already led, to an acute exacerbation of social and international conflicts.

So far as the labour market is concerned, the slowdown in productivity growth, increased cost-pressures and intensified competition, all result in attempts to change the balance of bargaining power and the procedures of industrial relations in favour of capital and to the detriment of labour. This can be seen clearly in the United Kingdom, where the pressure on profit margins has been most intense and where the new industrial relations legislation of 1980 and 1982 was explicitly designed to weaken the power of the trade unions in industrial disputes.

The danger of this approach, which is characteristic of the first phase of the long wave downswing, is that it may gather momentum and be pressed to extreme limits, as in the 1930s. As in the analogous case of the Third World debtor countries, 'immiseration' through reductions in real wages and living standards may generate such social tensions that it can be enforced only by repressive political changes.

It is in this context that Onuf's comments on the use of information technologies as 'control' technologies are highly relevant. We hardly need to be reminded in 1984 that the manipulation of public opinion through centralised control of the media, and the detailed control and regulation of the behaviour of the labour force through 'Big Brother' systems of computerised supervision, are both real possibilities. Although Onuf speaks of 'friendly fascism', it need not necessarily be 'friendly'.

Even without the benefits of computerised information and control systems, German fascism was successful in the 1930s, both in the suppression of the trade unions and in systems of 'thought control'. It was also successful in bringing about economic recovery. After Japan, which had already embarked on the invasion of Manchuria in 1931 and continued on the path of military expansion, Germany was the first major industrial country to recover from the 1930s' depression and to restore full employment. Schacht was the first effective Keynesian, albeit for rearmament and war. By contrast, Roosevelt's well-intentioned programme of New Deal reforms in the 1930s failed to resolve the problem of mass unemployment before the outbreak of the Second World War.

The notion that the deep crisis of the 1930s heralded the end of the capitalist system was quite widespread at the time, and the alternatives were sometimes posed as either authoritarian military-type systems or socialism. The search for social and political solutions to the crisis actually included many other possibilities, although in the early stages the experience of Germany and the Soviet Union seemed to dominate the stage.

Socialism or barbarism

In circumstances which are in some ways comparable today, Mandel and other Marxist economists have argued that the alternatives are *either* socialism or barbarism and war. However, as in the 1930s, this is to narrow too much the social and political alternatives and the complexity of the search. Moreover, the socialist countries of Eastern Europe are themselves experiencing problems of structural adjustment and adaptation to the potential of the new technological paradigm. Both in the capitalist countries and in the countries of Eastern Europe, it is essential to take into account the specific peculiarities of the new paradigm, in order to understand the peculiar problems of finding viable economic and social solutions.

The 'multiplier' with the new paradigm, which could generate very positive benefits in employment growth, depends on access to new information at all levels of society. As Schmookler[27] has pointed out, the effectiveness of any innovation depends on the number of people who use it and their capacity to improve on it. The full capital-saving and employment-generating potential of the new technologies can best be realised through a high level of participation in the design and implementation of new systems, whether they are flexible manufacturing systems (FMS) in industry, new office systems or new social services.

Consequently, the need for decentralisation and devolution of responsibility and control are likely to become paramount issues, whether in predominantly capitalist or predominantly socialist systems. The search for viable combinations of central co-ordination of the level of investment and employment with maximum local interest and participation in the design and development of new products and systems, is a fundamental challenge to social innovation. The problems of international co-ordination of world-wide economic expansion are even more daunting, since they also require arrangements for more rapid and effective international transfer of technology.

Nevertheless, the new technologies do offer exceptionally favourable possibilities for hitherto undreamt-of access to information at all levels of society, and enormous scope for active and creative participation at work. The 'control' systems which dominate the future need not be those of Big Brother. They could be those which go some way towards realising the humanistic and Promethean ideals of both liberals and socialists, for a combination of civil liberty and industrial democracy.

Notes

1. N.G. Onuf, 'Prometheus prostrate', *Futures*, Vol. 16, No. 1, February 1984, pp. 47–59.
2. D. Meadows *et al.*, *Limits to Growth*, Universe Books, New York, 1972.
3. H.S.D. Cole, C. Freeman, M. Jahoda and K.L.R. Pavitt, *Thinking about the Future*, Chatto and Windus, London, 1973 (first published as two special issues of *Futures*, Vol. 5, Nos 1 and 2, February and April 1973); C. Freeman (ed.),

'Technical innovation and long waves in world economic development', Special issue of *Futures*, Vol. 13, Nos 4 and 5, August and October 1981.

4. Onuf, *op. cit.*, reference 1, pp. 53–7.
5. *Ibid.*, pp. 59–50.
6. R.L. Meek (ed.), *Marx and Engels on Malthus*, Lawrence, London, 1954.
7. Onuf, *op. cit.* reference 1, p. 49.
8. See chapter 6 in Cole *et al.*, *op. cit.*, reference 3.
9. E. Mandel, 'Explaining long waves of capitalist development', *Futures*, Vol. 13, No. 4, August 1981, pp. 332–8.
10. Onuf, *op. cit.*, reference 1, p. 52.
11. G. Mensch, *Stalemate in Technology: Innovations Overcome the Depression*, Ballinger, New York, 1979.
12. C. Freeman, J.A. Clark and L.L.G. Soete, *Unemployment and Technical Innovations: A Study of Long Waves and Economic Development*, Frances Pinter, London, 1982, Chapter 3.
13. *Ibid.*, Chapter 4.
14. Mensch, *op. cit.*, reference 10.
15. J.A. Clarke, C. Freeman and L.L.G. Soete, 'Long waves, inventions and innovations', *Futures*, Vol. 13, No. 4, August 1981, pp. 308–22.
16. C. Perez, 'Structural change and the assimilation of new technologies in the economic and social system', *Futures*, Vol. 15, No. 4, October 1983, pp. 357–75; C. Perez, 'Micro-electronics, long waves and world structural change: new perspectives for developing countries', *World Development*, 1984 (forthcoming); G. Dosi, 'Technological paradigms and technological trajectories: the determinants and directions of technical change and the transformation of the economy', in C. Freeman (ed.), *Long Waves in the World Economy*, (2nd edition, Frances Pinter, London, 1984).
17. Onuf, *op. cit.*, reference 1, p. 51.
18. J.M. Keynes, *Treatise on Money*, Volume 2, Macmillan, London, 1930, p. 86.
19. M. Dobb, *Studies in the Development of Capitalism*, Routledge and Kegan Paul, London, 1946; 2nd edition, 1963.
20. See for example G.N. von Tunzelmann, 'The standard of living, investment and economic growth in England and Wales, 1760–1850', in L. Jörberg and N. Rosenberg (eds), *Technical Change, Employment and Investment*, Lund University Press, Lund, 1982.
21. N. Rosenberg, *Inside the Black Box: Technology and Economics*, Cambridge University Press, Cambridge, 1983, Chapter 2.
22. L.L.G. Soete and G. Dosi, *Technology and Employment in the Electronics Industry*, Frances Pinter, London, 1983.
23. L. Soete and C. Freeman, 'New technologies, investment and employment growth' (to be published by the OECD in the conference proceedings of Inter-Governmental Conference on Employment Growth in the Context of Structural Change, Paris, OECD, forthcoming).
24. R.J. Schonberger, *Japanese Manufacturing Technique: Nine Hidden Lessons in Simplicity*, Free Press, New York, 1982.
25. Dobb, *op. cit.*, reference 19, p. 302.
26. H.H. Glismann, H. Rodemer and F. Wolter, *Lange Wellen Wirtschaftlichen Wachstums*, Kiel Discussion Paper No. 74, 1980.
27. J. Schmookler, *Invention and Economic Growth*, Harvard University Press, 1966.

9 The human use of human beings and technical change*

1 Introduction

Although we have been debating the influence of computerisation on skills, employment, participation and working conditions intensively during the 1980s, this is not in fact a new debate. Norbert Wiener's book (1949) on the *Human Use of Human Beings* was written more than forty years ago in response to the perceived threat of mass unemployment through the widespread diffusion of computers. Wiener took this threat very seriously and at various times in the 1950s, 1960s and 1970s the issue again came to the fore. He also took very seriously the problem of deskilling of work, which has been repeatedly debated over the past forty years in relation to the diffusion of information technology as well as other types of technical change.

This chapter will attempt to summarise what can be learnt from these past debates and from our own more recent research in MERIT (Maastricht Economic Research Institute on Innovation and Technology) and in SPRU (Science Policy Research Unit). It will concentrate on two main issues: (1) skills; and (2) aggregate levels of employment. These issues are closely interrelated. If workers or managers fear the loss of employment, status or skill as a result of technical change, it makes positive participation far more difficult. If on the other hand they foresee increased opportunities for greater responsibility, training to enhance skills and good long-term employment prospects, a positive attitude to participation in technical change is far more likely.

The chapter will deal mainly with the diffusion of information and communication technology (ICT). Although this is not of course the only form of technical change, it is by far the most pervasive in the 1980s and 1990s. Norbert Wiener was certainly not wrong to foresee that the

*This chapter was originally presented as a paper for the European Foundation for the Improvement of Living and Working Conditions at a conference in The Hague on 9 October 1990.

computer would be ubiquitous in factories and offices. He only got the time-scale wrong.

Although the early pioneers of computerisation, such as Wiener, foresaw the general trend towards the automated factory and office, they made huge forecasting errors about the patterns of diffusion. The former head of IBM, T.J. Watson, Senior, greatly underestimated the potential of electronic computers for business applications; however, errors of overestimation were more characteristic of the technological enthusiasts of the 1940s and 1950s. Many estimates predicted big increases in labour productivity and widespread technological unemployment arising from computerised automation by the 1950s and 1960s. These fears were so widespread that international organisations, such as the Organisation for Economic Co-operation and Development (OECD) and the International Labour Office (ILO), commissioned special studies and convened international conferences on the employment effects of automation, and in the United States a special national commission produced a massive five-volume report on the topic.

In fact, the process of technical change in the early post-war period was mainly of an incremental type concerned with the improvement of mass production systems and affected especially the speed and accuracy of machining, and the use of new and improved materials. Automation was often little more than advanced mechanisation, rather than the use of telecommunication and computers. Productivity increases were high when economies of scale based on long production runs for standardised products could be attained. This was much more feasible with vehicles, consumer durables, oil and plastics, than with industries based on non-electronic engineering. Unemployment remained low throughout the 1960s.

It was only with the development of microelectronics (LSI and VLSI), and above all with the advent of the microprocessor in the 1970s, that the applications of the computer in every factory and office which had been foreseen by the visionaries in the 1940s, became an everyday reality. The new developments in telecommunications and computer technology meant that vast quantities of data could not only be recorded, processed and stored in a fraction of a second but they could also be transmitted world-wide extremely cheaply.

Almost everyone now agrees that the convergence of information and communication technology has led to a technological transformation, variously described as the 'information revolution', the 'microelectronic revolution' or the 'computer revolution'. However, this can mean very different things to different people (Table 9.1).

The first approach, pioneered by sociologists such as Daniel Bell and economists such as Fritz Machlup, puts the emphasis on information activities wheresoever they are performed. Machlup's (1962) pioneering book was entitled *The Production and Distribution of Knowledge*, and Bell (1973)

Table 9.1 Various ways of looking at ICT

Approach to Information technology	'Information society'	'IT' sector	Automation	ICT paradigm
Main focus of approach	Knowledge occupations	Microelectronics Computers Telecommunications	Process innovations	Pervasive technology
Representative work or analysis	Machlup Bell Porat	Macintosh IT industry Classification systems and lobbies	Wiener Jenkins & Sherman Craft unions	Diebold Imai Perez Petit
Major economic consequences	Informatisation Post-industrial society	Rise of electronics industry	Unemployment and de-skilling as main problems	New industries, new services *and* transformation of old
Representative strategies and policy proposals	Education	Support for sector: ISDN etc.	Shorter hours	Diffusion stratgies
Approach to software	Software as just another occupation	Emphasis on software *industry* and hardware suppliers	Software neglected	Emphasis on software *users*
Implications for technology policy	No special implications for technology policy	Support for electronic industry R&D	Slowdown Technical change	Generic technology programmes linked to diffusion networks

introduced the notion of the 'post-industrial society'. Sociologists and economists taking this route tend to stress the gradual growth of information-related occupations in every industry and service as a long-term trend characteristic of the twentieth century, and leading to what is often described as the 'information society'. This approach is not necessarily concerned with electronic or computer technology, although these have received increasing emphasis in recent times.

The second approach regards the IT 'industries' as major new branches of the economy capable of imparting an upward impetus to employment in their own right. Thus, for example, it is pointed out that as a result of its extraordinary growth in the 1960s and 1970s, the computer industry in the United States now employs more people than the automobile industry, once regarded as a typical 'engine of growth' of employment and economic activity more generally. The 'IT sector' in this approach comprises both manufacturing and service industries, whose growth may be analysed in the same way as that of vehicles, electrical machinery or garages and motor repair services, once the necessary reclassification of industrial output and employment statistics has been satisfactorily performed.

The third approach regards the debate about new technology as essentially a continuation of the 'automation' debate of the 1950s, and uses expressions such as 'factory automation' or 'office automation' as though they were virtually synonymous with information technology. Those who take this view consider all the important questions to have been resolved long ago by economists such as Einzig or others who contributed to the Report of the National Commission on Technology, Automation and Economic Progress. The emphasis in this approach is almost entirely on process innovation.

The fourth approach, which is my own, defines 'information technology' both as a new range of products and services and as a technology, which is capable of revolutionising the processes of production and delivery of all other industries and services. The scope for such a new technology itself is new, having emerged in the last couple of decades as a result of the convergence of a number of interrelated radical advances in the fields of microelectronics, fibre optics, software engineering, communications and computer technology. An approach to information activities which ignores the specific features of the new technologies is in danger of overlooking many of the economic and social consequences of these technologies including their employment and skill effects. This approach puts the emphasis on the new technology and not just on the information.

In my view, only this fourth approach can yield satisfactory results from the standpoint of the overall economic and employment effects of IT, since the third approach (automation) has an implicit bias towards job displacement, and the second (IT industries) towards job creation, and each is needed to complement the other. The first approach is more a theory of occupational trends than of employment. However, the new information technologies affect industrial structure, as well as occupational structure. Moreover, they have other specific features which cannot be ignored in considering the problems of structural change and skill change which have arisen in all the OECD member countries.

The pervasiveness of ICT is now more or less universally accepted and it can be measured with increasing accuracy. Measures of R&D show that in most leading industrial countries electronic and telecommunications R&D account for between 20 per cent and 30 per cent of total manufacturing and services R&D. However, these measures exclude most software applications development. Canada is the first country to attempt systematic measurement of this software R&D performed outside R&D laboratories. It amounted to 23 per cent of total industrial R&D in Canada in 1988. This means that in the leading industrial countries electronics plus software development accounts for about half of all new R&D in industry. Moreover, an increasing proportion of this is carried out in service industries.

Figures of investment tell a similar story. Work at MERIT for the HERMIT project shows that computer-related investment accounts for between 15 and 35 per cent of total investments in industry in the leading OECD countries, with Japan as the most advanced country.

ICT not only affects every industry and service but also every function within each industry i.e. R&D, design, production, marketing, transport and general administration. It is systemation rather than automation, integrating the various previously separate departments and functions.

For all these reasons, ICT is associated with major changes in company organisation and work structure (Table 9.2). It amounts to a change of 'techno-economic paradigm' to use the expression of Carlota Perez (1983;

Table 9.2 Change of techno-economic paradigm

'Fordist' Old	ICT New
Energy-intensive	Information-intensive
Standardised	Customised
Rather stable product mix	Rapid changes in product mix
Dedicated plant and equipment	Flexible production systems
Automation	Systemation
Single firm	Networks
Hierarchical structures	Flat horizontal structures
Departmental	Integrated
Product with service	Service with products
Centralisation	Distributed intelligence
Specialised skills	Multi-skilling
Government ownership and control and planning	Government information co-ordination and regulation; 'vision'

1985). We shall now examine the effects of this paradigm change on skills (Section 2) and aggregate employment (Section 3).

2. Skills

Perhaps rather surprisingly there is actually now a fairly high degree of consensus emerging from the numerous empirical studies of the skill effects of ICT. As Cressey and Williams (1990) show in their Report for the European Foundation it would be wrong to be deterministic about this question. There is scope for a variety of forms of implementation of technical change and the skill mix can be varied. Empirical studies do show on the whole that more skill-intensive solutions are often found in Scandinavia and Germany than in the United Kingdom or the United States. In particular craft skills have not been eroded to the same degree. These differences arise in part from the supply situation with both public and private training systems providing both a higher quality and a greater quantity of middle-range skills. They are also partly the result of different systems of industrial relations and management philosophies.

However, although there are certainly variations between countries, industries and companies, there are certain common trends which have been increasingly evident in the 1970s and 1980s as ICT has diffused more and more widely. On the whole these common trends vindicate the views of John Diebold (1952) in his vision of the 'factory of the future' rather than those of Norbert Wiener.

Wiener (1949) had argued:

It is a degradation to a human being to chain him to an oar and use him as a source of power: but it is an almost equal degradation to assign him purely repetitive tasks in a factory which demand less than a millionth of his brain power. But it is simpler to organise a factory or a galley which uses individual human beings for a trivial fraction of their worth than it is to provide a world in which they can grow to their full stature. (p. 163)

Diebold commented that he could not agree more fully:

It is easier to scoff at the possibility of workers doing tasks that demand a high level of ability than it is to train and adjust them for such work. The humility that management needs in order to understand why employees become hostile or 'ornery' is not taught in any school. Yet it is a quality that although always essential . . . will be of even greater importance in the future. (p. 163)

Diebold clearly recognised the full extent of the profound social transformation entailed in the shift from one type of techno-economic paradigm to another. He was aware of the huge scale of new investment required, the extent of the redesign of machines, factories and products, the dramatic changes in the skill profile of the work-force and above all, the change in attitudes needed throughout business organisations if participation was to become a reality.

Nevertheless, he believed that this prolonged redesigning of products and processes and the associated research activities would make enormous demands for new and enhanced skills. Moreover, the operation of computerised systems would in his view increase the need for greater responsibility and initiative at all levels and for greater communication between all functions:

One of the impediments to re-thinking of products and processes has been that the traditional division of responsibilities has the effect of localising the areas in which re-thinking is done. Almost by definition however, re-thinking must be done on an extremely broad basis—viewing the objectives of the entire organisation as a whole. It cannot be confined to the product design engineering department. It must be an attitude, a state of mind, permeating the entire organisation (Diebold, 1952, p.53)

The findings of empirical research in this field can be divided into three categories: (1) national statistics of occupational change; (2) industrial statistics of skill composition; and (3) case studies and surveys of management and workforce opinions. All three categories support the Diebold analysis and were summed up well in the Sundqvist Report (OECD, 1988). Table 9.3 gives the results for the first category for an 8–10-year period in the main industrial countries. It shows clearly that without exception there has been a strong growth in technical, scientific and related professional occupations. It also shows in many countries a growth of managerial and administrative occupations although Japan is an interesting exception. One possible explanation here is that the rationalisation of management structure has gone further in Japan than almost anywhere else with horizontal structures replacing vertical hierarchies. At the other end of the spectrum 'production workers', labourers and agricultural workers have declined in many countries or grown only very slowly. In the middle there is a tendency for sales and service employment to grow fairly fast though not as quickly as technical and scientific employment.

Disaggregated industrial employment and training statistics provide a clearer indication of what underlies these very broad categories. Perhaps the strongest indication comes from a comparison of the occupational composition of employment in the electronics industry with that of other older sectors of the engineering industries (Figure 9.1). The pattern of the electronics industry shows the shape of things to come, both because it is the fastest growing sector and because much of its technology is slowly diffusing through the rest of industry. The main feature here is the very high proportion of technical and scientific personnel in electronics and the

Table 9.3 Annual growth of employment by major occupational groups (per cent)

Major occupational groupings	Australia 1978–85	Canada 1976–86	Finland 1977–86	Germany 1976–84	Japan 1976–86	Netherlands 1977–85	Norway 1975–85	Spain 1976–86	Sweden 1976–84	United States 1976–86
0–1 Professional, technical and related	3.4	2.9	3.7	2.5	3.7	3.7	4.6	2.7	2.9	2.5
2 Administrative and managerial workers	3.0	8.1	5.7	1.4	-0.1	4.6	6.3	-0.5	2.7	3.0
3 Clerical and related workers	2.2	1.5	1.6	0.1	2.2	1.0	1.4	0.0	0.7	1.2
4 Sales workers	1.8	0.9	2.5	1.2	1.6	0.9	1.4	-0.1	0.1	9.0
5 Service workers	1.7	3.1	1.6	1.0	1.2	2.6	1.7	1.3	1.7	1.9
6 Agricultural, animal husbandry and forestry workers, fishermen and hunters	1.4	0.2	-1.5	-1.6	-2.6	-0.5	-1.5	-4.1	-1.9	1.9
7–9 Production and related workers, transport equipment operators and labourers	-0.1	0.5	0.1	-0.4	0.8	-1.8	-0.7	-2.2	-1.6	0.4
Total employment	1.5	2.1	1.5	0.4	1.1	0.9	1.3	-1.2	0.5	2.1

Source: ILO, *Year Book of Labour Statistics*, 1986 and 1987.

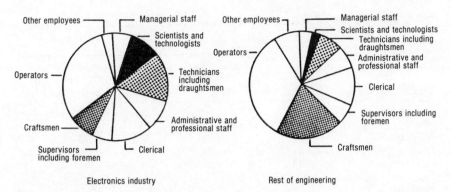

Electronics industry   Rest of engineering

Figure 9.1   Employment by occupational category in the electronics industry
and in the rest of engineering
Source: EITB

smaller proportion of craftsmen. However, this figure is based on British
data and for reasons which have already been described, German or
Scandinavian data would show a higher proportion of craftsmen.

Finally, there is survey evidence. The Sundqvist Report points out:

> Data from the United Kingdom are particularly valuable. Given the widespread
> inclination of management towards Taylorist methods, that country might be
> expected to have one of the least skill-using environments for IT application. Yet
> only a small minority of British installations have been accompanied by reductions
> in skill and autonomy. In the great majority of cases, job requirements either
> remained unchanged or (particularly in terms of skills in nonmanual jobs)
> increased. Only in work pace and freedom from supervision did the overall picture
> of enriched jobs fail to find support, and even there the typical situation was 'no
> significant change' (Table 4). These findings reflect the perceptions of managers.
> Union officials hold similar views, however; if anything they suggest more
> widespread increases in skill and responsibility requirements than do managers.
> (OECD, 1988, p. 73)

Other survey evidence from particular industries points to the growing
importance of multi-skilling, particularly in inter-country comparisons
involving Japan. A good example are the studies of the Japanese
automobile industry which identify the capacity of line workers to deal
with repair and maintenance problems and one of the main competitive
advantages of Japanese firms (Altshuler *et al.*, 1985; Womack *et al.*, 1990).
These studies also frequently point to the growing importance of
communication skills and their role in Japanese training.

This general picture of an increased demand for scientific, technical and
communication skills is strongly borne out throughout the OECD area by
the evidence of labour market shortages. Whereas unemployment is
heavily concentrated among unskilled and less educated segments of the
work-force, persistent shortages of technical and scientific skills are

Table 9.4   Managers' accounts of the impact of advanced technical change upon jobs

Direction of change	PERCENTAGES					
	Job interest	Skill	Range of activity	Responsibility	Pace of work	Super-vision
Manual jobs						
More	46	42	38	33	22	16
No change	40	42	46	54	48	64
Less	11	15	15	12	28	19
Not stated	3	1	1	1	2	1
Non-manual jobs						
More	60	55	59	39	34	10
No change	27	39	29	55	45	70
Less	5	2	8	2	16	17
Not stated	8	4	4	4	5	3
Change score	+120	+110	+110	+80	+40	+10

Source: OECD (1988)

present even in periods of high aggregate unemployment. In particular, software skills have been an acute problem for a long time in almost all OECD countries throughout the 1980s and future projections show supply lagging behind demand for a long time to come.

However, this picture of increased demand for higher level skills and qualifications and reduced demand for unskilled workers needs to be qualified in two important respects: First, there is considerable uncertainty about the trend of demand for middle-level craft skills and for middle management skills. Much depends then on the mode of implementation of ICT, although from a purely technical point of view it is possible in some areas to reduce both the craft skill requirements and the numbers of middle managers. Second, changes in occupations and skills take place over a very long time and are notoriously difficult to measure. It is possible that the picture will change over the next few decades as ICT becomes a more familiar and possibly a more standardised set of technologies. Efforts are being made all the time both in hardware and in software to overcome skill shortages by developing new types of standardised tools and equipment. In some areas, such as maintenance of telecommunications equipment, these have proved rather successful. It is therefore still possible that eventually Braverman and Wiener's ideas will appear rather more plausible than they do at present. This will depend largely on the pattern of social and educational change and of industrial relations over the next twenty years or so. It will also depend on the new technologies which succeed ICT in the twenty-first century.

3. Aggregate employment

As with skills, so with unemployment, a remarkably high degree of consensus has emerged from the debates of the 1970s and 1980s (see for example; Katsoulacos, 1986; Julien and Thibodeau, 1991; Cyert and Mowery, 1988; Freeman and Soete, 1987). The naïve view of Wiener (1949) and the automation debate of the 1950s that computerisation would automatically lead to mass unemployment has been discarded. This was based on a view of computerisation as simply a set of labour-saving process innovations (Table 9.1). It is generally recognised that ICT both displaces some older types of employment and generates much new employment, as well as facilitating a further reduction in working hours. The balance between job creation and job destruction will vary depending upon the speed of structural adjustment, the strength of world-wide demand growth and specific national and regional employment policies.

However, within this broad consensus there are still important areas of disagreement which are in turn related to basic theories of economic development and change. Traditional neo-classical theory emphasises above all the compensation mechanism. Loss of jobs from technical change in one firm, industry or town, may be compensated or more than compensated by the creation of new jobs elsewhere in the system. It is also essential to remember that case studies which demonstrate increases in employment in innovating firms (e.g. because of the increased market share which they win as a result of technical innovation) may also give rise to misleading conclusions if the results are generalised. It is often the case that any employment displacement effects occur not in the innovating firms, but in the *non*-innovating firms, which lose out in technological competition and may be located thousands of miles away. This does not mean of course that case studies of individual firms, departments, industries or sectors are worthless. On the contrary, they are absolutely essential in order to identify the nature of technical innovations and the real problems which are created. The difficulties arise when attempts are made to generalise about the behaviour of the entire system from inadequate or unrepresentative cases, which, however accurately described, cannot possibly take into account all the linkages, feed-back effects, compensation mechanisms, and counter-tendencies of the system as a whole.

However, this does not mean that such mechanisms operate instantaneously, automatically, or painlessly. From the classical economists onwards, and in particular from Ricardo's famous comments on the introduction of new machinery, economic theory has explicitly recognised the time-lags of adjustment and in particular the structural problems resulting from the shift towards more capital-intensive techniques of production. The naïve pessimists have their counterpart in the naïve optimists who disregard the complexities of the adjustment.

The emphasis on the effectiveness of the compensation mechanisms, as well as their time-lags, varied with different schools of economic thought. Whereas the classical economists, particularly Ricardo, tended to stress some of the structural rigidities, neo-classical economics with its emphasis on capital–labour substitution mechanisms, tends to postulate a smoother adjustment, provided all prices are flexible.

The Keynesian school can probably best be distinguished from the neo-classical school by its rejection of the notion that equilibrium necessarily implies full employment. To Keynesians, equilibrium in markets can be reached below 'full employment' levels, if aggregate demand is inadequate. More generally it can be said that Keynes did not carry his inquiry into the relationship between technological change and employment. He related unemployment directly to underinvestment— through liquidity preference.

In contrast to Keynes and neo-classical economic thinking, technological progress was for Schumpeter and structuralists at the centre of the dynamics of the economic system. Whereas in the previous two schools of thought, growth was simply accompanied by the emergence of new industries and technologies, for Schumpeter the system was driven by such technical innovations and their diffusion. The contemporary rapid growth of the software industry and all kinds of related information services are good examples of what Schumpeter had in mind.

Whereas some economists place great emphasis on the 'structural' problems of adjusting the capital stock and the skills of the labour force to the introduction of new technologies, others, following the neo-classical tradition, tend to minimise these problems and stress price rigidities as the main problem of adjustment. Present-day economic views on technical change and employment tend to correspond to neo-classical 'general equilibrium' theory. Furthermore, with the exception of the US automation debate in the 1960s, there has been a general disinterest in the subject of technological unemployment on the part of the academic economics community.

Part of this neglect is simply a reflection of the more widespread neglect of the analysis of the technical change factor in macro-economics over the last decades. The concentration has been on general equilibrium as the main approach to the understanding of the operation of economic markets and economic agents. From a general equilibrium point of view the technology/employment issue is reduced to a simple one of distribution. In so far as technological change increases productivity, this will be reflected in an increase in real aggregate income. The only relevant question about employment within such a framework is how this increase in real income will be distributed and spent. In labour market failure the increased real income could indeed become wasted in the form of unemployment for the 'marginal' workers.

A major cause of disequilibrium in the economy such as technological change, resulting in the creation of new products and the rise of entirely new industries does not fit well into such contemporary economic analyses. Furthermore, the measurement and definition of technological change have not yet benefited from general economic approval. There is, consequently, a broad consensus among most contemporary economists to treat the technology factor as a black box, not to be opened except by scientists and engineers or occasionally by economic historians. For the short-term problems with which most economic analysis is concerned, it becomes reasonable to treat this long-term, 'messy' technology variable as something outside the system.

Nevertheless, almost all economists agree that problems of structural adjustment to the rise of new industries and technologies (and the decline of some old ones) are an important part of the agenda for overcoming unemployment problems. Disagreement arises from the difficulty of assessing the relative significance of factor–price mechanisms on the one hand and overcoming institutional and structural rigidities on the other hand. I myself believe that these inflexibilities are exceptionally important for the far-reaching changes which are involved in the adoption of information technology.

Thus, just as in the Braverman debate, the last word has not been said. The world-wide diffusion of ICT is an extremely uneven and often disequilibrating process. The rise of Japan to global technological leadership has been accompanied by severe adjustment problems in the United States and the EEC. The rise of NICs like South Korea and Taiwan has been accompanied by the relative and absolute decline of other areas like Latin America and Africa. Income distribution both within and between countries is becoming increasingly unequal. Severe problems of indebtedness and weaknesses in the banking system are present both in Third World countries and in Japan and the United States. The experience of the 1930s cannot be simply written off in this connection (Freeman and Perez, 1988). These problems are compounded by military and political problems such as the present crisis in the Middle East. To emerge from these problems will require rather better global steering mechanisms than the present G7 and International Monetary Fund (IMF) provide.

4. Conclusions

This chapter has argued that the evidence of the 1980s points to two main conclusions:

1. The diffusion of ICT has led to an increased demand for high-level skills, some intermediate-level skills and new skill combinations.
2. The diffusion of ICT depends on a process of structural and institutional change whose rate and characteristics vary greatly between countries.

Table 9.5 Old and new models of industrial organisation

Fordist model	New model
(1) Rationalisation of labour by mechanisation	Global optimisation of whole production flow
(2) Design and then manufacture and organise work	Attempt to integrate R&D, design, production
(3) Indirect mediated links to consumers	Close ties between producers and users
(4) Low cost by standardisation quality comes second	'Zero defect' objective at each stage
(5) Mass production for stable rising demand and total production for unstable	Flexible fast response to market whether batch or mass
(6) Centralisation of the production management	Decentralisation of production decisions
(7) Vertical integration with circles of subcontractors	Networking and joint ventures to reap gains of specialisation and co-ordination
(8) Use subcontractors to stablise cyclical demand fluctuations	Long-run co-operation with chosen subcontractors
(9) Divide and specialise production tasks for productivity gains	Integrate some production maintenance and management tasks ('recompose')
(10) Minimise skill and training and education requirements	Effective training plus general education to maximise competence
(11) Hierarchical control of higher wages to achieve consent to poor job content	Human resource policies to spur the competence and the commitment of workers
(12) Adversarial industrial relations Collective agreements to codify provisional armistices	Explicit long-term compromises between management and workers: via job tenure and/or sharing dividends
(13) 'Full employment'	'Active society'

Source: Boyer (1990)

These institutional changes are occurring at all levels and successful adjustment in OECD societies will depend very much on the type of factors identified by Cressey and Williams (1990) and are summed up at the micro-level in Table 9.5 based on Boyer's summary. Whether the 'new model' displaces the old, how rapidly it does so and whether it does so with a high level of participation depends on industrial and social policy and the public response to the problems identified by Cressey and Williams.

However, for these policies to succeed at the *micro*-level, *macro*-level policies to achieve high levels of employment and high levels of education are essential. These will differ from traditional Keynesian full employment policies in several important respects (Table 9.5). The most important difference was summed up in the Sundqvist report as the 'active society'.

References

Altshuler, A. *et al.* (1985), *The Future of the Automobile*, MIT Press, Cambridge, Mass.

Bell, Daniel (1973), *The Coming of Post-Industrial Society: a Venture in Social Forecasting*, Basic Books, New York.

Boyer, R. (1990), Synthesis Report to OECD Helsinki Conference, OECD, Paris.

Cressey, P. and Williams, R. (1990), *Participation in Change*, European Foundation for the Improvement of Living and Working Conditions, Dublin.

Cyert, R.M. and Mowery, D.C. (1988), *The Impact of Technological Changes on Employment and Economic Growth*, Ballinger, Cambridge.

Diebold, J. (1952), *Automation: the Advent of the Automatic Factory*, Van Hostrand, New York.

Freeman, C. and Perez, C. (1988), 'Structural crises of adjustment: business cycles and investment behaviour' in (eds G. Dosi et. al.) *Technological Change and Economic Theory*, Pinter Publishers, London.

Freeman, C. and Soete, L.L.G. (eds) (1987), *Technical Change and Full Employment*, Blackwell, Oxford.

International Labour Office (1986, 1987), *Year Book of Labour Statistics*, Geneva.

Julian, P.A. and Thibodeau, J. (1991), *Nouvelles Technologies et Economie*, Presses de l'université de Québec.

Katsoulacos, Y. (1986), *The Employment Effort of Technical Change*, Wheatsheaf, Brighton.

Machlup, F. (1962), *The Production and Distribution of Knowledge*, Princeton University Press.

Organisation of Economic Co-operation and Development (1989), *New Technologies in the 1990s: A Socio-Economic Strategy* (Sundqvist Report), OECD, Paris.

Perez, C. (1983), Structural change and the assimilation of new technologies in the economic and social system, *Futures*, Vol. 15, No. 5, October, pp. 357–75.

Perez, C. (1985), Micro-electronics, long waves and structural change, *World Development*, Vol. 13, No. 3, pp. 441–63.

Wiener, Norbert (1949), *The Human Use of Human Beings: a Cybernetic Approach*, Houghton Mifflin, New York.

Womack, J.P. *et al.* (1990), *The Machine that Changed the World*, MIT Press, Cambridge, Mass.

10 A green techno-economic paradigm for the world economy*

I. Introduction

It is now twenty years since the appearance of the international best-seller *Limits to Growth* (Meadows *et al.*, 1972). Over the past twenty years public awareness has grown about various global pollution hazards. Undoubtedly the work of Jay Forrester and of Denis and Donella Meadows and their colleagues in the Systems Dynamics Faculty of MIT played a very big part in awakening public interest and arousing public concern. Their computer models of the global economy demonstrated to many people for the first time that there were indeed limits to growth of materials production and consumption as well as the traditional Malthusian limits of food supply and population growth.

Their models showed that if the world economy continued to expand over the next fifty years on similar lines to the growth of the US economy over the previous fifty years then there would probably be such severe problems as to engender a collapse of the entire system. This collapse would come about either through the exhaustion of the supply of some critical materials or, if that mode of collapse should be averted, through the pollution effects of the massive increase in materials-intensive industrial production.

The models did not deal specifically with energy and were developed before the greenhouse effect was taken seriously by the world scientific community, governments and world public opinion. In subsequent debate and discussion on world models of economic growth it was also recognised that the MIT method of aggregating all pollution hazards was not a very satisfactory way of representing the hazards or the policy implications.

Nevertheless the MIT models (Forrester, 1971; Meadows *et al.*, 1972) and the subsequent debate (Cole *et al.*, 1973; Freeman and Jahoda, 1978) did help to alert world public opinion to some of the dangers of a highly materials

---

*This chapter is based on a talk given to the Netherlands Directorate-General for the Environment in Leidschendam on 5 February 1992.

and energy-intensive pattern of economic growth if extended to the entire world economy and projected over two or three generations.

In the debate on *Limits to Growth* the 'pessimists' tended to argue on the basis of the MIT models that disaster could be averted only by zero population growth and zero economic growth from the year 2000 onwards, if not sooner.

The 'optimists' (who included the Science Policy Research Unit) argued that growth should and could continue into the twenty-first century on two conditions:

1. If a combination of institutional changes led to a different path of world development (i.e. what came to be called 'sustainable development'). Such changes would require the effective regulation of pollution hazards as well as major modifications to the pattern of inputs.
2. If the world R&D system was reoriented so that these environmental objectives were given a high priority in the work of industrial, university and government laboratories. This reorientation would be needed to assure the rate and direction of technical change necessary to achieve the first objective (sustainable development).

Most of the participants in the debate came to agree that both types of change would be needed and indeed that they interact with each other (e.g. new recycling technologies need good waste-collection systems; new regulations or laws to limit hazards need accurate measurement and detection technologies, etc.). Most of those concerned with world models also came to agree that it was both politically impossible and ethically unacceptable to deny to the peoples of the Third World the possibility of raising their living standards to catch up with those of the OECD countries, even though their specific patterns of production and consumption would undoubtedly differ from those of the United States. A revised version of the MIT models (Meadows *et al.*, 1992) was published in 1992 which amended some of the assumptions relating to technical change and envisaged the possibility of a much more optimistic scenario (Chapters 7 and 8).

However, with the increasing concentration on the greenhouse effect more and more attention has been paid to institutional change and rather less to technical change. In particular economic incentives and penalties have moved to centre stage. Economists, such as Pearce (1988) have argued persuasively that in a market economy it is essential that prices in the market should reflect the true long-term costs of environmental degradation: 'the polluter must pay'. Taxes and subsidies should be used to realign market prices to conform more closely to long-term social costs (Kemp and Soete, 1991). It is of course recognised that some hazards are so severe and so immediate that continuing pollution simply cannot be allowed at all and outright prohibition is the only course. Still other pollutants such as chlorofluorocarbon (CFC) may be tolerated for a short period until industry finds alternative methods, and may then be prohibited.

In practice most countries have begun to use a combination of economic incentives and legal regulations. However, the effectiveness of most of these methods depends on:

1. the degree of public support for the policies. Consequently methods of public persuasion and mobilisation of public opinion also play an important role. Historically, voluntary groups and organisations have made the major contribution to this mobilisation and this was indeed the major achievement of the MIT models and many other similar publications and activities. The success of the environmentalist movement in the 1970s and 1980s has meant that now governmental agencies also often participate in public advocacy and persuasion, albeit not to the extent nor with the same degree of conviction as some 'Greens' might wish.
2. a continuing high rate of technical change. In the debate on the MIT models the critics argued that the introduction of a technical change factor of 1 to 2 per cent per annum in the industrial and agricultural subsystems would be sufficient to avert catastrophe or postpone it for a long period.

During the 1970s and 1980s the countries of the European Community did actually achieve useful reductions in the energy intensity of final output through a combination of institutional and technical change. Even greater reductions were achieved in Japan. These reductions do show that the pattern of inputs and outputs can indeed be changed in a desirable direction over a long enough period.

Numerous examples could be quoted to illustrate the type of change which is taking place. In the early stages (in the 1970s), mainly as a result of the oil price shock, energy savings were largely the result of institutional changes and retrofitting of known technologies, e.g. regulatory limits on petrol consumption, subsidies for insulation of existing houses, etc. In the later stages more fundamental and lasting changes began to be made as a result of the redesign of industrial processes, new design of vehicles, boilers, buildings, etc. Much of this was based on new research, design and development. Here it is possible to give only a few illustrative examples.

In one of the most energy-intensive industries, aluminium, a substantial shift is taking place towards the recycling of aluminium products. According to one of the major producers, Alcan, the new plant in Warrington (Lancashire, England) with a capacity of 90,000 tons p.a. will use less than 10 per cent of the energy needed for regular aluminium products. The proportion of aluminium cans which are recycled in Britain is still far below the Swedish level (85 per cent) or the United States (60 per cent) although it is expected to reach 50 per cent by 1996.

The new hospital which is being built in Ashington, Northumberland (England)—Wansbeck General Hospital—is designed to reduce energy costs by 60 per cent compared with older hospitals. It will incorporate a 40-metre high wind turbine. Heat exchangers will ensure that no heat from generators or air conditioning goes to waste.

These two examples one from manufacturing and one from a major service industry both illustrate the type of energy-saving which can be achieved when there is a determination at the top level, whether in a private or a public sector industry to give energy-saving a high priority in new design. The savings are far greater than can be achieved by retrofitting in old buildings or manufacturing processes.

Nevertheless, such examples can give a misleading impression of the aggregate trends in an industrialised economy. The replacement of old buildings, old plant and machinery with new designs using less energy is a very prolonged process. Moreover, in most cases the energy savings which are achieved are considerably less than in these two examples. Primary aluminium production processes are still extremely energy-intensive, and although energy efficiency has improved, the savings are far less than those achieved in plants based on recycling.

In many areas there is a problem of diminishing returns to energy-saving and material-saving based on existing technologies or minor improvements to existing technologies. It is certainly necessary to keep up the pressures towards incremental improvements in all directions. However, much greater results will be necessary to achieve absolute reductions in materials and energy consumption over the next fifty years, as opposed to the relative reductions in energy and materials inputs per unit of output which have so far been achieved. Taking into account that since Third World countries will almost inevitably increase their consumption of energy and materials as they industrialise and raise their living standards, the need for radical innovations in the energy industries and energy and materials-intensive activities is quite evident, as well as continuing incremental improvements. Rather slow progress has been made with the development of renewable energy technologies, such as solar and wave power, and the resources devoted to these and to other more radical innovations are still relatively small. The second and third sections of this chapter will therefore discuss the broad patterns of technical change in industrialised societies, the relationship between various types of innovation and how these change over time. The fourth section discusses the specific characteristics of information and communication technology and the final section discusses policies which might accelerate a desirable pattern of technical change.

2. A taxonomy of technical innovation

So far we have used such terms as 'incremental' and 'radical' innovations without defining them or their interrelationships. It is now necessary to introduce some definitions and a taxonomy of innovations in order to assess the feasibility of an accelerated orientation of the science–technology system in the desired direction. We may distinguish four main categories of innovation: incremental innovations; radical innovations; new technology systems; and changes of techno-economic paradigm. Each of these categories is now briefly described:

(i) *Incremental innovations*

These occur more or less continually in any industry or service activity, although at a varying rate in different industries and at different times. They may be stimulated by continuing pressures to reduce costs as well as to improve quality, design, performance and adaptability. They may often occur, not so much as the result of any deliberate research and development, as of the outcome of inventions and improvements suggested by engineers and others directly engaged in production ('learning by doing'), or as a result of initiatives and proposals by users ('learning by using'). Many empirical studies have confirmed their great importance in improving efficiency in the use of all factors of production (for example, in Hollander's (1965) study of Du Pont rayon plants). Incremental innovations are particularly important in the follow-through period after a radical breakthrough innovation (see below) and frequently associated with the scaling up of plant and equipment and quality improvements to products and services for a variety of specific applications. Although their combined effect is extremely important in the growth of productivity, including economy in the use of materials and energy, no single incremental innovation has dramatic effects, and they may sometimes pass unnoticed and unrecorded. The combined effects of numerous incremental innovations show up in changes in the input/output coefficients in the input/output tables and other measures of factor intensity.

(ii) *Radical innovations*

These are discontinuous events and in recent times are usually the result of deliberate research and development in enterprises and/or in university and government laboratories. The discontinuity is in the production system. The changes within the science–technology system may be (indeed often are) incremental. However, the transfer of the results to the economic system means a radical departure from previous production practice. No incremental improvements in cotton or woollen textiles would lead to nylon, nor (as Schumpeter pointed out) would improvements in stage coaches lead to railways. As Schumpeter insisted, such innovations are unevenly distributed over sectors and over time. Whenever they may occur, however, they are important as the potential springboard for the growth of new markets, or in the case of radical process innovations, such as the oxygen steelmaking process, of big improvements in the use of inputs and hence in the cost and quality of existing products. Strictly speaking, at a sufficiently disaggregative level, radical innovations would constantly require the addition of new rows and columns in an input/output table whereas incremental innovations change only the coefficients. In practical terms, however, such changes are introduced only in the most important innovations and with long time-lags, when their economic impact is already substantial. It generally took about thirty years for statistics of electronic computers and related industries to enter the regular statistical system and even now the process is far from complete. Although in the early stages teething problems and skill shortages may lead to very low productivity gains, once experience and learning accumulate, productivity increases may be very great with a 'virtuous circle' of learning effects and many incremental innovations and complementary innovations.

(iii) *Changes of 'technology system'*

These are far-reaching changes in technology, affecting several branches of the economy, as well as ultimately giving rise to entirely new sectors. A cluster of radical innovations may be linked together in the rise of entire new industries and services, such as the railways or the semiconductor industry. Keirstead (1948), in his exposition of a Schumpeterian theory of economic development, introduced the concept of 'constellations' of innovations which were technically and economically interrelated. Obvious examples are the clusters of innovations in synthetic materials and petrochemicals introduced in the 1930s, 1940s and 1950s with the associated developments in machinery for injection moulding and extrusion and later with numerous complementary innovations in packaging, construction, electrical equipment, agriculture, textiles, clothing, toys and other applications unforeseen when the materials were first developed. Another example is the cluster of innovations in electrically driven household consumer durables, where the availability of electric power and very cheap electric motors combined with new marketing techniques and financial innovations transformed the patterns of household expenditures in high income countries as well as the organisation of production in many industries.

(iv) *Change in 'techno-economic paradigm' (technological revolutions)*

These are the 'creative gales of destruction' or 'successive industrial revolutions' which are at the heart of Schumpeter's long wave theory. They represent those new technology systems which have such pervasive effects on the economy as a whole that they change the style of production and management throughout the economy. The introduction of electric power or steam power are examples of such profound transformations. A change of this kind carries with it many clusters of radical and incremental innovations, and may eventually embody several new technology systems. This fourth type of technical change not only leads to the emergence of a new range of products, services, systems and industries in its own right, it also affects directly or indirectly almost every other branch of the economy. Perez (1983) was the first to develop the concept of 'techno-economic' rather than 'technological paradigm' (Dosi, 1982), because the changes involved go beyond specific product or process technologies and affect the input cost structure and conditions of production and distribution throughout the system. The electronic computer and microelectronics are at the heart of such a paradigm change today. In the Perez model a new techno-economic paradigm develops initially within the old technological regime and becomes dominant only after a crisis of structural adjustment entailing deep social and institutional changes as well as the replacement of the leading motive branches of the economy. It is essential to bear in mind the long time required for the diffusion of a new economic paradigm. Some of the early pioneers of electronic computing thought that it would have a revolutionary effect on investment, unemployment and economic growth already in the 1950s. However, it is clear now that an enormous amount of further technical development and training of large numbers of skilled people was necessary before the costs and convenience of computing came down to a level where the new technology could be diffused widely not just in a few leading edge industries, but in all branches of manufacturing and services.

In considering materials and energy-saving innovations it is particularly important to stress the third and fourth categories in this taxonomy, since we are looking for pervasive technologies with effects throughout the economy. It is obviously essential to consider how far the present change of techno-economic paradigm is in itself promoting the type of technical change which is desirable and how far, if at all, it might be steered further in this direction. Or if this is not feasible, then what type of paradigm change might be needed to switch the world economy on to a path of sustainable development (see Kemp and Soete, 1991; Opschoor, 1991; Soete and Ziesemer, 1991; Van Weenen, 1992). In order to address these questions it is first necessary to clarify a little further the concepts of technological paradigms, technological trajectories and technological determinism.

3. Technological trajectories and techno-economic paradigms

Once evolutionary economists began to study the development of technology, using patent data and other historical sources, they became increasingly aware of the importance of clustering phenomena (categories (iii) and (iv) in the above taxonomy) and of the emergence of ordered patterns of technical change. It was quite evident to historians of science and technology, as to evolutionary economists, that the activities of scientists and technologists have their own internal dynamics even though the way in which a particular technology develops is heavily influenced by economic circumstances and by the social milieux (often described as the 'selection environment'). Thus Nelson and Winter (1977) in their seminal paper 'In search of a useful theory of innovation', which set the research agenda for a whole generation of neo-Schumpeterian economists, spoke of 'natural trajectories' in technology and of generalised natural trajectories for some especially influential technologies. Dosi (1982) systematically developed both the idea of technological trajectories and the concept of 'technological paradigms' by analogy with Kuhn's (1962) scientific paradigm. Sahal (1985) followed a parallel path in developing his concepts of 'technological guideposts' and 'innovation avenues'.

They and other authors point to such examples as aircraft and microelectronic technology where over a considerable period new developments followed a more ordered (and to some degree predictable) pattern. 'In micro-electronics technical change is accurately represented by an exponential trajectory of improvement in the relationship between density of the electronic chips, speed of computation, and cost per bit of information' (Dosi, 1984).

Moore's Law of the annual doubling of the number of components on successive new generations of microchips was first formulated in 1964 and proved reasonably accurate for at least thirty years from the first planar process transistor in 1959. Even in areas where the pattern of technical change is less clearly evident and regular, it is fairly obvious that the search for new advances is not completely unconstrained but starts from the neighbourhood of past achievements and present knowledge. In other words it is path dependent.

However, the idea that such trajectories are in some sense natural or pre-determined has been effectively criticised by sociologists, especially Donald MacKenzie (1990). He pointed out that although the idea that a trajectory showed a persistent pattern is unexceptionable, a trajectory can never have a momentum 'of its own'. Patterns are persistent partly because scientists, technologists, designers and others believe they will persist and act accordingly. Trajectories are self-fulfilling prophecies based on the actors' decisions and expectations of the future. Like any institutions they are sustained not by 'naturalness' but by the interests that develop in their continuance and the belief that they will continue. This belief of course is not arbitrary for it is founded on previous knowledge, experimental work, discoveries, 'paradigms' and self-interest.

This insistence by sociologists on the role of beliefs and institutions in sustaining trajectories is an important corrective to the economists' tendency to classify observed regularities and patterns in social phenomena as natural, whether the rate of unemployment, the rate of interest or a technological trajectory. It is all the more important when we come to consider the interrelationships between a variety of trajectories and the prevailing social institutions governing the behaviour of the system as a whole.

A satisfactory evolutionary theory in economics has to be 'Lamarckian' rather than 'Darwinian' and take into account the role of purposive action and beliefs of individuals and social groups. Furthermore it must recognise that the 'selection environment' for technical change includes not only firms in competition, but also the internal workings of the science and technology system and the policies of governments. That is not all; it must also include both the natural and built environments comprising the capital stock embodying past innovations, and the interaction between this capital stock, social institutions and new technological trajectories (see Chapter 6). Thus, it must go well beyond the selection of individual 'mutations' and deal with new technological systems and the conditions under which they emerge to dominance. Finally, it has to take into account changing values (Opschoor, 1991).

The idea of a techno-economic paradigm is one such attempt to develop a more comprehensive evolutionary theory. A techno-economic paradigm is a set of common-sense guidelines for technological and investment decisions as pervasive new technologies mature. It introduces a strong bias in both technical and organisational innovations which are increasingly embodied in capital equipment and software. This cumulative bias tends to lock out alternative technological innovations and trajectories. However, it is driven not by predetermined natural forces but by economic and social institutions and actors.

The advantages of conforming to a particular pattern of technical change are related to the falling costs and scale economies of key inputs to production and their numerous externalities and complementarities. Examples are the use of steel in the 'third Kondratieff wave' (1880s–1930s), oil in the fourth wave based on Fordist mass production (1930s–1980s), and microelectronics in the present wave. Some aspects of the locking-in mechanisms which tend to reinforce an established technology have been analysed by Brian Arthur (1988) and Paul David (1985). Their work and that of Perez show why the combined influence of standards, textbooks, availability of low-cost components and materials, fashions, training-systems, management routines, technological expectations, advantageous infrastructure and scale economies is so great that, once established, a techno-economic paradigm becomes a dominant technological regime for several decades (corresponding to the upswing and boom period of the Kondratieff long waves). The new paradigm is so strongly entrenched that it appears as the only natural common-sense path of development.

The dominance of each regime is reinforced by a variety of political and social institutions, including government policies to promote particular infrastructures, research programmes, sectoral privileges, management systems, educational and training activities, and so forth. We now turn to consider how far the present change of techno-economic paradigm is facilitating a shift towards material and energy-saving technologies and how much further this shift may go.

4. Information and communication technology

There are several ways in which information and communication technology (ICT) does already conform to the needs of reducing energy and materials intensity and has begun to make a contribution to a path of sustainable development.

In the first place ICT provides the possibility for far more accurate monitoring and control of a wide variety of industrial processes, including the consumption of energy and materials. Thus energy-saving technologies in many industries and increasingly also in buildings and households depend on the incorporation of electronic sensors and monitors interacting with feedback control systems and small computers. In this role ICT is complementary and often essential to process control innovations throughout the economy. The same is increasingly true in the fuel systems of motor vehicles, railways, ships and aircraft. In this role of a universal sensing and monitoring system ICT is also essential for many regulatory purposes and measuring instruments for detection of pollution hazards.

In the second place, ICT goes beyond process control and monitoring by offering greater possibilities of quality and inventory control and the reduction or elimination of defective or substandard products. In some respects this is the diffusion of a management philosophy associated with ICT and the paradigm change rather than a feature of the technology itself. Although many of the ideas for 'zero defects' and raising quality were originated by Demming and other American consultants and engineers, they found the most receptive environment in the Japanese electronic and automobile industries. The new management common sense characteristic of the new techno-economic paradigm is now diffusing from Japan world-wide (see, for example, the MIT studies of the autombile industry: *The Machine that Changed the World*, (Womack, Jones and Ross, 1990). The importance of this new management philosophy is that in some respects it reverses the rather wasteful attitudes and traditions of the old mass production paradigm, which was often prepared to tolerate a rather high scrap and reject rate and loss of inventory during production. This extends beyond the single plant to the integration of networks of plants, whether they are independent subcontractors or part of one large multinational firm with plants in many countries. The computer control of refinery mix and tanker operations of the major oil companies is one such example. However, it should be noted that 'just-in-time' systems may have negative effects on the environment as in the transfer of stocks from warehouses to lorries choking up roads in Japan. In their anxiety to be on time subcontractors park lorries close to delivery points.

In the third place, ICT is in many ways a miniaturising technology. As the successive generations of computer-controlled instruments, processes and equipment are introduced, each one is based on VLSI technology which is constantly increasing the number of components on one chip. Compared with the old valve technology, semiconductor technology is already greatly superior in terms of energy and materials consumption. All kinds of electronic products, such as TV sets, now use far fewer discrete components because of the availability of VLSI. However it is not only in the electronics industry itself but also more widely in the engineering industry that ICT is leading to a substantial reduction in the number and weight of components. Many electro-mechanical engineering products (such as Black and Decker DIY power tools) have been redesigned to reduce the number of components, often by as much as 50 per cent. Industrial statistics of all major countries show the benefits of this wave of technical change in the reduction of metal consumption in the engineering industries (Figures 10.1 and 10.2) over the past twenty years.

In all these ways and others ICT has already demonstrated that it can make a substantial contribution to a more energy and material-saving pattern of production and distribution, although this is far from exhausting the potential of this technology. On the contrary, the most revolutionary possibilities opened up by ICT have yet to be realised. This is partly a question of political and social change associated with the technical and economic changes. As we have seen, the technology itself, although it has intrinsic technical possibilities, is shaped and directed by a variety of institutions. Thus for instance, the Gulf War demonstrated beyond all reasonable doubt the immense potential of the technology for military purposes. This was based on an immense R&D effort, especially in the United States, directed towards the exploitation of this military potential. Similarly in the case of space technology, the former Soviet Union and the United States also showed what could be achieved in the way of remote control, sensing and communication across enormous distances.

However, as Nelson (1977) pointed out in his book *The Moon and the Ghetto*, the same interested institutions either did not exist or lacked the necessary resources and political muscle to realise the potential of new technologies in many other areas of potential application. This is still true of environmentally-friendly technologies.

This inevitably raises the question of the market mechanism and market

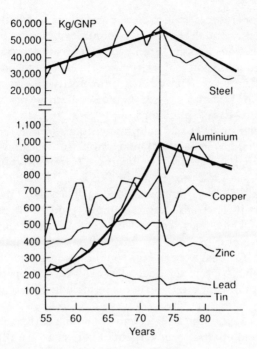

Figure 10.1 Metals consumption per unit of GNP in Japan, 1955–84
Source: Cohendet *et al.*, 1988.

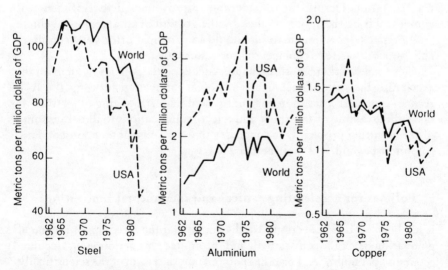

Figure 10.2 Trends in the intensity of metal usage
Source: Sousa, 1988.

failure. The impetus to develop, diffuse and adapt ICT in the economies of both developed and underdeveloped countries undoubtedly came mainly from the market mechanism. Both producers (computer, semiconductor, telecommunications and software firms, etc.) and users (all other industries and firms) gradually realised the profit-making and cost-saving advantages of ICT; they also realised the competitive disadvantages of *not* adopting various ICT applications.

However, non-market mechanisms were also important, both in the generation of the original radical innovations (often in university or public laboratories) and their early applications (often in civil and military government organisations or in public service). This interplay of markets and other institutions was important for each change of paradigm though especially for ICT. Each new paradigm requires a modification to infrastructure which can only occur as a result of institutional and regulatory changes in each country. Particularly important in the evolution of ICT have been the public programmes for computer technology going back to the Second World War and public policies for the telecommunications infrastructure (including deregulation in the 1980s).

The development of the ICT techno-economic paradigm resulted in the emergence (and partial convergence) of two parallel streams of innovations in computers and in communications. It is the *potential* of the paradigm associated with this convergence which is so far largely unrealised.

Although materials and energy consumption in manufacturing industry have already been considerably affected by ICT, this is far less true of transportation. Despite the considerable improvement in fuel efficiency of engines, this has been outweighed by the growth of air and motor vehicle traffic. Yet telecommunications should in principle offer very considerable possibilities for reducing the movement of people.

The final section of this chapter deals with policies which might accelerate the rate of technical and social innovation in using the ICT techno-economic paradigm for energy and material-saving objectives. It takes the example of transport and telecommunications to illustrate some of the resulting problems. It concludes that a change of techno-economic paradigm beyond ICT will be needed.

5. Policies for accelerating radical and incremental innovations

It has been argued in Sections 3 and 4 above that the direction of technical innovation is both constrained and promoted by a dominant techno-economic paradigm. As Perez has pointed out, the realm of the scientifically conceivable is infinitely greater than the realm of the technologically feasible and the realm of the technologically feasible is far greater than the realm of the economically profitable and the socially acceptable. There are very powerful constraining forces in our societies which channel, promote and limit the main directions of scientific and technical effort and advance. These have been primarily economic and military influences in the past interacting with the internal forces within the science–technology system. The reason that a paradigm has such a great influence is because of the systemic characteristics of both the economy and technology. The lock-in mechanisms are extremely strong and make it difficult to embark on an entirely different trajectory. For the next ten to thirty years, therefore, most technical change is likely to be within the dominant ICT techno-economic paradigm. Over a longer period a new paradigm (for example, based on nanotechnology and biochemistry) could displace the ICT paradigm.

However, as the potential of the ICT paradigm is far from being exhausted, some opportunities lie in the further exploitation of its material and energy-saving possibilities. The ICT paradigm can be shaped and steered in an environmentally-friendly direction. This was not true of the previous paradigm which was based on mass production and the exploitation of cheap oil. The displacement of this older paradigm is far from complete. We are still in the midst of a structural crisis of adjustment.

Almost every government has some R&D support programmes in ICT and many have incentives to develop and adopt recycling and cleaner technologies. The EC also has such programmes. These are valuable in promoting a wide variety of incremental improvements and in some cases more radical change, as in the PROMETHEUS programme. This seeks to promote the use of electronic systems in automobiles and in traffic movement and control. However, although these are desirable objectives, they will not contribute to the fundamental problem: there is too much motor vehicle traffic and it has to be reduced. The same is true of air travel. The ICT paradigm does not in itself lead to solutions for these problems and in some cases could even exacerbate them.

How could a trend be set in motion which would reduce the absolute volume of passenger road and air travel? To attempt to address this question necessarily requires some speculative ideas and the following paragraphs are intended to be a stimulus to debate and research rather than the advocacy of a particular solution.

Two different types of movement are at issue: work-related journeys and leisure-related journeys or tourism. We shall first discuss work-related journeys.

One obvious way is to improve public transport within and between urban areas so much as to eliminate both the need and the desire to use private cars for the journey to work for most people. It is only a half-century or so since the great majority of people in Europe did *not* travel to work by car so that a reverse movement should be quite feasible. However, in that half-century patterns of urban settlement and industrial location have changed enormously and new attitudes have become entrenched. A change back to public transport is therefore necessarily a prolonged and difficult transition. It can be accelerated on the one hand by dramatic improvements in transport systems, such as high-speed trains, and on the other hand by strong economic incentives and disincentives. A combination of these two methods is clearly the most desirable.

However, radical innovations in transport systems are unlikely to emerge from the automobile industry, the electronic industry or the railway industry alone. They require some independent promotion and funding. Although superconductivity offers promising long-term possibilities, other systems using monorails and magnetism offer more immediate prospects. However, none of these changes emerges directly from ICT even though computerised traffic control, signalling and scheduling systems will become increasingly important in achieving the necessary flexibility if public transport services are to recapture a considerable proportion of road passenger and goods traffic.

A second way to reduce traffic is to enable people not to travel to work at all. This is indeed the preferable solution to the environmental problem. Here ICT would appear to offer great potential although it is a potential which is so far unfulfilled. Early dreams of the 'electronic cottage' which would eliminate the need for the journey to work have clearly not been realised (Miles, 1988). Rather few people are able to work entirely from home using computerised telecommunications to meet their work commitments. Nevertheless, the total demise of this idea is premature. Technologies such as FAX, E-Mail and mobile telephones have advanced enormously since the 'electronic cottage' was first mooted and much has been learnt about why people need to journey to work. The need for direct personal contact was very much underestimated in the first glow of enthusiasm for home terminals, teleconferencing, etc. It is now evident that whereas rather few (although by no means a negligible number) of people can work *entirely* from home or with very little work-related travel, a great many people could work *partly* from home and partly in an office or other place of work. People in a variety of occupations do already travel to work on only one, two, three or four days a week and work at home for most of the remaining time. Such an arrangement is often personally advantageous for other reasons not related to work, so there are social incentives to extend these arrangements as well as environmental advantages. However, the change is extremely slow and offset by increases in other types of travel. The problem is to reduce the economic, social and technical barriers to the widespread use of homework on one or more days of the week. This requires big changes in employment practices, working hours and management control systems, and is clearly an area where organisational and social innovations are more important than technical innovations. Nevertheless, further reductions in the cost of FAX, E-Mail and other types of telecommunications would clearly be helpful and it may be that the videophone will represent a breakthrough technology at some point. There is clearly a spectrum of work-related activities extending from those which absolutely necessitate personal contact with other people or goods to those where there is no need for this at all. In the intermediate area the videophone and improved and cheaper tele-conferencing could make a big difference to their acceptability.

The other type of movement of people—tourism and leisure movements—is in many ways more difficult to limit or reduce even though it is of course not essential for the efficiency of the productive system. Many countries, including those of the Third World, now depend on receipts from tourism to finance their external payments and huge numbers of people have now grown accustomed to holidays abroad. As real incomes rise even greater numbers of people are likely to wish to take holidays abroad. Is there any way to reconcile this trend with the environmental objectives of reducing energy and materials consumption and the conservation of nature?

In her highly original analysis of ICT and world tourism, Auliana Poon (1989, 1992) distinguishes a group of technical, social and institutional changes which together combined to create the phenomenon of mass tourism in the 1950s and 1960s. The most important were:

1. cheap chartered jet aircraft services;
2. paid holidays in the northern industrial countries of two to three weeks for very large numbers of people;
3. the belief that sun-bathing promoted health; and
4. the standardised packaged holiday provided by tour operators on similar lines to other service innovations influenced by mass production philosophy.

She shows that ICT has dramatically changed the tourist industry in a variety of ways:

1. computerised airline booking systems linked to travel agents, enabling far greater flexibility in choice and timing of destinations;
2. customisation of tours to meet specific needs of special groups, e.g. ornithologists, archaeologists, etc.;
3. 'Diagonal integration' of various service industries—airlines, financial services, travel business, hotels, etc.; and
4. New tourist centres no longer relying on sun associated with (2) and with the growing belief that sun-bathing is not good for health.

However, important as these changes are, they do not lead to energy and materials-saving or reduction of air travel. Rather the reverse since the combination of still longer holidays (four to six weeks) with customisation and wider choice of destination leads both to more and to longer journeys.

It is true that tourism is characterised by high income elasticity of demand and is highly sensitive to political events (terrorism, wars, etc.); nevertheless, if the long-term trend of rising personal incomes continues for thirty to forty years, it is likely to lead to a huge increase in tourist air travel which could be very damaging to the environment. This danger is reflected in the growth of a number of specialised campaign groups to promote a 'green' approach to tourism.

Similarly for business travel. The new ICT paradigm has facilitated 'global networking' although so far, this has led to an *increase* of travel rather than a reduction. Thus the new ICT paradigm does not in itself lead to environment-friendly outcomes and may indeed still tend to stimulate contrary types of development.

The most fruitful method of changing this outcome is likely to be one which combines both institutional and technical changes as occurred with the mass tourism of the previous generation. However, the problem is so vast that it would amount to a change of techno-economic paradigm.

To reduce the absolute consumption of energy and damage to the environment, it is essential not just to improve the design of aero-engines but also to switch very large numbers of people away from jet air travel to sea travel. Fortunately, this is already the choice of many in the high income groups who have always preferred cruise-type holidays. It is also highly compatible with the lengthening of holidays towards four to six weeks and with the reduction of pressures on particular historical sites and hotel accommodation.

However, it would not be enough to persuade millions of people to travel by sea rather than air, although this in itself could achieve enormous savings in energy and reductions in atmospheric pollution. It would also be necessary to use computer-controlled sailing technology so that wind-assisted ships would become the norm. Toy yachts and Japanese experiments with larger ships have already pioneered in this direction.

For those who continued to travel by air despite powerful financial and social incentives to change their behaviour, and for air freight traffic, airships rather than aircraft would probably offer the best possibilities of technical and social change.

6. Conclusions

From this brief discussion of one very important area—the possibilities of energy-saving in transport systems—certain general conclusions can be drawn which are relevant also for other major economic activities. The discussion has been purely illustrative and in no way exhaustive. Nor is it claimed that other sectors share exactly the same problems as the transport sector. Construction differs in many important respects from transport and manufacturing differs from both. Transport was chosen as an example because it is in many respects the most difficult area to tackle. The conclusions which emerge are that the incremental improvement of existing systems will not be enough to achieve the scale of reduction in energy and materials consumption which will be needed in the industrial countries during the twenty-first century. Radical innovations will be needed including new transport, construction and industrial systems. Although ICT does indeed greatly facilitate many incremental improvements in existing systems and could be used also to facilitate more radical changes, it does not in itself embrace radical environmental objectives.

What is needed therefore is on the one hand to continue and reinforce a wide range of existing policies nationally and internationally, such as those set out in the Dutch National Environmental Policy Plan ('To choose or to lose'). As Kemp, Olsthoorn, Oosterhuis and Verbruggen (1991) argue, there is no single optimal policy for stimulating innovation. Many different methods are needed, some of which are entirely sector-specific and some of which are general.

In addition to all of these measures, there is a need to anticipate and to some degree stimulate the next change of techno-economic paradigm (which can be expected to occur in the early decades of the twenty-first century). The time scale of paradigm change is measured in decades rather than years and it is certainly not too early to begin moving in this direction. In every change of a techno-economic paradigm (TEP) which has so far occurred, the new TEP already emerged and developed within the previous paradigm. A set of technologies cannot indeed become dominant in a system unless they have already been proven and advantageous. Thus the second TEP (steam power) was based on a technology already well established, even though on a small scale in the eighteenth century. The third TEP (electric power) was developing over half a century before the generation and transmission of electricity became widespread towards the end of the nineteenth century. The fourth TEP (mass production) was already established in such industries as meat-packing and automobiles decades before it became the dominant system. The fifth ICT paradigm has been developing since the Second World War to the point where it is achieving dominance today.

It is therefore not too soon to start thinking about and designing and building institutions and technologies which are likely to combine in a sixth (environmental) TEP. Some features of course cannot be forecast since technical and commercial uncertainty remain. However, since the establishment of a TEP is largely a *diffusion* phenomenon comprising a variety of novel applications of technologies which already exist, at least in embryonic form, it is quite possible to make a start two or three decades ahead. It is in any case clear that the sixth TEP can already make use of many features of the fifth TEP although in novel ways. Thus for example:

1. It will be essential to stimulate the substitution of telecommunications

for work-related journeys on a far greater scale than at present conceived. This applies to both the daily travel to work and world-wide business travel by air.
2. It will be essential to move traffic from road and air transport to sail, canal and sea transport. This applies both to goods and people and will require radical systemic innovations.

The implications of these conclusions for technical and social innovations are as follows (essentially the same arguments apply to manufacturing and construction as to transport):

1. Changes of this magnitude require a substantial long-term policy embracing environmental, social and technological objectives. Institutional and technical changes are intimately associated in a change of TEP.
2. Although the ICT techno-economic paradigm did not develop primarily with environmental objectives, it can in fact be adapted to these objectives given the political will. The technology itself can be helpful in a very broad range of applications (see, for example Table 3 in Chapter 5).
3. However, the scale of the problems requires a broad stream of both radical and incremental innovations going far beyond ICT. Although economic pressures and incentives are already stimulating many desirable innovations, these pressures have less effect on long-term research and development. They need to be strongly reinforced both by a more radical realignment of prices to reflect true long-term environmental costs and benefits and by a long-term technology programme directed to a new TEP.
4. Such a technology programme should be based on a networking approach because of this huge variety of participants. It is essential to include potential users of new products and systems as well as innovators and to include universities as well as industry to ensure that the most imaginative and radical solutions are explored.
5. An essential feature of the technology programme would be a strong directorate with high-level government support and funds and capable of co-ordinating a variety of activities. Also essential would be a leading role for one or more public laboratories with experience of working with universities and industry. (The number of laboratories would vary in different countries depending on the degree of EC participation and the size of country.) The MITI/NEDO Research Institute for Innovative Technology for the Earth (RITE) may well be a prototype for such lead laboratories.
6. This does not mean that such lead laboratories would do all the R&D themselves. Far from it: they would perform some of the work themselves and the greater part would be subcontracted. They would also

assemble temporary teams of people seconded from a variety of sources on the model of the Japanese engineering programmes or the British wartime radar programme. Although in this latter case the highly successful TRE (Telecommunications and Radar Establishment) did perform a great deal of R&D in-house, they also worked very closely with the end-users of ground, marine and airborne radar systems as well as with industry and universities.

7. In view of the global nature of most of the problems international networking would be essential and wherever possible international agreement on lead laboratories on an international scale. However, the diversity of the problems and the institutions means that some national initiatives would probably bear fruit more quickly and have strong demonstration effects. An element of pluralism and competition is in any case essential to promote good results.

8. A system of national and international awards (including if possible appropriate Nobel Prizes) should be set up to promote top class scientific and technological work in this field.

9. Strong capability in ICT would be a valuable feature of the public laboratories taking part, and nanotechnology and biotechnology would also be important. In fact multi-disciplinarity would be an essential feature of the programme and it would be vitally important to include social scientists together with natural scientists from the outset.

10. In some cases entirely new initiatives would be needed, in others the enhancement or reinforcement of existing activities. Since success depends on the strong support of public opinion world-wide as well as on new technology, the strategic importance of the programme would need a high profile, nationally and internationally, and the commitment of the UN and other international organisations. It would be especially necessary to bring in Third World countries and to enlist the support of the World Bank for major projects in the Third World and Eastern Europe, including demonstration projects.

This last point is the most important one of all. The most threatening environmental hazards are intrinsically global. They cannot be counteracted without the strong commitment of Third World countries. This commitment and understanding will not be forthcoming without the active participation of the Third World science and technology community and Third World governments. A leading role for Third World laboratories could also greatly help that strengthening of scientific and technical competence which is necessary for any form of sustainable development.

This conclusion is the direct opposite of that proposed in an internal memorandum within the World Bank (*Economist*, 8 February 1992). This document suggested that such continents as Africa were 'under-polluted' and would 'benefit' from the transfer of heavily polluting industries from the OECD countries to the Third World. This memorandum from the World Bank chief economist (fortunately now disowned) is a good example of the short-term, parochial, market-oriented thinking which needs to be displaced by an entirely different orientation of international initiatives for the twenty-first century. Nothing could demonstrate more clearly the need for a paradigm change.

The Rio Conference on the Global Environment provided some further grounds for hope that the necessary international consensus of governments and world public opinion can be achieved despite the equivocal position of President Bush. But, as the architect of the Conference success, Maurice Strong, observed, it is the practical world-wide follow-up which matters. This will at some point in the 1990s have to include an 'Environmental Bretton Woods' i.e. an imaginative attempt to re-structure the global institutions set up after the Second World War. Even at the time Keynes considered them to be under-resourced and now, half a century later, with the growth of the world economy and the new problems of sustainable development we need a much stronger World Bank, stronger regional institutions and an International Technology Agency to support them.

References

Arthur B. (1988), 'Competing technologies: an overview', Chapter 26 in G. Dosi, C. Freeman, R.R. Nelson, G. Silverberg and L.L.G. Soete (eds), *Technical Change and Economic Theory*, Pinter Publishers, London.

CEC (1990), *Panorama of Industry*, EC, Luxembourg.

Cohendet, P., Ledoux, M.J. and Zuscovitch, E. (1988), *New Advanced Materials*, Springer-Verlag, Berlin.

Cole, H.S.D., Freeman, C., Jahoda, M. and Pavitt, K. (eds) (1973), *Thinking about the Future: A Critique of Limits to Growth*, Chatto & Windus, London.

David, P. (1985), 'Clio and the economics of QWERTY', *American Economic Review*, Vol. 76, No. 2, pp. 332-7.

Dosi, G. (1982), 'Technological paradigms and technological trajectories', *Research Policy*, Vol. 11, No. 3, pp. 147-62.

Dosi, G. (1984), *Technical Change and Industrial Transformation*, Macmillan, London.

Economist (1992), 'The World Bank's green gaffe: let them eat pollution', 8 February, p. 82.

Forrester, J. (1971), *World Dynamics*, Wright-Allen, New York.

Freeman, C. (1990), 'Innovation, changes of techno-economic paradigm and biological analogies in economics', *Revue Économique*, Vol. 42, No. 2, pp. 211-31.

Freeman, C. and Jahoda, M. (eds) (1978), *World Futures*, Martin Robertson, London.

Hollander, S. (1965), *The Sources of Increased Efficiency: A Study of Du Pont Rayon Plants*, MIT Press, Cambridge, Mass.

Keirstead, B.G. (1948), *The Theory of Economic Change*, Macmillan, Toronto.

Kemp, R., Olsthoorn, A., Oosterhuis, F. and Verbruggen, H. (1991), 'Policy Instruments to stimulate cleaner technology', Paper for the EAERE Conference, Stockholm (mimeo).

Kemp, R. and Soete, L. (1991), 'The greening of technological progress: an evolutionary prospective', MERIT, Maastricht, Netherlands (mimeo).

Kuhn, T. (1962), *The Structure of Scientific Revolutions*, Chicago University Press, Chicago.

MacKenzie, D. (1990), 'Economic and sociological explanation of technical change', Paper given at Manchester Conference on Firm Strategy, 27–28 September, Sociology Department, University of Edinburgh, (mimeo).

Meadows, D.H., Meadows, D.L., Randers, J. and Behrens, W.W. (1972), *The Limits to Growth*, Universe Books, New York.

Meadows, D.H., Meadows, D.L., Randers, J. (1992), *Beyond The Limits*, Earthscan Publications Limited, London.

Miles, I. (1988), 'The electronic cottage: myth or near-myth? A response to Tom Forester', *Futures*, Vol. 20, No. 4, pp. 355–66.

Nelson, R.R. (1977), *The Moon and the Ghetto*, W.W. Norton, New York.

Nelson, R.R. and Winter, S. (1977), 'In search of a useful theory of innovation', *Research Policy*, Vol. 6, No. 1, pp. 36–77.

Opschoor, J.B. (1991), 'Sustainable development', (mimeo).

Pearce, D., Markandy, A. and Barbier, E.B. (1989), *Blueprint for a Green Economy*, Earthscan, London.

Perez, C. (1983), 'Structural change and the assimilation of new technologies in the social and economic system', *Futures*, Vol. 15, No. 5, pp. 357–75.

Poon, A. (1989), DPhil thesis, University of Sussex.

Poon, A. (1992), *Tourism, Technology and Competitive Strategies*, CAB International, London (forthcoming).

Sahal, D. (1985), 'Technological guideposts and innovation avenues', *Research Policy*, Vol. 14, No. 2, pp. 61–82.

Soete, L. and Ziesemer, T. (1991), 'Meritocracy for sustainability. Comments on J.B. Opschoor's "Sustainable development"', MERIT, Maastricht (mimeo).

Sousa, L.J. (1988), *Problems and opportunities in metal and materials; an integrated perspective*, United States Department of the Interior and United States Bureau of Mines, Washington, DC.

Van Weenen (1992), 'Lost and new environmental policy paradigms', Lecture for DGE, Leidschendam, 5 February.

Womack, J.P., Jones, D.T. and Ross, D. (1990), *The Machine that Changed The World*, Rawson Associates, New York.

11 Technology, progress and the quality of life*

I. Introduction

In a time of cholera, AIDS, earthquakes and volcanic eruptions, renewed famine in Africa, assassinations, nationalistic, sectarian hatred and killings, wholesale corruption in numerous governments and business enterprises, it is difficult to find grounds for optimism about the quality of life or the possibility of progress.

After the terrible Lisbon earthquake of 1759 and in the midst of the Seven Years' War, when, as Voltaire put it, men were ready to slaughter each other enthusiastically for sixpence a day, people were driven to reflect in a similar way on natural and social disasters. Frederick II, who provoked the war if not the earthquake, remarked that wars, devastations and plagues would always be with us. Others maintained that in spite of these disasters this was still the best of all possible worlds. Whatever is, is good. This facile, complacent optimism drove Voltaire to write his classic masterpiece, *Candide*, although even before that he asked rhetorically, 'If this is the best of all possible worlds, what are the others like?'

If this chapter nevertheless indicates some grounds for optimism, this is not so much because of what the quality of life actually is for most people, but because of what it might become. Policies for science and technology must always be a mixture of realism and idealism.

The chapter will first of all briefly discuss the development of science and technology policies since the Second World War. During the lifetime of SPRU, the emphasis has shifted from an essentially science-push framework in the 1950s, through a phase of preoccupation with economic growth and management of innovation in the 1960s, and on to a wider concern with the environment and quality of life since the 1970s. Within this context, the second part of the chapter will discuss some quality of life issues which are only indirectly related to economic growth: civil liberty, quality, variety and choice in new products and services, and social equity.

On an occasion such as the twenty-fifth anniversary of SPRU and

*Originally published for the twenty-fifth anniversary of SPRU in *Science and Public Policy*, Vol. 18, No. 6, December 1991.

dealing with such a topic as 'quality of life', where subjective values are ever-present, much of what I say will be in the nature of personal comments, rather than the results of any organised research.

I first heard of 'research and development' when I was a student at the London School of Economics. However, it was not from economists. The first lecture I ever heard which dealt specifically with the links between organised research and development, technological competition and the associated growth and decline of firms and industries was by an Irish physicist, J.D. Bernal. In 1939 he wrote his classic book entitled *The Social Function of Science* which attracted the attention of Keynes and included the first systematic attempt to measure the total research activity in British industry, government and universities.

More than Schumpeter, Bernal perceived that the allocation of resources to the various branches of organised and professionalised R&D and related scientific and technical services and their efficient management had become crucial for the development and performance of enterprises and nations in war and peace alike. Around this central idea he was able to build up a critical analysis of the use and misuse of science and technology in Britain and other countries, and thereby to establish 'science policy' and 'technology policy' as important issues of public debate and government policy. To this day, his book represents an agenda for research in social studies of science.

Half a century later groups like SPRU in various parts of the world have done much to fill in the picture which Bernal sketched out in the first part of his book: 'What science does'. The tenfold increase in resources for R&D which he advocated in 1939 seemed at that time absurdly Utopian to many people. Nevertheless, it has in fact been realised and exceeded in most industrial countries on approximately the time-scale which he envisaged. We have learned to define and measure the R&D system a little more accurately than he and his colleagues so that the 'map' of the world science–technology system is both more comprehensive and more detailed, even though there are still many gaps and inaccuracies.

We have also learned much more about other areas which were neglected by Bernal and his contemporaries, for example, the diffusion of innovations and the uses and limitations of a variety of output measures for the science–technology system. In all of this work SPRU has made original contributions which go well beyond what Bernal achieved. However, when it comes to the second part of Bernal's agenda ('What science could do'), the position is different.

II

In the twenty-five years after the Second World War GNP grew at a high rate in Europe, Japan and North America and also in some Third World countries. Increased investment in science and technology (S&T) certainly played an important part in this accelerated growth, which was probably more rapid than in any previous period of world history. To this extent Bernal's hopes and expectations were vindicated.

However, the improvements in human welfare which he had hoped would be associated with increased prosperity have only been partly realised and in many parts of the world not at all. Moreover, the high expectations which he had of the communist countries have manifestly not been fulfilled, as he himself recognised in the 1950s despite the very big investments in R&D which most of them made, especially the Soviet Union. In part of course this was for the very reasons that he analysed: the vast increase in the world's military R&D. From the recent work of Soviet colleagues it seems that this bias was even greater in the Soviet Union than previously estimated. To keep up in the arms race, the Soviet Union seems to have devoted about three-quarters of its R&D budget to military–space objectives, leaving less than 1 per cent of GNP for civil objectives. The high growth rates achieved in Eastern Europe in the 1950s and 1960s gave way to stagnation and decline in the 1970s and 1980s and many environmental and social problems became more acute. In the OECD countries too, growth slowed down, unemployment once more became a serious problem and environmental issues came to the fore. In the Third World the structural crisis was far more severe. However, technology policy and science policy have still not fully responded to the new issues and still make more connections with military and economic problems than they do with wider social problems and quality of life issues.

In the first phase of post-war science policy, (Table 11.1) the experiences of the war still dominated public policies. Not only did the Cold War mean that military expenditures predominated in the superpowers, as well as in Britain and France (although not in Japan and Germany), but civil science and technology were also profoundly influenced by the military model and especially the Manhattan Project. The devastating weapon systems achieved by this and other projects, such as rocket and radar projects, led people quite naturally to think that big science and technology and big government laboratories could achieve similar results elsewhere. Physics enjoyed enormous prestige and most science advisers to governments were physicists in this period. Nuclear physics and nuclear energy occupied far more government attention and accounted for far greater expenditures than agriculture or other civil technology. Stefan Dedijer, who established the first academic Science Policy Unit in a European university in Lund in Sweden, and helped to inspire the establishment of SPRU, left his own country, Yugoslavia, in the 1950s in protest against the extreme distortion of R&D by huge nuclear projects. The Studiengruppe für Systems Forschung in Heidelberg (which also preceded SPRU) made a number of studies, which, like Dedijer's work showed the extreme imbalance in science and technology towards military objectives.

Table 11.1   Three phases of science policy

1	2	3
Manhattan Project, military aircraft, V1, V2, missiles, radar, guidance systems	Nuclear reactors, CERN, ESRO, NASA, ELDO, etc. Civil aircraft	ERAs (Japan), ESPRIT, 'Human Frontiers' Programme
Science Advisory Councils	Science and Technology Councils and Ministries	Science, Technology and Industry Departments. Technology Assessment bodies
Physicists Chemists	Physicists Economists Engineers Chemists	'Hard sciences' Biology, ecology Economics Social sciences
Military R&D Basic research Government labs Universities	Applied research Industrial R&D Big science & technology Universities	'Generic technologies' Networks Systems University–industry links
J. Bernal, *Social Function of Science* (1939) V. Bush, *Science the Endless Frontier* (1948)	I. Svennilson, *Science, Economic Growth and Government Policy* (1963) Brooks Report (OECD, 1971), *Science, Growth and Society*	R. Nelson and J. Salomon, *Science and Technology in the New Economic Context* (1979) Sundqvist Report (1989), *New Technologies in the 1990s: A Socio-Economic strategy*
Weapon systems	Economic growth Weapon systems	Environment Weapon systems Economic growth Quality of life

Of course the Science Advisory Councils, dominated by physicists as they were, were not altogether unmindful of economic and social issues. However, as in the case of nuclear weapons and nuclear power, they tended implicitly to assume a science-push model, in which the benefits of scientific discovery would almost automatically flow through into technology (often revealingly called 'Applied Science', as at that time in our own School of Engineering here in Sussex), and thence into the economic system. It was also commonly assumed that there would be major 'spin-off' or 'spill-over' benefits from military R&D to the civil economy.

However, already in the 1950s, economists such as Dick Nelson and Nathan Rosenberg in the United States, Charles Carter and Bruce Williams in this country, Perroux in France, Dahmen and Svennilson in Sweden began to transform this situation. Moreover, the large civil aircraft projects, such as Concorde, and the various nuclear reactor projects which imitated the military model began to run into serious problems of cost overrun. Derek Price (1963) in his book *Little Science, Big Science* pointed out that the exponential growth of scientific activities, so successfully advocated by Bernal, could not continue indefinitely into the future. Both industry and government began to recognise the need for far more careful project evaluation than had been the case in the days of headlong expansion which followed the Second World War.

During the second phase of post-war science policy, at both the national and international level, in the UN, the OECD and the EEC economists began to be seriously involved in the debates on science and technology policy, the writing of reports and the advisory bodies. Svennilson played the leading part in writing the OECD report on *Science, Economic Growth and Government Policy* in the early 1960s, to which both Keith Pavitt and I also contributed; Bruce Williams became an adviser to the British Ministry of Technology, and most countries began to appoint economists to similar positions. Growth and economic performance became the main concern of science and technology policy, even though in many countries military influences remained extremely strong.

Economists, although sometimes more cautious than physicists, certainly did not advocate wholesale curtailment of R&D and other S&T expenditures. On the contrary they often provided hard evidence of the beneficial effects of these activities. However, they probably did succeed in injecting greater discrimination into the allocation of resources, through a more careful consideration of potential costs and benefits. They also largely succeeded in their critique of the hitherto prevalent 'science-push' model and in putting technology policy more firmly on the agenda as well as science policy more narrowly conceived. Indeed some of them went too far in their emphasis on 'demand-pull' until corrected by Mowery and Rosenberg (1979) in their classic piece in *Research Policy*.

In retrospect, the 1960s were a golden age of growth although by the end of the decade many social and environmental problems began to cast a shadow over the triumphs of economic growth and growth-oriented R&D. The oil-based energy and materials-intensive mass production system, which had been so successful in the post-war period and indeed during the war itself, began to bump against limits of various kinds. Dissatisfaction became widespread with working conditions in large mass production factories (as so evident in France in 1968), with the quality of many consumer durables, and the philosophy of 'consumerism' itself, with the destruction of urban and rural amenities and quality of life brought about by mass use of automobiles, the threats to wildlife from mass tourism and unrestrained commercialism, and the poor quality of the mass media and mass education. All these and other unpleasant consequences of growth led to widespread questioning and criticism. The MIT study on *Limits to Growth* (1972) became the best-known general critique of growth policies, although there were many other manifestations of this dissatisfaction, including of course the rise of the 'Greens' and Scitovsky's (1976) critique of *The Joyless Economy*.

All of these developments contributed to a third phase in science and technology policy, which was also associated with a radical shift towards information and communication technology, gathering force in the 1970s and 1980s. Environmental and ecological issues became more prominent in policy-making. Quality of working life and worker-participation in technical change began to be taken more seriously. Biologists and even sociologists began to be invited to join top-level government advisory bodies. OECD reports such as the Brooks Report (OECD, 1971) and even more the Sundqvist Report (OECD, 1989) both reflected and stimulated these developments.

III

From 1 July 1991 SPRU began work on one of the most difficult and challenging projects: 'Global Perspective 2010: Tasks for Science and Technology'. This project, led by Tom Whiston and sponsored by the European Community through its programme on 'Future Applications of Science and Technology' (FAST) enabled us to take up again some of the main quality of life issues which we began to research in the 1970s in our own programme for the Research Councils on Social and Technological Forecasting. In that programme we were involved in a critique of the MIT work on *Limits to Growth* (Cole et al., 1973) and a wider comparative analysis of many different computer models of the future development of the world economy (Freeman and Jahoda, 1978). Now, nearly twenty years later, in embarking on our new EC project, it may be useful to look back as well as forwards and try to see what can be learnt from our earlier work.

In the 1960s it was commonly assumed that high economic growth rates could be extrapolated into the future and that unemployment was a thing of the past. It was also often assumed that high rates of energy production and consumption could be extrapolated with fixed energy coefficients related to gross national product (GNP).

Simple extrapolation is of course a dangerous technique in forecasting.

A trend is a trend, is a trend, is a trend,
But when and how does it bend?
Does it rise to the sky?
Or lie down and die?
Or asymptote on to the end?

The validity of extrapolation of the trends of the 1950s and 1960s was one of the main points of the controversy with Denis and Donella Meadows (1972) and their colleagues at MIT in the early 1970s. In our books and papers we criticised some of the basic assumptions used in the MIT models and their main conclusion that zero growth was the only way to avert collapse. We argued that there was too much extrapolation of earlier trends and that both technical change and social change were underrepresented in the MIT models. Since in any computer modelling the assumptions determine the outcome ('Malthus in, Malthus out') the extrapolation of exponential trends in population growth, materials and energy consumption and pollution would necessarily lead to the collapse of the system. We maintained that a combination of technical and social changes could lead to a different pattern of growth and that the MIT models had confused a particular mode of materials and energy-intensive growth with the problem of economic growth in general.

We also argued that the pattern of growth which was especially characteristic of the US economy in the nineteenth and twentieth centuries would not necessarily be the standard for other countries in the next century. If materials became scarce and expensive, or if their use created unacceptable pollution hazards, we argued that technical changes could (and very likely would) facilitate reduction in materials intensity, substitution between materials, innovation in processes, recycling and other changes which would lead to a different pattern of growth. There has in fact been a change in materials intensity and energy intensity of production in the 1970s and 1980s (Table 11.2), which suggests that our ideas about a new pattern of growth were not too far removed from reality, even though we still have a long way to go. Information and communication technology can greatly facilitate reduction of energy and materials intensity.

We did not use the expressions 'sustainable growth' or 'sustainable development' in our books in the 1970s. These expressions entered the debate somewhat later, but they convey the sense of what we were suggesting in our comments on the 'composition' of growth and the distribution of the fruits of growth (Cole et al. 1973: p. 10).

Table 11.2 Energy intensity of GDP
(tonnes per 1000 ECU)

	1973	1988
Denmark	0.46	0.31
France	0.44	0.36
Germany (FR)	0.51	0.40
Italy	0.46	0.36
Netherlands	0.59	0.47
Spain	NA	0.42
UK	0.62	0.45
EC	0.52	0.41

Source: CEC, *Panorama of European Industry*,
1990.

IV

Economists have always maintained that growth of GNP is quite distinct from happiness or improvement in the quality of life. Nevertheless the objective of increasing per capita GNP has often been equated with improvement in the standard of living or even quality of life. Nor is this transposition entirely misplaced. For people suffering from malnutrition, homelessness, disease and poverty on a vast scale, it is difficult to conceive of a substantial improvement in the quality of life without the kind of growth in per capita production and consumption which is measured, however crudely, in GNP indices. To continue world-wide economic growth, especially in the Third World, is a necessary condition for the achievement of many other quality of life objectives. Therefore in our work we should continue to pay attention to long-term sustainable forms of economic growth.

However, in the SPRU contributions to the debate on *Limits to Growth*, in the 1970s we insisted on two important qualifications to simplistic growth policies. These qualifications concerned both the distribution and the composition of GNP. Clearly it is possible to have quite high levels of per capita GNP growth, as in Brazil in the 1960s and 1970s, whilst leaving a large proportion of the population in the direst poverty and even becoming worse off. In Britain between 1979 and 1989 the income of the richest households increased 40 per cent whereas that of the poorest fell by 5 per cent. Again, some increases in measured GNP, as in military production, may bear no relationship to improvements in the standard of living. In polluting forms of growth, damage to the environment and loss of amenity may be so great as to create a general deterioration in quality of life, even though GNP growth rates are high.

Finally, people do not live by bread alone. Many other factors affect perceptions of the quality of life as well as the production and consumption of food and other necessities. Among these are civil liberty, social equity, opportunities for satisfying employment, conditions at work, standards of design, leisure amenities, the urban and rural environment, personal and group relationships, women's rights, the state of the arts, levels of crime, international relationships, and personal and public health standards. For many people some combination of these factors may often be more important than increases in per capita income and expenditure. Some forms of economic growth may of course promote the improvement of many aspects of the quality of life. For example, there is generally a connection between higher standards of living, health and life expectancy. But the correspondence is not automatic and cannot be taken for granted, either in this or other areas. It is therefore essential to pursue quality of life objectives for their own sake and not to pursue the reductionist path of trying to fit everything into the growth and measurement of GNP.

The lack of one-to-one correspondence between GNP and quality of life and in particular concern with environmental damage and other negative externalities of economic growth led to many attempts in the 1970s to improve GNP measures with quality of life indicators (see for example, Miles, 1985). Other attempts were made to develop composite indices of social welfare or new types of revised GNP indicator which took greater account of environmental and social issues. It must be said that these attempts did not prove very successful and perhaps they were misconceived from the outset. Almost by definition some of the most important indicators of quality do not lend themselves to quantitative measurement. Even when quantitative measures of quality or life can be used, they are not easily combined. The separate consideration and assessment of various quality factors is therefore essential in developing both policies for economic growth and for science and technology, as well as their interrelationship. The arts and humanities necessarily play a much bigger role in quality of life issues.

It might appear at first sight that quality of life objectives bear little or no relationship to science and technology policies, but by taking a number of examples I hope to show that there are very important connections in almost all instances. Clearly, the direction and scale of some types of R&D may have a great influence on health, conservation, pollution prevention and the efforts of Third World countries to overcome poverty. Twenty years ago a group of us in SPRU and IDS advocated a major reorientation of global R&D in this direction and away from a predominantly military emphasis. This became known as The Sussex Manifesto and a version of it was published in *Science Studies* (Cooper *et al.*, 1971). However, the most important connections are not simply in R&D expenditures but also in the organisation of scientific and technical activities and the methods of evaluation, assessment and regulation of discoveries, inventions and innovations. These were the main concern of Part 2 of Bernal's book. The examples which I shall take are: civil liberty, choice, quality and variety in the design of new products and systems and social equity.

One of the few generalisations in political science which has stood the test of time is Lord Acton's dictum: 'Power corrupts and absolute power corrupts absolutely'. It has been demonstrated time and again that the concentration of economic and political power can be extremely dangerous. Since the time of Aristotle or earlier human beings have been concerned to devise checks and balances in social institutions to guard against the abuse of power. History shows only too well that this is not easy since the restraints are constantly in danger of being circumvented or destroyed. This is just as true in the area of science and technology policy as any other. Even in the small world of SPRU we have learnt in the last twenty-five years that government departments and industrial organisations sometimes do attempt to suppress evidence and critical comments and to manipulate reports. It does not come easily to any powerful organisation to welcome informed public criticism of its policies. Nevertheless, this spirit of toleration and encouragement of alternative points of view is fundamental for a civilised way of life.

Among the most important constraints on the abuse of power are freedom of speech, freedom of publication and freedom of information. These freedoms are also fundamental to the science system and over the years scientists have by and large succeeded in establishing sophisticated self-regulating institutions to maintain these freedoms and the quality of scientific research. Harold Laski and other political scientists have shown that the rise of these norms in the scientific enterprise was very closely associated with the rise of civil liberty in general in the seventeenth, eighteenth and nineteenth centuries. The accepted norms in the science system recognise, just as John Stuart Mill argued in his essay on Liberty, that no one has or ever can have a monopoly of truth, that all theories and hypotheses benefit from a continual process of critical debate, re-examination and testing, including whenever possible experimental validation. The world-wide diffusion of these norms in the science system represents a recent and an extremely important reinforcement for those wider institutions which promote civil liberty in society at large, thus giving new grounds for hope for the future of democratic institutions.

C.P. Snow (1961) in his essay on 'Science and government' expressed the more cynical view that science could flourish just as well in the totalitarian political systems of Nazi Germany or Stalinist Russia as in liberal democracies. He was wrong. Whereas some results can of course be achieved by the application of established technologies, especially in the military area, in the long run both science and technology depend on iconoclastic challenges to established theories and methods, on freedom of criticism and open debate.

Anyone who imagines that nothing has changed in the Soviet Union, has forgotten or never knew what life was like under Stalin. They should read or reread the *First Circle*, or the Reports of the Genetics Conference, or the trials of Trotskyists and Bukharin in the 1930s, or see the film of *A Day in the Life of Ivan Denisovich*, or read *Darkness at Noon*. All of us would of course like to see higher living standards in the Soviet Union and less queueing, no one more than the Russians, but so far as civil liberty is concerned the shadows which still remain are small compared with the horrors of the first half of this century. Sakharov and his colleagues made a very important contribution to this change.

The change from the first half of this century is even more remarkable in Germany and the countries which were occupied during the Second World War. Moreover, this also applies more recently to many countries of the Third World. The rejection of military regimes in many countries of Latin America as well as in Southern Europe is especially notable. Even in South Africa and Haiti there are now real grounds for optimism.

Of course there are still repressive regimes in various parts of the world and there are still countries like my own, with a long tradition of civil liberty where ugly abuses of police power have recently occurred. Nowhere can the very real gains in civil liberty be taken for granted. Nevertheless there are legitimate grounds for optimism. Social innovations such as Amnesty International reinforce world-wide public opinion, which now finds constant expression in the international institutions of the world community of nations. This is something new and hopeful in the world, even though the last report of Amnesty International in 1991 points to many countries where torture of prisoners and the work of 'death squads' are still everyday occurrences.

This conclusion has been challenged in relation to the recent industrialisation of the Asian NICs and China. Much of this took place under authoritarian regimes. But one of the authors and advocates of rather authoritarian policies in that period, Lee Kuan Yiew, the former Prime Minister of Singapore, has recently acknowledged that further progress of these countries too depends increasingly on democratisation, because the complexity of modern technology requires a highly educated and more participative work-force, who will not easily accept authoritarian norms (*Economist* magazine interview, 9 June 1991, pp. 18–19). An essentially similar argument was put with even greater conviction by Slater and Bennis (1990) in their article 'Democracy is inevitable' in the *Harvard Business Review*. This was originally published in 1964, and was recently republished with the legitimate claim that events over the last quarter century have vindicated the views they put forward.

It is true, however, that when it comes to technology, even though many of the same principles apply, as in science, there are also some big differences. It is not only a matter of open discussion and free criticism but also a matter of choice based on a variety of physical artefacts and systems, which can be seen, tested and used. Organised markets provide the opportunities to select, accept or reject new and old products and processes, for both individuals and organisations. Markets also provide incentives to develop and improve such products and processes. As both Marx and Schumpeter insisted, the capacity to generate a continual flow of innovations has proved one of the greatest evolutionary advantages of capitalism. Hegel described history as the 'world court of judgement' but it is the world market which performs this function in many ways.

However, the freedom to choose between alternatives in the market, rightly extolled by Milton Friedmann (1980) as an important extension of human freedom, has to be qualified in several important respects. The first and most obvious is the case of safety and environmental standards. The problems which have arisen in almost every industry, but especially in food, chemicals, energy, construction and transport, have shown that it is quite impossible to promote quality of life objectives without some form of public regulation of quality and safety standards and of the hazards and externalities which are inevitably associated with diffusion of innovation. This means that choice in technology will always have a political and social as well as an economic dimension.

The scale and intensity of these problems has led in many countries to the development of some form of 'technology assessment' (TA). Sometimes it has a different name but this function is likely to become increasingly important with the growing complexity of new technologies. This complexity means that parliamentary institutions may lack the expertise to assess what are often conflicting claims about the merits and dangers of new technologies. Sometimes this function can be devolved to those primarily and directly concerned. Often this is not possible, however, because of conflicts of interest, the scale of the problems or the dangers of 'expertocracy' and monopoly.

This means that technology policy research must be increasingly concerned with the problems of TA and international comparative studies can be especially valuable. The idea of 'constructive' TA first introduced by Arie Rip, Wiebe Bijker and their colleagues (Bijker *et al.*, 1987) and by the Netherlands OTA seems to be especially interesting. TA has too often been viewed as a negative way of safeguarding society against dangers or even as a form of 'technology harassment'. It must of course have the role of reducing hazards; however, it also has a very important positive function—to help in the face of great uncertainties, difficulties and conflicts to find constructive solutions so that society benefits from potential innovations. The research of Van de Wen (1991) and his colleagues in the University of Minneapolis has shown how important this role of institutional innovation can be in the case of Cochlea implants and many other innovations, especially in the medical field. The systematic representation of potential users and other affected groups is especially important.

It is here too that sociologists have made an important contribution to technology policy studies with their concept of social construction of technology (Mackenzie, 1990) and their critique of the idea of 'natural' trajectories. Economists often make use of the expression 'natural' to describe phenomena which are far from natural, such as the 'natural rate of unemployment', 'natural rate of interest', 'natural monopoly' and 'natural trajectories in technology'. All of these are social and not natural phenomena; all of them are the result of human actions, human decisions, human expectations, human institutions.

It is of course possible to discuss this as a purely semantic issue. Shakespeare in *King Lear* used the word 'natural' in two completely different senses. On the one hand he used it to describe the traditional norms of behaviour in a feudal hierarchical society: it was 'unnatural' for daughters to behave towards fathers in the way that Goneril and Regan behaved. This is the way that economists use the expression 'natural'—to describe stable norms of social behaviour. However, Shakespeare also used the word 'natural' to describe a totally different phenomenon—the rebellion, like that of Edgar, against archaic and outdated institutions. Both continuity and discontinuity can be described as 'natural'.

The sociologists of science have compelled us to face this semantic problem and to decide which (if any) kind of 'naturalness' we are talking about. In doing so, they have pointed to the extremely important role of institutional development which surrounds the emergence of any major new technology and enables us to shape and influence it before it hardens into a standardised system, which we then (too late) regard as a 'natural' system.

This leads to a second general problem of the market as a form of selection and improvement of new products and systems: this is the locking-in effects and concentrations of power which may result and may for a long time inhibit the development and introduction of alternative and possibly superior technologies. The example of QWERTY, thanks to the work of Paul David (1985) will forever be quoted in this context, although he and Brian Arthur have shown that standardisation and lock-in effects go far beyond this beautiful example. Because of scale economies, complementarities and institutional inertia (Perez, 1983), lock-in effects are pervasive throughout the economy as any major technological system matures.

Scitovsky (1976) in his book *The Joyless Economy* tried to account for the existence of widespread consumer dissatisfaction side by side with the huge growth of per capita incomes. One part of his explanation related to the loss of choice represented by such lock-in effects of mass production. He describes the mass production lifestyle as one where millionaires are satisfied because they can afford to indulge all kinds of eccentric tastes. Conformists who share their tastes with millions of others can also be satisfied by a mass production lifestyle. However, that still leaves many people deeply dissatisfied with the design and quality of mass-produced articles and services and the conditions under which they are produced. He concluded: 'Modern technology creates great possibilities but it also pushes us towards standardisation and uniformity, both of which inhibit our ability to exploit the possibility it creates.'

That was written in 1976. Since then we have seen considerable progress in the flexibility of production systems, including more flexible mass production systems able to provide a wider product mix, a better quality of product and a more rapid response to changes in consumer tastes. This is another break in trend. Nevertheless, it still does not mean that all the problems to which Scitovsky drew attention have been resolved. Small variations in the existing product mix and lifestyle may be less important than substantial variations which are still inhibited by lock-in effects and lifestyle pressures of conformism. The preservation of the capacity for more radical innovations remains extremely important. In part this can be achieved by the kind of small firm policies adopted in many countries as awareness grew of the importance of promoting alternative sources of technical change. Innovative small firms must be complemented by the preservation and enhancement of the university tradition of path-breaking innovative R&D.

Piore and Sabel (1982) may be right in thinking that networks of small firms provide greater work satisfaction to those who work in them as well as to consumers. However, it cannot be assumed that the change of techno-economic paradigm towards information and communication technology automatically ensures that the days of giant oligopolistic firms are over and that a new era of small networking firms has begun. On the contrary, much evidence points to a new wave of concentration precisely within the IT heartland industries, especially computers and telecommunications. In the 1970s there was a burst of small firm start-ups associated with the microprocessor and the new generations of computers. Firms like Nokia, Nixdorf and Norsk Data flourished in Europe, Wang and Apple in the United States and many small cloning firms in Asia. Now a reverse process of reconcentration is taking place. It is true of course that the biggest firm of all, IBM, is experiencing severe problems in adjusting to the decline of its mainframe business and in making a flexible response to the new types of competition. However this competition comes increasingly from large Japanese firms. Jim Utterback (1991) has shown that the number of firms associated with the emergence of such diverse products as automobiles, typewriters and television in the United States fell very rapidly as each industry matured. ICT is unlikely to be exempt from the concentrating and scale economy effects which have affected other new waves of technology in the past (see Table 4 in Chapter 5).

In the preparation of our recent book *Technology and the Future of Europe* (Freeman, Sharp and Walker, 1991), we found that there were strong tendencies towards oligopolistic concentration in many of the new industries and concluded that some major international social innovations will be needed to cope with these world-wide oligopolies in the Triad of Japan, the United States and the European Community. This was also a major concern of Luc Soete (1991) and his colleagues in the recent TEP Project for OECD.

V

As in the case of political power, the dangers of abuse of concentrations of economic power are ever-present and the need for appropriate checks and balances is also a continuing one (Whiston, 1990). Nor are the two unconnected. The past evidence is very strong that those wielding large concentrations of economic power frequently abused their position to reinforce political movements which sought to destroy civil liberties. Consequently the integrity and independence of those making technology assessment and competition policy will be a key issue in the development of new institutions, both nationally and internationally.

Not only is civil liberty essential to a satisfactory quality of life; so too is the element of social equity. Extreme disparities of wealth and income not only jeopardise civil liberty and inhibit technological choice, they also endanger industrial and national security and are offensive to common decency. In particular, the disparity between rich and poor countries is so great that almost everyone accepts the need to reduce this gap and many international institutions have this as one of their main goals.

In most parts of the world absolute as well as relative poverty constrains choice to a bare minimum and talk of freedom of choice is often empty air. As Anatole France ironically remarked: the rich and the poor are equally free to sleep under the bridges of the Seine. (Today, you do not have to go to Paris to find people sleeping under bridges. There are even more in London.)

The satisfaction of very elementary human needs for shelter, nutrition, health and clothing is still the most urgent priority for huge numbers of people in the Third World as well as for substantial minorities in the richer countries. This does not mean, however, that they all have to accept the same pattern of consumption or way of life.

Two apparently contradictory principles have to be reconciled: the biblical principle 'Do unto others as you would be done by' and the Bernard Shaw principle: 'Do not do unto others as you would be done by because their tastes may be different'. They are not so irreconcilable as they might appear at first sight. The biblical principle recalls our common humanity and shows us a way to develop a sympathetic insight into the needs of others by prohibiting discrimination against people because of race, nationality, gender or other attributes. The Shaw principle recalls the fact that people have a great variety of tastes and needs and just as we should not want someone else to force their tastes upon us, so we ought not to try to enforce our pattern of consumption or way of life on others.

In our work on *World Futures* we calculated that it would be possible for many Third World countries to catch up in living standards with the OECD countries by growing more rapidly for half a century or so. What in fact occurred in the 1980s was that only a few of the NICs in Asia succeeded in achieving these high growth rates whereas most of the Latin American and African countries suffered severe setbacks, and so too did the Soviet Union and many East European countries. Whereas in the 1960s and 1970s Brazil, Venezuela and Mexico had vied with South Korea and Taiwan in their rate of growth, a stark contrast between Latin America and East Asia emerged in the 1980s (Table 11.3). In many Latin American countries both education and R&D expenditures have been cut in response to the international financial pressures to reduce budget deficits, thus further undermining the prospects for future growth. The scenario of the Third World catching up with the richer countries seems in many ways more remote than in the 1970s.

Table 11.3   Divergence in national systems 1980s

East Asia	Latin America
Return to high levels of economic growth	Stagnation or negative growth
Moderate inflation	Galloping inflation
Debt burden reduced or eliminated	Persistent heavy burden of debt
Major wave of Japanese investment	Low level of US and other investment
High rate of technical change and productivity growth	Low rate of technical change and productivity growth
Rapid growth in total R&D (1–2% GNP)	Stagnation or decline in R&D ($<0.5\%$ GNP)
Industrial R&D growing most rapidly and proportion of total reaching 40–65%	Industrial R&D low and stagnant ($<30\%$ of total)
Strong and fast-growing electronic industries with strong exports	Weak electronic industries with very little export
Expanding higher education with output of engineering graduates per 100,000 population >Japanese	Deteriorating higher education with output of engineering graduates per 100,000 population much <Japanese
Relatively low income disparities	Very high disparities of income distribution
Universal access to education	Big disparities in access to education

However, the East Asian countries do demonstrate that given the right combination of economic, science, technology and education policies, considerable catching up is possible even in rather unfavourable global economic circumstances. Andrew Tylecote (1990) has shown that greater equity in income distribution and education in East Asia has been an important factor in their growth, and there is a remarkable unanimity about the beneficial effects of radical land reform after the Second World War (e.g. Wade, 1990; Lee Kuan Yiew, 1991). Nevertheless, the later stages of catching up will probably require further major political and social reforms, as already foreshadowed in South Korea.

Since its inception, SPRU has maintained an active research programme in Third World technology. From early on this programme, led by Geoff Oldham, Charles Cooper and Martin Bell, pointed to the need for Third World countries to develop an autonomous capability in science and technology, which, although not eliminating the need for technology imports, would enable the importers to make better choices and to make some independent contribution to the development and modification of the technology to meet local needs in a more satisfactory way. This research was always conducted jointly with colleagues in Latin America, Asia and Africa, and it has made a small contribution to new institutional developments in various parts of the world.

Side by side with these new and hopeful developments, even though they are still at an early stage, there are some parallel changes in international agencies and institutions. Within the World Bank, as Francisco Sagasti indicated, there is an increasing recognition that the development of autonomous scientific and technological capability is a fundamental necessity for development and a growing readiness to provide support for projects aiming to strengthen scientific and technological infrastructure. Within the UN system there is also a renewed interest in an idea put forward in one of the first papers ever produced in SPRU by Geoff Oldham, Ergun Türkcan (a Visiting Fellow from Turkey) and myself (1967). We proposed a new International Technology Agency which would provide an independent assessment of alternative technologies and licensing proposals for Third World clients. This would be achieved through an international network of consultant experts, whose consultancy fees together with any royalty and know-how payments, would be paid by the international agency, although financed by the country of origin of the technology with a small contribution from the client. This would thus be a positive sum game.

The need for a greatly enhanced role for independent consultants has been very widely recognised during the change of techno-economic paradigm towards information and communication technology. This is one of the fastest growing service industries in the world. Both technical and organisational changes are of such novelty and complexity that few organisations either in rich or poor countries have been able to dispense with the services of outside consultants. It is a crucial issue for reconstruction in Eastern Europe. While developing their own capability Third World countries urgently need access to independent advice and help. Such an agency as we proposed would specialise in the assessment of alternative technologies especially suitable for Third World countries and would also be a vehicle for the selection of environmentally superior technologies, whose application should be subsidised for investment projects financed through the World Bank and other international agencies.

Other social innovations will be needed in the world's international economic institutions, including reform of the World Bank and IMF themselves. Keynes already thought them to be inadequately resourced forty-five years ago and today they clearly need a greater role for other countries in their management, especially Japan, Germany, Russia and China, and also Third World countries.

All these are truly complex problems, although I have tried to give in this chapter a number of examples of changes in trend, influenced by and sometimes closely related to changes in science and technology which give some grounds for hope. The book by Gabriel Garcia Marquez, *Love in the Time of Cholera*, can be read at many different levels; however, I take the message to be: 'Never give way to cynicism or despair. Remain true to the ideals of youth.' If we do this, and like Voltaire, we cultivate our gardens, improve industrial technology, use science intelligently and uphold civil liberty, we can realise some of his hopes and those of the Encyclopaedists and Bernal for a better world, if not the best of all possible worlds.

References

Bernal, J.D. (1939), *The Social Function of Science*, Routledge, London.

Bijker, W., Hughes, T.P. and Pinch, T. (eds) (1987), *The Social Construction of Technological Systems: New Directions in the Sociology and History of Technology*, MIT Press, Cambridge, Mass.

Brooks Report (1971), *Science, Growth and Society*, OECD, Paris.

CEC (1990), *Panorama of EC Industry*, Luxemburg.

Cole, H.S.D., Freeman, C., Jahoda, M. and Pavitt, K.L.R. (eds) (1973), *Thinking about the Future*, Chatto and Windus, London.

Cooper, C.M., Freeman, C., Oldham, G. and Singer, H. (1971), 'The goals of R&D in the 1970s (The Sussex Manifesto)', *Science Studies*, Vol. 1, No. 3, pp. 357–406.

David, P.A. (1985), 'Clio and the Economics of QWERTY', *American Economic Review*, Vol. 75, No. 2, pp. 332–7.

Freeman, C. and Jahoda, M. (eds) (1978), *World Futures*, Martin Robertson, London.

Freeman, C., Oldham, G. and Türkcan, Ergun (1967), *Trends and Problems in World Trade and Development: The Transfer of Technology to Developing Countries*, GE 67-22954, UNCTAD, Geneva.

Freeman, C., Sharp, M. and Walker, W. (eds) (1991), *Technology and the Future of Europe: Global Competition and the Environment in the 1990s*, Pinter Publishers, London.

Friedmann, M. (1980), *Free to Choose—a personal statement*, Harcourt Brace, San Diego, Ca.

Mackenzie, D. (1990), 'Economic and sociological explanation of technical change', Paper presented at Manchester Conference on Firm Strategy and Technical Change.

Marquez, G.G. (1988), *Love in the Time of Cholera* (English Edition), Jonathan Cape, London.

Meadows, D. *et al.*, (1972), *Limits to Growth*, Universe Books, New York.

Miles, I.D. (1985), *Social Indicators for Human Development*, Frances Pinter, London.

Mowery, D. and Rosenberg, N. (1979), 'The influence of market demand upon innovation: a critical review of some recent empirical studies', *Research Policy*, Vol. 8, No. 2, pp. 102–53.

OECD (1971), *Science, Growth and Society* (Brooks Report), OECD, Paris.

OECD (1980), *Technical Change and Economic Policy: Science and Technology in the New Economic Context*, OECD, Paris.

OECD (1989), *New Technologies in the 1990s: A Socio-Economic Strategy* (Sundqvist Report), OECD, Paris.

OEEC (OECD) (1963), *Science, Economic Growth and Government Policy*, OECD, Paris.

Ostry, S. (1990), 'Beyond the border: the new international policy arena', OECD Forum for the Future, Paris, 30 October.

Perez, C. (1983), 'Structural change and the assimilation of new technologies in the economic and social system', *Futures*, Vol. 15, No. 5, pp. 357–75.

Piore, M. and Sabel, C.F. (1982), *The Second Industrial Divide*, Basic Books, New York.

Price, D.J. de Solla (1963), *Little Science, Big Science*, Columbia University Press, New York.

Scitovsky, T. (1976), *The Joyless Economy: An Inquiry into Human Satisfaction and Consumer Dissatisfaction*, Oxford University Press.

Slater, P. and Bennis, W.G. (1990), 'Democracy is inevitable', *Harvard Business Review*, September–October, pp. 167–76.

Snow, C.P. (1961), *Science and Government*, Oxford University Press, London.

Soete, L.L.G. (1990), 'National support policies for strategic industries: the international implications', OECD Forum for the Future, Paris, 30 October.

Sundqvist Report (1989), *New Technologies in the 1990s: A Socio-Economic Strategy*, OECD, Paris.

Tylecote, A. (1990), *Long Waves in the World Economy*, Routledge, London.

Utterback, J. and Suarez, F.F. (1991), 'Innovation, competition and industry structure', *Research Policy*, Vol. 20.

Van de Wen A.H. *et al.* (1989), *Research on the Management of Innovation: The Minnesota Studies*, Harper and Row, New York (Ballinger Division).

Whiston, T.G. (1991), 'Forecasting the world's problems: the last empire, the corporatisation of society and the diminution of self', *Futures*, Vol. 23, No. 2, pp. 163–78.

Epilogue

Requirements for science and technology policy in the 1990s*

1. Introduction

When Lew Branscombe asked us to speak at this symposium he asked us to address the question of the adequacy of science policy research for policy-making in the 1990s. This we have done, drawing heavily on our experiences in the Science Policy Research Unit at the University of Sussex; a group which we started jointly twenty-five years ago.

The relationship between policy-makers and the policy research community has always been a delicate and difficult one, even though both need each other. In fact the requirements of both communities often broadly coincide in terms of data, models, dialogue and even publications. Nevertheless, there are tensions and dangers in the relationship which require careful attention and mutual understanding. The pressures of government are usually short-term and often nationalistic, and as we shall see, this can lead to problems.

Our unit has been concerned with policy analysis in all parts of the world from its earliest days. We have carried out many projects for various departments and agencies of the British government and learnt a great deal from them. The same applies to projects for the European Community. However, we have never thought about our work in nationalistic or even in European terms. On the contrary, from the very outset we deliberately planned a substantial programme on science and technology policies in the Third World including China and this was our first major research programme (with the support of the Ford Foundation). We have always tried to understand the special problems of these countries and there is little doubt that the *influence* on policy-makers has been greater in the Third World than in Europe. We have viewed science and technology as a global system and much of our work has been for international organisations such as the UN, the OECD and the European Community; and some has been for multinational companies, such as ALCAN, IBM, ICI or BP.

*This chapter was written with Geoffrey Oldham of SPRU for the 75th Birthday Symposium for Harvey Brooks.

All of this experience has led us to some fairly definite conclusions about relationships between researchers and policy-makers, whether in Europe or the Third World, and about the requirements for good research and policy-making. Nevertheless, these requirements do vary between countries and they are also changing over time. This chapter is therefore a review of the special needs and problems of science and technology policy in the 1990s in the light of our experience over the past twenty-five years. We shall look first of all at requirements for data on an internationally comparable basis; then at the development of models and theories to guide understanding and policy-making; and finally at the relationship between researchers and policy-makers. Each is an essential ingredient if good research is to be done and the results used.

2. Data requirements for science and technology policy (STP)

Although there have been many improvements in the available statistics about science and technology over the past twenty-five years, they still leave much to be desired in range, speed of availability, reliability and international comparability. Here it is possible to point to only a few of the key problems and make a few suggestions for improvements in the 1990s.

Probably the most widely used statistics in STP research and policy-making are still those relating to R&D and the derived statistics of R&D intensity of countries, industries and firms. Since the OECD Frascati Conference in 1963 which standardised international definitions and conventions, great progress has been made in extending the range of countries producing these statistics and improving their quality. The Science and Technology Indicators group at the OECD deserve great credit for these achievements both before and since the untimely death of Yvan Fabian. More than fifty countries now measure R&D activities, and almost all use the Frascati conventions.

However, no one recognised more clearly than Yvan Fabian the limitations of R&D statistics, and no one worked harder to extend the scope of OECD activities beyond the range of R&D to other science and technology indicators, and especially to output measures. We were happy in SPRU to collaborate in a series of international seminars organised by Fabian and his colleagues which were a good example of constructive collaboration between academic researchers, policy-makers and statisticians. As a result of hard work in many countries (for example, the initiative of the NSF in its work on S&T Indicators), we now have a greatly extended range of quantitative indicators. Despite this, however, no one in the field has any doubt that they still have many shortcomings and gaps.

For example, last year one of us (Geoff Oldham) chaired a working group of a Science Advisory Committee to the British government. The objective was to investigate the experiences of other countries in international collaboration in science and technology. It might have been expected that the percentage of a country's R&D budget spent on international collaboration would have increased in recent years and that from the statistics it would prove possible to identify each country's favoured partners for collaboration. No such statistics existed.

This is just one example of the deficiencies of existing statistics. The main improvements and innovations which are required are:

(a) Harmonisation of definitions and measurement capability with the Soviet Union, China and Eastern Europe. Regular measurement of the world-wide R&D and related activities of multinational corporations (MNCs).
(b) Extensions of the range and coverage of S&T activities beyond R&D to include other scientific and technical services.
(c) Systematic use of Japanese and European patent data in conjunction with US statistics to create a global patent data base.
(d) Development and improvement of international citation analysis, especially in relation to scientific networks and co-authorship.
(e) Extension of the range of output indicators by the widespread international development of regular measures of innovation and above all of *diffusion*.
(f) Establishment of experimental task forces to work with national statistical offices and other data collection agencies in pioneering new types of indicator and measurement, and in speeding up the rate of appearance of preliminary indicators.
(g) The measurement of indicators of international collaboration in science and technology.

Already at the first Frascati Conference in 1963 and in the manual on R&D measurement (which one of us helped to write), it was clearly stated that R&D statistics themselves measured only part of a wider spectrum of S&T activities, all of which were important for the healthy development of any country's science and technology system. These activities were defined as 'related activities' and their characteristics were briefly described. They included testing and standardisation; geophysical exploration work; scientific and technical information, documentation and abstracting services; design and engineering, technical and market consultancy services; the work of Patent Offices and Patent Departments; education and training, and so forth.

Although these related activities are especially important in the Third World and in the transfer of technology, they are essential everywhere. The time has come in the 1990s to make a big push forward to extend the range of S&T statistics to encompass a variety of related activities in addition to R&D. Of course there are big problems of definition and scope, and there is great inertia and resistance in some national statistical systems.

However, the difficulties are certainly no greater than those encountered with R&D statistics in the 1950s and 1960s.

International action in this field can be greatly facilitated by the need to achieve comparability with the Soviet Union, other East European countries and China. This must be a top priority for S&T indicators in the 1990s and it should not be too difficult since there is now much goodwill on both sides. We took part in the first abortive efforts to achieve this international harmonisation in the 1960s. Although these early efforts failed, they enabled us to identify the key problems and the main advantages. The Soviet Union and similar economies have a long tradition of measuring scientific and technical activities and in their rubric they include many related activities as well as R&D. Several of the East European countries have moved to the narrower Frascati definitions and have disaggregated the other services. Thus international standardisation could proceed by *extending* the range of measurements in the OECD area and making them more precise in the East. In the end the UN is probably now the appropriate body to take the responsibility for global harmonisation, but the OECD has shown far more capability in this area, so as a first step we hope that they will continue their initiatives by regularly inviting Russian and other statisticians to the new Frascati Conferences in the 1990s. Consultants should be invited to prepare manuals of measurement and defintions of R&D and related S&T activities to be implemented world-wide during the 1990s.

Not only do we need better input measures, we also require better measures of the output of the science and technology system. One of the biggest changes in our own policy-related work in the 1980s has been a great increase in the use we make of output indicators in SPRU. These indicators are still highly controversial, although as a result of continuing dialogue and debate between policy-makers, statisticians and the research community and open publication, the problems are now much better understood than they were when the first pioneering attempts were made by scientists like Derek Price in the 1960s and 1970s.

The two main types of indicator which are in use are patents (including patent citations) and bibliometric (or scientometric) indicators. We are happy that SPRU researchers have made some original contributions to the development and use of both these types of indicator. Irvine and Martin were among the pioneers of the second generation of scientometric indicators and their work has been much in demand for both large and small countries in policy-related consultancy work all over Europe and beyond. Pavitt and Soete helped to establish the use of patent statistics in policy analysis and international trade performance. In particular we have benefited greatly from the US Department of Commerce data base and the technique of using patenting in the United States to achieve a rough international comparability of patenting activity. However, despite the considerable international experience in the use of these indicators in the

1980s, there are still some serious problems associated with their use.

Irvine and Martin have always insisted that bibliometric indicators should be used in combination with a variety of other indicators and that citation measures are an indication of *impact* of scientific work, not necessarily of *quality* of output. With these qualifications, scientometric data can be a valuable input to policy-making, especially peer review of the performance of research groups and institutes.

However, there are many problems to resolve and interesting new developments, such as the use of multiple authorship indicators; analysis of networks and mobility of scientists; regional concentrations of scientific effort; and above all the interaction between science and technology, universities and industry. There is still enormous scope for enlarging and improving the range of applications of citation and publication analysis; however, the associated time-lags are an intrinsic element of this type of indicator, which limits their value and means that great care is always needed in their policy applications.

The same problem is present in patent citation work which is so far undeveloped by comparison with scientific citations. This is an area where much further research and testing is needed before reasonably reliable indicators can be confidently used by policy-makers. Nevertheless, the early results by Narin and his co-workers on the citation analysis of Japanese patents are promising.

However, the biggest problem for policy-makers and researchers in the 1990s is not the further improvement of existing indicators but the development of new indicators to extend the range of measurement. Just as it was always recognised that R&D statistics were only one part of a wider spectrum of scientific and technical activities, so too it has always been recognised that scientometric and patent statistics measure only part of the outputs, albeit a very important part. For technology policy as for industrial policy more widely, it is indicators of innovation and diffusion of innovations which are most urgently needed.

Good research and good inventive work do not necessarily lead to efficient and successful innovation. Even being the first to innovate with a world-class new product or process does not necessarily lead to a competitive and successful diffusion of these innovations. Technology policy-makers both in the United Kingdom and in the United States have had very good reasons to reflect on the truth of these propositions in the 1970s and 1980s.

3. Models and theories in science and technology policy

It would be absurd and wasteful of course to invest large resources in the development and collection of quantitative indicators just to accumulate statistics. The suggestions which have been made for new and improved statistics in the 1990s are the result of experience in developing models and theories of the science–technology system and the needs of policy-makers.

Good analysis of empirical data must be guided by hypotheses, models and theories. For the most part in SPRU we have borrowed our methodologies from relevant social sciences in an eclectic way. Even so, there are problems with this. With a few exceptions economists in the past have been notoriously neglectful of technology and technological change in their models and theories, although in the past few years there have been welcome signs of change. We are well aware of the need to contribute to theory as well as draw on that developed by others.

The interplay between statistics and theory for the benefit of policy can be illustrated by two examples. The first is the case of diffusion statistics where there is a demand for international comparable statistics of the rate of diffusion of new technologies. Policy-makers are well aware that it is the rapid and efficient diffusion of new technologies which leads to economic and social development and contributes to international competitiveness.

Models of diffusion have developed considerably in the past twenty years. The pioneering work of Mansfield concentrated primarily on the diffusion of individual products and processes and measuring various characteristics of the adopter population. Using such models with their characteristic sigmoid curves of adoption provided reasonably good forecasts for diffusion and in some cases made it possible to develop policies to influence this pattern favourably.

More recent studies of diffusion pointed to the importance of changes in product characteristics and the environment *during* the diffusion itself, requiring measurement of these changing characteristics of successive generations of new products. However, they also demonstrated the interdependence of many diffusion processes. The *systemic* characteristics of new technologies came to the fore in assessing such new developments as CAD, CNC, FMS or CIM in manufacturing or data banks and VANs in the telematic service industries. Useful and reliable statistics are rarely available in such cases because the problems of measurement and comparability are much more complex.

The second case we wish to mention (where the interest of policy-makers has outstripped the ability of existing statistics and theory to enable researchers to provide solutions) is what is sometimes referred to as the globalisation of technology. *Business Week* has had a special issue this year on the 'Stateless corporation', and the *Economist* and the *New York Times* have featured the forthcoming book by the Japanese writer, Mr Ohmae, on *The Borderless World*.

This type of analysis points to the role of multinationals in increasingly rapid diffusion of new technologies throughout the OECD area and in the NICs too. Japanese investment in the United States and the European Community (especially the United Kingdom) is growing rapidly in the electronic industries as well as in South-East Asia and China. European firms have also been investing heavily in the United States in the 1980s, and US investment has long been considerable in the countries of the European Community, especially in electronics, computers and automobiles. As the Japanese capital market is opened up and even Eastern Europe and the Soviet Union attract a wave of foreign investment, so it will become more and more difficult to distinguish 'national technological systems' from one another. The new telecommunications infrastructure with digitalisation of the international network means that companies like Hewlett-Packard are able to link design and development in several different countries so closely that it is hard to trace the national origin. The same is true of the world-wide chemical plant contractors who may switch work between Frankfurt, London, Milan and Singapore more or less instantaneously, depending upon the work-load of the various design offices.

Internationalism has long been a characteristic of basic science, and through scientific publications, abstracting, translation and information services new advances in any country are rapidly made known everywhere. Moreover, with the enormous growth in numbers of foreign graduate students in the universities of the United States, Europe and Japan, another and ultimately more powerful method of diffusing international scientific capacity is also at work. Multiple authorship of scientific papers is one type of measurement which helps us to keep track of this 'globalisation' in science.

However, other work at SPRU shows that globalisation of science and technology is by no means such a strong tendency as is sometimes suggested. Pavitt and Patel have used patent statistics to show that during the 1980s inventive work in the major multinational corporations was still overwhelmingly concentrated in the home base of the corporation. Only Belgium and Holland showed really strong internationalisation and much of this was due to the forthcoming Single European Market rather than true globalisation. Japanese corporations have yet to develop major R&D facilities outside Japan to match their investment in production and sales or the much larger overseas investment in R&D of companies like IBM. Like Brazil and other NICs the European Community must now decide whether to make R&D performance a condition for foreign investment.

This points to another area where major improvements are needed in S&T indicators. Our information about the world-wide R&D, licensing agreements and related activities of MNCs is still very spasmodic and weak, despite its acknowledged importance. It is essential to improve this data base in the 1990s and this is an obvious area for international co-operation through the OECD.

Nor can it be simplistically assumed that the technologies which are being transferred to Third World countries are either appropriate or up to date. It is more likely that the export of technology is quite logically intended to spread R&D and design costs incurred in the home country over a wider world market. Consequently quantitative analysis of R&D, licensing and know-how agreements and the so-called 'technological balance of payments', valuable though it is, can never be a substitute for qualitative analysis of the specific needs and experience of Third World countries in technology transfer. Particularly in Europe in the 1990s the issue of national systems and globalisation will be one of the most exciting and important research areas.

We have given a number of examples to illustrate the point that improvements in international quantitative indicators are essential to improve the quality of policy research and policy advice. However, only if there are good theories and models to guide the use of this data will this investment yield a worthwhile return. The reciprocal relationships between policy-makers, policy-researchers and data collection agencies are therefore a fundamental issue and it is to these relationships that we now turn in the final section of this chapter.

4. Policy researchers and policy-making

The problems of forging linkages between those who do policy research and those who make policy are not unique to science and technology. Social science researchers have studied those problems in many areas of policy, especially those pertaining to health and education. Systematic analyses of the problems of science and technology policy are few, and in this section of our talk we draw heavily on our own experiences in SPRU.

The impact of policy research on policy-making can be either direct or indirect. With the direct impact there is a clear link between the research and a change in policy. Our own experiences suggest that such instances are rare. Researchers can often facilitate impact by accepting appointments as advisors to governments or serving on advisory committees. In this way a direct channel is provided between one's own research, or the research of colleagues, and policy-making. However, such close association between researchers and policy makers poses its own set of problems. To what extent, as an adviser, does one recommend incremental changes to policy rather than the radical changes which the policy research might suggest, in the expectation that incremental changes are more likely to be accepted than radical ones?

In our own knowledge of the effects of SPRU research it seems that our impact has been greater on foreign governments and international organisations than on the British government. A few examples will illustrate.

1. Early SPRU research on developing countries was directly fed into the design of the Canadian International Development Research Centre through one of us (Geoff Oldham) bring a member of the task force

which drafted legislation. Its emphasis on helping to build research capacity in developing countries was in contrast to the approaches being followed by UK and US aid programmes at the time, although it followed the needs identified by SPRU researchers.

2. The Organisation of American States technology transfer studies. This programme was designed in the late 1960s to investigate the conditions under which technology was transferred from North America and Europe to Latin American countries. Most of this research was carried out by teams in Latin America although a SPRU team also participated. This research yielded new understanding and knowledge about the transfer process which was used as a basis of policy by many Latin American governments. Indeed the time from the initiation of the research to the issue of international technology transfer appearing on the agenda of a meeting of Latin American foreign ministers was less than four years.

It is interesting to note that the policy response of Latin Americans was largely defensive. Mechanisms were introduced to monitor and control the inflow of foreign technology. By contrast South Korea, faced with the results of similar research carried out in that country, decided to opt for a more offensive strategy whereby technology needed by the country was sought for aggressively.

3. A third example of a fairly direct link between SPRU research and policy-making was the impact of our early work on the effects of information technology on employment. These results were reported on a television programme seen by Jim Callaghan, the then Prime Minister. A programme of research on IT was then formulated following cabinet instructions. In this instance we were told of the link between the TV programme and policy. There may be other instances, of course, where our research has had a direct impact although we are unaware of the connection. Some government policy advisers have suggested that these 'direct hits' may be more frequent than we realise.

Of the cases where there seem to be direct impacts there seems to be little correlation between the academic quality of the work and impact.

Let us turn now to those cases where impact has been indirect. This is defined by some social scientists as the 'limestone model'. The knowledge generated by research may be published although this may then 'disappear', perhaps being merged with other streams of knowledge, perhaps hidden in underground pools for many years before finally re-emerging and being found useful by some policy-maker. In these cases it is often impossible to trace the connection between the research and its impact.

Also in the indirect category is that research which influences a climate of opinion within which policies are made. This is the way in which we believe that our research has had greatest impact and we make a substantial effort to communicate the results not only through articles in journals or through books but also by making sure our work is reported in the quality press and broadcasting media.

Despite all these efforts we believe there is still a major gap between the production of knowledge and its utilisation by decision-makers. We have still not solved the problem of knowledge transfer. Decisions are made on the basis of only a fraction of the knowledge which is relevant. For policy research to be adequate for the needs of science policy-making in the 1990s we must do more to disseminate information so that it is accessible to policy-makers in a way that they can assimilate—and in a timely manner. Studies of this problem in Australia and China showed the need for a science and technology briefing service. The Library of Congress puts out such a service in the United States. What is needed is an international version of this.

The more direct links between researchers and decision-makers may have more immediate impact but they also carry greater risks of censorship. There have been several occasions in SPRU when research which has been supported by government departments has yielded results which the department did not wish to hear and then attempted to stop publication. One such case was where our work showed that technical change in some sectors of British industry was less than in many of our competitors' and that this was inimical to our economic competitiveness. The chief scientist of the relevant department publicly called the work 'treasonable'. Fortunately there is a higher turnover of government officials than SPRU researchers so that even in cases of censorship and cool relations, after a year or so when new officials are in post, good relations have been rebuilt. It is now a common occurrence for ministers and opposition spokesmen to visit the unit for briefing sessions, even in those ministries where a few years earlier their officials had attempted to suppress publication of its work.

To conclude. In this talk we have drawn on our experiences over the past twenty-five years to address the question of the adequacy of science policy research for effective policy-making. We have attempted to show that although substantial progress has been made over these twenty-five years in each of the three elements of data, theory and communication there is still much more to be achieved if the full potential of science policy research is to be realised.

Stephen Toulmin played an important part in the initiatives which led to the establishment of SPRU. In the *New Scientist* in 1963 he made the case for a British university replicating something like the 'Harvard seminar on science and public policy' which brought together natural scientists, sociologists, psychologists, economists, historians of science and students of public administration as well as officers from the armed services and government agencies. Toulmin went on to say:

If the example of economics is any guide, discussion of the problems of scientific policy should not be confined to government ministries and research councils. It should become a subject for continuing work in the universities also. By now the existence of a body of professional economists who can criticise the Treasury's financial and economic policies has become an essential element in democratic control. Unless decisions about scientific policy are to be left to be made by *eminences grises* we shall need a corresponding body of independent informal opinions about the natural history of science: men whose business is to undertake academic research on the intellectual foundations of scientific policy and who are engaged continuously in a critical exchange of ideas with the actual policy making agencies of government.

Harvey Brooks is the epitomy of such a man, and we are grateful for the opportunity to salute his contributions to science, to science policy research, and to policy-making.

Index